How the Land Lies

FIGURE 1. Map of case study locations.

How the Land Lies

The Origins of Regular Landscapes in the English Lowlands

Adrienne C. Compton

Windgather Press is an imprint of Oxbow Books

Published in the United Kingdom in 2025 by
OXBOW BOOKS
81 St Clements, Oxford OX4 1AW

and in the United States by
OXBOW BOOKS
1950 Lawrence Road, Havertown, PA 19083

© Windgather Press and the author 2025

Paperback Edition: ISBN 978-1-914427-45-9
Digital Edition: ISBN 978-1-914427-46-6 (epub)

A CIP record for this book is available from the British Library

All rights reserved. No part of this book may be reproduced or transmitted in any form or by any means, electronic or mechanical including photocopying, recording or by any information storage and retrieval system, without permission from the publisher in writing.

Printed in the United Kingdom by Halstan & Co Ltd.
Typeset in India by DiTech Publishing Services

For a complete list of Windgather titles, please contact:

United Kingdom	United States of America
OXBOW BOOKS	OXBOW BOOKS
Telephone (0)1226 734350	Telephone (610) 853-9131, Fax (610) 853-9146
Email: oxbow@oxbowbooks.com	Email: queries@casemateacademic.com
www.oxbowbooks.com	www.casemateacademic.com/oxbow

Oxbow Books is part of the Casemate group

Cover: Landscape near Tea Green, Bedfordshire in October 2021. Taken by author.

The Publisher's authorised representative in the EU for product safety is Authorised Rep Compliance Ltd., Ground Floor, 71 Lower Baggot Street, Dublin D02 P593, Ireland.
www.arccompliance.com

Contents

List of figures — vii
Acknowledgements — xi
Introduction: interpreting patterns — xiii

Part 1: Reassessing relict field systems — 1

1. 'Rough grids': prehistoric boundaries and 'ancient' fields — 3
    Prehistoric fields — 4
    The first relict field systems — 10
    Relict fields in the Midlands — 15
    Alternative arguments — 17
    Conclusion — 20
2. The relict field systems in west Cambridgeshire — 23
    Relict field systems in the Bourn Valley — 27
    Roman roads and slighted field boundaries — 40
    The Saxon proto-common field — 44
    A Bronze Age field system in Tadlow — 50
    Conclusion — 52
3. Revisiting some famous relict field systems — 53
    The beginning: relict landscapes in southeast Essex — 53
    Relict field systems in East Anglia — 58
    Late Iron Age or Romano-British field systems in the Arrow Valley? — 66
    'Bronze Age' landscapes on the London Clays — 75
4. Summary and conclusion to Part 1 — 83

Part 2: Planned open fields — 85

5. The origins of open fields — 87
    Planned open fields — 89
    Alternative explanations for 'planned settlements' — 92
    Conclusion — 93
6. Open fields and 'planned' agricultural landscapes — 95
    Long furlongs in the East Riding of Yorkshire — 95
    Long furlongs in the Midlands — 105

vi Contents

        Regular landscapes in the open fields of North Yorkshire   108
        Conclusion   118

7. Northamptonshire and its open fields   121
        Case study: The Orlingbury Hundred   123
        Case study: The Central Nene Valley   130
        Conclusion   140

8. Marshland: a planned landscape?   143
        The Marshland environment and soils   146
        Medieval reclamation of the Silt Fen   152
        Marshland's landscape framework   155
        The regular field pattern   168
        Conclusion   170

9. Conclusion   173

Bibliography   177
Index   183

List of figures

Figure i	Map of case study locations	ii
Figure 2.1	The topography and parishes of the West Cambridgeshire Clay Plateau Environment	24
Figure 2.2	The 'ancient alignments' (north–south) and 'proto-common field' commons (east–west) in the Bourn Valley	29
Figure 2.3	Soil type and churches in the southeastern Bourn Valley	30
Figure 2.4	The distribution of the named sites within the Cambourne Development Area	31
Figure 2.5	Phases of the Lower Cambourne site	33
Figure 2.6	Illustrating the location of The Fields site at the head of a dry valley	34
Figure 2.7	The field ditches excavated at The Fields, with the two phases identified by the archaeologists	35
Figure 2.8	The field ditches excavated at The Fields, overlain with the medieval ridge and furrow identified by the archaeologists	36
Figure 2.9	The features excavated at The Fields	37
Figure 2.10	The First Edition Ordnance Survey 6-Inch map covering the northwestern Bourn Valley	38
Figure 2.11	LiDAR plot of the northwestern Bourn Valley	39
Figure 2.12	The pre-Roman boundaries identified by Oosthuizen, overlaid on First Edition Ordnance Survey 6-Inch map	41
Figure 2.13	The pre-Roman boundaries identified by Oosthuizen, overlaid on LiDAR Composite DTM 2 m	42
Figure 2.14	Plan of the ridge and furrow in Caxton	43
Figure 2.15	Caxton ridge and furrow plan	44
Figure 2.16	Elements of Oosthuizen's Bourn Valley relict field system over LiDAR	46
Figure 2.17	Linear commons west of Toft	47
Figure 2.18	Pre-Inclosure Commons in Toft	48
Figure 2.19	Pre-Inclosure Commons in Toft, and Oosthuizen's 'proto common field'	49
Figure 2.20	The stepped parish boundaries in Tadlow	50
Figure 3.1	Pre-Roman field boundaries near Little Waltham, Essex	54
Figure 3.2	Supposed Pre-Roman field boundaries near Little Waltham, Essex	55
Figure 3.3	The nineteenth-century field pattern around Little Waltham, Essex	56

List of figures

Figure 3.4	The landscape around Yaxley, Suffolk	58
Figure 3.5	Detail of the northwestern portion of Yaxley, Suffolk	59
Figure 3.6a	Detail of the field pattern south of Yaxley, Suffolk from the Tithe Map	61
Figure 3.6b	Detail of the field pattern south of Yaxley, Suffolk on the First Edition Ordnance Survey 6-Inch map	61
Figure 3.7	Detail of the First Edition Ordnance Survey 6-Inch map showing Yaxley Road, Braisworth, Suffolk	62
Figure 3.8	The topography close to Yaxley, Suffolk	63
Figure 3.9	Rowe Ditch in the Arrow Valley	66
Figure 3.10	Archaeological features near Leen Farm, Pembridge	69
Figure 3.11	LiDAR covering the area of Rowe Ditch in the Arrow Valley	70
Figure 3.12	Wider topography of the environs of Rowe Ditch in the Arrow Valley	71
Figure 3.13	Offa's Dyke near Lyonshall	73
Figure 3.14	Offa's Dyke crossing the river Arrow	74
Figure 3.15	Wormley, Hertfordshire from the First Edition Ordnance Survey 6-Inch map	75
Figure 3.16	The earthworks in Wormley	77
Figure 3.17	The Wormley earthworks overlying a terrain map	79
Figure 3.18	The semi-regular field pattern around Saffron Green in Arkley	80
Figure 3.19	The 'co-axial' pattern in the area of Saffron Green	81
Figure 3.20	The Arkley co-axials identified by Hunn and categorised by type	81
Figure 3.21	The First Edition Ordnance Survey 6-Inch map over a modern LiDAR Composite DTM 2 m	82
Figure 6.1	*A Copy of the Enclosure Plan of Preston in Holderness by John or William Iverson* and strip orientations	97
Figure 6.2	*A Copy of the Enclosure Plan of Preston in Holderness by John or William Iverson* and the approximate location of the main 'bydale' boundaries	99
Figure 6.3	LiDAR Composite DTM 50 cm for Preston in Holderness	101
Figure 6.4	Detail of the First Edition Ordnance Survey 6-Inch for Preston in Holderness	102
Figure 6.5	*A Copy of the Enclosure Plan of Skeffling in Holderness by John or William Iverson* and strip orientations	104
Figure 6.6	Long furlongs in Raunds	106
Figure 6.7	Long furlongs in Wollaston	107
Figure 6.8	First Edition Ordnance Survey 6-Inch map for part of the parish of Middleton in Ryedale, Yorkshire	109
Figure 6.9	*A Plan of the Tyth Land at Middleton in the County of York*	112

List of figures

Figure 6.10	Detail of *A Plan of the Tyth Land at Middleton in the County of York*	113
Figure 6.11	The village of Middleton in Ryedale	114
Figure 6.12	Detail of *A Plan of the Tyth Land at Middleton in the County of York*	115
Figure 6.13	Fields to the south of Middleton and Aislaby in Ryedale	117
Figure 6.14	Detail of *A Plan of the Tyth Land at Middleton in the County of York*	117
Figure 7.1	The topography of the modern hundred of Orlingbury	124
Figure 7.2	Soils of Orlingbury Hundred	125
Figure 7.3	Phases of settlement in Great Harrowden	127
Figure 7.4	The landscape of Old and Walgrave at the time of Parliamentary Enclosure	128
Figure 7.5	Detail of the furlong pattern in Old	130
Figure 7.6	The topography of the Central Nene Valley	131
Figure 7.7	Soil types in the Central Nene Valley	133
Figure 7.8	Detail of the furlong pattern in Warmington	137
Figure 7.9	Detail of the *Map of the Manor of Warmington in 1621 by Richard Norwood*	138
Figure 7.10	Detail of the greens and furlongs of Warmington	139
Figure 8.1	The landscape to the south of King's Lynn, Norfolk	144
Figure 8.2	The Norfolk Fens before reclamation from the Sea	147
Figure 8.3	Late Saxon settlement activity in Marshland from archaeological fieldwork	151
Figure 8.4	Twelfth-century settlement activity in Marshland	153
Figure 8.5	The sixteenth-century landscape near Terrington St Clement	154
Figure 8.6	The thirteenth-century landscape	156
Figure 8.7	Topography of the Marshland vills	158
Figure 8.8	The relationship of common droves and the Silt Ridge settlements in Tilney, Terrington and the Walpoles	159
Figure 8.9	a) Walpole East Drove after Hayward; b) detail of the First Edition Ordnance Survey 6-Inch map showing the field divisions in East Field, Walpole	160
Figure 8.10	Township banks in Marshland	162
Figure 8.11	Castor or the Old Fendike	164
Figure 8.12	Newfendike and twelfth-century settlement	165
Figure 8.13	Orientation of the strips	169

Acknowledgements

This research could not have been carried out without using the data created by the Environment Agency National LiDAR Programme, which underlies the case studies both large and small. I would like to thank the various archives and libraries I have visited in the course of this research, and particular I would like to thank the staff at Cambridgeshire Record Offices (Cambridge and Huntingdon), Cambridge University Library, East Riding Archives, Norfolk Record Office, Northamptonshire Archives and North Yorkshire County Record Office for their patience in retrieving numerous large maps from the storerooms. I am very grateful to the Northamptonshire National Mapping Programme for making the wealth of data used in the project of the same name freely available through the Archaeology Data Service. I would also like to thank Jon Gregory for his guidance on how to successfully add the ADS data into the GIS mapping software, saving me hours of frustrating tinkering. I would like to thank my supervisor Tom Williamson for his enduring advice, guidance and support during the research and writing of the thesis upon which this book is based. I am grateful for my friends and family and their encouragement over the last few years. Finally, I would like to thank my parents for their support and understanding.

Introduction: interpreting patterns

In *The Making of the English Landscape*, W.G. Hoskins (1988, 19) explained to his readers that evidence for the everyday lives of countless generations of rural people was hidden in plain sight. The informed observer was able to identify and interpret features that belonged to earlier ages whether this was through examining maps, photographs or simply being present in the countryside. Understanding what these features were and what roles they played in the past illuminated the landscapes inhabited by our ancestors.

A key method of interpretation of landscape is the identification of patterns and, most importantly, those features that do not appear to conform to the expected arrangement. An example would be a modern field that contained a discontinuous line of mature trees; a casual observer may see a tree or even several trees in the midst of a crop, the student of the countryside will perceive evidence of a former boundary hedge, preserving the line of earlier enclosures. The distinct and often multi-layered patterns that form the English landscape led to it being described as a historical 'palimpsest' by F.W. Maitland (1907, 15).

Patterns lend themselves to categorisation, and one of the principal divisions in the understanding of historic landscapes is between regular and irregular arrangements of fields, lanes and settlements. Within landscape studies there has been a general presumption that regular landscapes originate from deliberate planning, while irregular patterns are believed to arise from organic development. Hoskins briefly touched upon this when he described the rectilinear grid of prehistoric fields of Horridge Common, Dartmoor as a 'planned Bronze Age enclosure'. There was no mention of planning in his descriptions of roughly contemporary but irregular patterns of prehistoric enclosures (Hoskins 1988, 27–9).

During the 1970s a number of regular prehistoric field systems had been identified in England and these were interpreted as being the result of deliberate, large-scale planning by the archaeologists who worked upon them (Fleming 1988; Pryor 2013). Several of these archaeologists commented how they observed correlations between the prehistoric fields and boundaries and features visible in the adjacent modern field pattern (Fleming 1988; Pryor 2013). In the later 1970s and 80s the concept of 'relict field systems' developed. This was based upon identifying fossilised elements of ancient, frequently prehistoric, planned landscapes still visible in the modern countryside (Drury and Rodwell 1980). Over time the study of relict field systems suggested that large areas of the English countryside had been planned and laid out, before the Middle Ages, with regular boundaries and divisions (Rackham 1986).

The survival of Late Prehistoric and Romano British fields into the modern field pattern is frequently used to argue for continuity of society, particularly in the centuries following the withdrawal of the Roman troops from England (Rippon *et al.* 2015). The link between planning and regularity has also been used in the study of medieval field systems. Regular landscapes have been used to support arguments for seigneurial, ecclesiastical and tribal control, influence and links between settlements where there is little or no surviving documentary evidence (Oosthuizen 2006; Hall and Coles 2014). Villages in England have been categorised based upon their morphology and those with the most regular layouts of tofts and crofts have been interpreted as characteristic of planned settlements (Roberts 1982). Similarly uniform arrangements of strips, furlongs and parish boundaries have been used as evidence for planned landscapes, and in examples that range in scale and detail from the sharing of resources between multiple vills, to the order of open field strips and crofts within a single township (Harvey 1978; Harrison 2002). The interpretation of the origin of these arrangements also varies, from an inheritance of boundaries from prehistoric fields to land allocation schemes devised by Norse colonisers (Harvey 1983). The consistent theme remains that regular landscapes must result from deliberate planning and laying out of boundaries. The following chapters set out to investigate the reliability of that presumption.

Part 1

Reassessing relict field systems

CHAPTER ONE

'Rough grids': prehistoric boundaries and 'ancient' fields

In *The Making of the English Landscape*, Hoskins explained that the underlying structure of the modern countryside has been inherited from the early medieval or Saxon period. However, by the late 1970s this understanding of the development of field, village and road patterns was being challenged by archaeologists and historians who identified landscapes both small and large that they believed contained the fossilised traces of ancient systems of land division. Since then, so-called 'relict field systems' – that is, traces of prehistoric and Roman patterns of land division that survived into the medieval and modern landscape – have been identified all over lowland England, comprising apparently regular and frequently grid-like patterns of boundaries, tracks and roads (Christy 1926, 85–100; Rodwell 1978, 89–98; Williamson 1987, 419–31). The characteristic relict field system extended across large areas encompassing numerous parishes, providing further confirmation of their great antiquity by being unaffected by medieval territorial divisions. Many examples were apparently identified through their disharmonious relationship with a Roman road or other dated linear feature, which cut through the field pattern at an awkward angle, providing a *terminus post quem* for the establishment of the relict landscape (Rodwell 1978, 93).

In locations where there is no conveniently datable feature in the vicinity, the origin period for the relict field systems has been established through morphological comparison with known prehistoric fields (Bryant *et al.* 2005, 15). As a result, the historical understanding of relict field systems is closely aligned with archaeological research into prehistoric fields; the examination and interpretation of the archaeological evidence has been extrapolated and applied to analogous landscape patterns that have been identified in the modern landscape. The importance of prehistoric fields to the understanding and development of the subsequent study of relict field systems is such that this chapter will begin with a review of prehistoric fields before examining the historiography of relict field systems in the British Isles, particularly those found in lowland England.

The first farmers who established permanent settlements in what would become England, did so within a landscape that had already been altered by human activity. Mesolithic hunter-gatherer societies manipulated their landscape to attract prey species and increase the likelihood of a successful hunt. This they could only have achieved with a thorough understanding of the natural environment they inhabited. Early farmers developed, and ultimately passed on, an even more detailed knowledge of the environmental influences that affected their territories and how to successfully manipulate them in order to prosper, if only because they remained in one place for longer (Fowler 1981, 2).

Despite the profound influence of humans on the English landscape during the Neolithic period, there is very little physical evidence of farms for the first millennia after farming arrived in Britain. Evidence obtained from ethnobotanical investigations does provide some insight and indicates that there was a dramatic change in flora after settled farming was introduced. Unfortunately, no evidence for fields, whether pasture or arable have been found in relation to the few Neolithic farmsteads and villages that have been identified (Fowler 1981, 8). It is likely that early arable fields were impermanent, regularly shifting when the soil nutrients were exhausted, or the land became infested with weed species. No fences were required to keep domesticated livestock out of the arable fields; they could simply be tethered or grazed at a distance from the arable land and overseen by a herdsman (Fowler 1981, 8).

Prehistoric fields

The oldest known physical field boundaries in Northern Europe are the Neolithic stone walls found in Co. Mayo, Ireland. In England the earliest prehistoric fields date to the Bronze Age. An early example of surviving anciently farmed landscape is visible in the field lynchets found across the chalk downs of Southern England. These have been dated to the Middle Bronze Age and are evidence for fields becoming increasingly permanent (Fowler 1981, 8). Field lynchets are created by regular and repeated ploughing along the same alignment on the side of a slope. Over many years the action of the plough gradually caused the edge of the upper field to bank up and simultaneously the lower field was cut away leading to the creation of a scarp. The gradual development of the lynchet reduces the overall slope of both fields and eventually the field pattern comes to resemble the deliberate terracing of a hill side, but it is generally considered to be an unavoidable consequence of ploughing across a slope (Fowler 1981, 108).

The development of field lynchets provides several significant pieces of information about the land use of the area during the period in which they formed. The first is that the field was regularly being ploughed, which indicates that it was being used for arable cropping and the second, that a fixed boundary line between the two parcels either predated the ploughing or was contemporary with it (Fowler 1981, 108). As a lynchet is created through repeated ploughing to the same border it can only be created once a field boundary is permanent (Bowen 1978, 117). As the earthwork was formed by repeatedly ploughing along a slope up to a pre-determined point, a lynchet could therefore be formed during any historical period. The notion that prehistoric fields in part, preserve earlier organisation and one apparently without physical boundaries will be discussed later in this chapter.

The prehistoric fields found on the South Downs sometimes form regular sub-rectangular patterns, frequently described as a 'cohesive' arrangement. The apparent regularity of these patterns convinced scholars that they originated from societal planning, but to early observers at least they did not argue for great antiquity (Crawford and Keiller 1928, 10). By contrast, irregular patterns of boundaries, forming so called 'aggregate' field systems, were consistent with ideas of piecemeal enclosure and this was supported by early origin dates provided by archaeological excavation of the features and associated settlement sites (Fleming 1988, 112). 'Cohesive' field systems provide the models for supposed relict field systems, as well as the distinctive prehistoric boundary patterns exemplified by the so-called Dartmoor 'reaves'.

Although the long stone walls of the Dartmoor reaves have been visible for millennia, the first records of interest in early field systems on Dartmoor date from the early nineteenth century. In 1825 Thomas Northmore published several articles on the discovery of the reaves in Dartmoor, in which he identified the regular pattern of stone walls as ancient boundary features. Although Northmore was unsure of their date, his collaborator the Rev John Pike argued that they had very early origins on the basis of their physical relationship with standing stones and other prehistoric archaeology (Fleming 2008, 20–1). This early flurry of interest in Dartmoor's regular stone field walls waned and the subject declined in popularity, with little notice being paid to these curious features again until the 1970s.

So little notice that when Andrew Fleming discovered the reaves in 1972, he was unaware of any previous research (Fleming 2008, 7). He independently came to many of the same conclusions as Northmore and Pike and suggested that the reaves were an extensive system of prehistoric land division, embracing much of Dartmoor. Like Pike, Fleming was aware there was little evidence of Roman activity on the high moorland. Furthermore, he argued – like Pike before him – that the physical relationship between the reaves and nearby prehistoric monuments meant that they must be contemporary, and that the reaves were therefore of Bronze Age date. Fleming also emphasised the relationship between the reaves and the natural landscape and topography. The earliest elements of the reave system were the stone walls that were found to maintain a roughly level path along the hillside as if they were following a contour line. Above this 'terminal' reave, as Fleming called it, was open moor and below the enclosed landscape of parallel stonewalls. The 'terminal reave' was the end point of the 'axial reaves', again Fleming's terminology. The axial reaves began at the watercourse to which they were set at right angles; from the stream they took a direct path up the hill slope until they met the terminal reave. The relationship between the axial reave and the terminal reave was also perpendicular and the importance of the angle was such that some of the long axial reave walls even contained a kink in their course to enable them to meet both the watercourse and terminal reave at a right angle. Other reaves appeared to ignore the local topography entirely in their path between the start and end point, cutting across valleys and streams and even the deep fissure of the Dart Gorge in order to maintain a straight path between river and terminal reave. The reaves, in Fleming's words, were 'terrain oblivious' (Fleming 2008, 29).

Fleming described the parallel pattern of the axial reaves as 'co-axial' (Fleming 2008, 29). Further analysis identified several discrete co-axial systems running up onto Dartmoor. The morphological similarity between them convinced Fleming that all the reave systems originated from a single planning decision; one that illustrated cooperation between neighbouring prehistoric communities (Fleming 1988, 50). An organic development of the reave systems over time, Fleming concluded, would not have produced so regular an arrangement of divisions (Fleming 1988, 67). He considered that the regularity of the reaves itself constituted evidence for planning, for how could a system that developed in an organic and piecemeal way eventually appear so consistent in layout (Fleming 1988, 60)? However, he also noted that if the separate reave systems were not exactly contemporary, it was likely that the presence of a nearby pre-existing boundary would influence the alignments of the neighbouring reaves (Fleming 1988, 50).

The purpose of the reaves is not well understood. Dartmoor certainly enjoyed a more favourable climate in prehistory, which would have encouraged settlement and farming at a higher altitude than would be viable today. There is also some evidence that the reave systems were not limited to the areas of moorland but had originally extended in places onto what was now enclosed farmland at lower altitudes. Fleming identified modern field boundaries that appeared to align with the upland reaves (Fleming 2008, 71). The deterioration in climate from the later Bronze Age, combined with a reduction in soil quality, is likely to have caused a reduction in settlement activity on the moor.

During the medieval period many parishes in Devon had rights to upland grazing on the moor. It is possible that the co-axial alignments preserved by the reaves originated as features in a landscape of transhumance, but as Fleming noted the stone walls would have hindered transit from valley to upland (Fleming 1988, 70). Instead, Fleming suggested that the reave fields were enclosed to allow arable production within a wider grazing landscape. Fleming considered but dismissed the argument that the reaves resulted from cultural change with regard to private property rights in the Bronze Age, as he noted that some of the enclosures bounded by the reaves contained groups of hut circles. Fleming further concluded the construction of the reaves was evidence against the fields being private territories, as only a community of shared resources could have cooperated to construct the Dartmoor reaves (Fleming 1988, 64).

Although the purpose of the reaves is still subject to debate, their regularity of form as proof of prehistoric planning is widely accepted, although there are some critics of this conclusion, particularly Johnston, which will be discussed later in the chapter (Fleming 2008, 1–21). Fleming believed that there was a grand plan of reaves to cover the moorland and beyond, which in places was never fully realised. The original layout, Fleming suggested, was eventually found to be too complex, required too much labour and ran into conflict with neighbouring territories (Fleming 2008, 136).

In Co. Mayo in the Republic of Ireland, a morphologically similar field system was being excavated at the same time that Fleming was rediscovering the reaves. It too had suffered abandonment when the climate and soil became less favourable, but unlike Dartmoor where the reaves remained visible in the grazing landscape, in Co. Mayo the whole system had been buried under several metres of peat. The Behy/Glenrulha field system is now more commonly known as the Céide Fields. It is a co-axial field system comprised of stone boundary walls running upslope from the modern cliff edge. The field walls have been found to extend at least 800 m up the hillside and possibly much further: as they still lie beneath the peat, with only a few small sections of the walls that have been excavated and left exposed, their full extent is unclear, although partially revealed by careful probing through the peat and the excavation of keyhole trenches. This revealed an arrangement of co-axial walls, each separated by between 150 to 200 m and with an overall morphology that is strikingly similar to that of the Dartmoor reave systems (Caulfield 1978, 138). The Céide Fields, although on a much smaller scale than the Dartmoor systems, also contain similar evidence for transverse field walls, hut circles and funerary monuments lying within the wider regular landscape (Caulfield 1978, 142). The Behy/Glenrulha field system was initially dated to the Neolithic period, although recently it has been suggested that it might be significantly younger (Whitefield 2017, 273).

In Co. Mayo the overlying peat has preserved the Neolithic soil *in situ*. Analysis has shown that there is evidence for widespread burning before the stone boundary walls were built, implying the clearance of woodland (Caulfield 1978, 138). Soil analysis also indicated that the walls were constructed, and the fields utilised, within a pastoral landscape with no evidence for crop production or ploughing. Archaeologist Seamus Caulfield concluded that the Céide Field System must have been associated with stock farming which in the warmer climate of the late Neolithic could have supported a relatively large local population. Caulfield suggested that the walled fields allowed selective livestock breeding to take place and facilitated rotational grazing management both probably associated with cattle farming. Caulfield interpreted the fields as belonging to a society with very high levels of agricultural sophistication (Caulfield 1978, 200).

Like Fleming, Caulfield concluded that the regularity of the Céide Field System could not have originated organically but must have been planned in a single event (Caulfield 1983, 200). Caulfield noticed that local topography strongly influenced the course of the stone walls, which run directly up slope just as they do on Dartmoor. Caulfield, like Fleming, considered the suggestion that the stone walls were built to separate individual private farmsteads, but like Fleming dismissed it on the basis that the construction of the local mortuary monuments found in some of the enclosures would have required the cooperation of the whole community (Caulfield 1983, 200).

Only 7 km from the Céide Field System lies a contemporary field pattern that had a strikingly different morphology. This system, called Belderg Beg, is much less extensive than the cliff top fields and topographically the sites are very different, with the Belderg Beg fields being located within a sheltered hollow. But they were covered with many metres of peat that preserved the former soil surface and the stone field walls just as it has on the upland Céide Fields site. The layout of the two systems differs significantly: while the Céide Fields are an example of a 'cohesive' field pattern, the irregular enclosures of Belderg Beg are 'aggregate' in character. Further analysis of the irregular field system found evidence for crop production at Belderg Beg including plough marks and lazy (raised) beds (Caulfield 1978, 140). When considered in combination, the differences between the sites raised many questions and Caulfield suggested that the Neolithic agricultural landscape in Co. Mayo might have incorporated specialist farms focused on different forms of production (Caulfield 1983, 200).

In the 1970s archaeological excavations at Flag Fen, near Peterborough on the edge of The Fens, proved that evidence of Neolithic land organisation could survive in lowland Britain. The wetland environment on the fen edge had preserved evidence of the earlier landscape. Unsurprisingly in a region prone to waterlogging the Neolithic boundaries were formed by ditches. The spine of the landscape was a ditched drove-way that led down the very muted slope to the contemporary fen edge, which it met at right angles. The wider landscape contained only a few other field boundaries, but these all ran parallel to the drove-way. Studies of the preserved pollen found in the peat indicated that the surrounding landscape was pastoral with no evidence for crop production. Francis Pryor interpreted the Neolithic landscape of Flag Fen as one of transition between the higher ground that would provide drier pasture in the winter and the summer grazing on the fen (Pryor 2013, 406).

In addition to the Neolithic drove-ways Flag Fen also contained Bronze Age field systems. These were found on a slightly different alignment to the earlier Neolithic landscape. Like the Neolithic landscape the Bronze Age drove-ways and boundaries were arranged at right angles to the contemporary fen edge and travelled up the slight slope leading to drier ground (Pryor 2013, 408). The Bronze Age field system at Flag Fen was far more extensive than the Neolithic arrangement, including many more boundaries and drove-ways. Although Bronze Age field systems were found at other sites Pryor was investigating near Peterborough at the time, none of these were found to contain evidence for Neolithic field boundaries or lanes, suggesting that the Bronze Age saw an increasing intensity of land use in the area (Pryor 2013, 406). Palaeobotanical analysis of the pollen preserved in the waterlogged ditches included some evidence for cereal production in the Bronze Age although the levels found do not suggest a substantial amount of arable production in the vicinity. The discovery of a complex landscape of drove-ways and associated features at Storeys Bar, which lay on the edge of the Flag Fen basin, led Pryor to conclude that this was evidence of a sophisticated stock handling system, intended to facilitate husbandry of the animals as they were moved from the summer grazing on the fen to the winter pasture grounds (Pryor 2013, 414). His conclusions mirrored those of Caulfield in Ireland, albeit for a later date, envisaging a society where livestock equated to wealth and perceiving the establishment of co-axial boundaries as an element of a livestock management system (Pryor 2013, 401).

Following the publication of the archaeological research from the 1970s and 80s discussed above, there was an increase in discoveries of organised prehistoric field systems that led to what Fleming described as a 'cornucopia of co-axials' (Fleming 2008, 159). In 1999 David Yates summarised the results of numerous archaeological excavations, which showed that during the Bronze Age co-axial arrangements were common along the alluvial terraces of the Thames and its tributaries (Yates 1999, 157). Yates noted that the prehistoric fields that lay inland and upstream of the river Thames appeared to be focused upon rearing of livestock and Yates concluded that the co-axial boundaries were used to manage stock possibly in a manner similar to that proposed by Pryor for the Flag Fen landscape. By contrast several of the co-axial systems identified further downstream appeared to be associated with the production of flax into textiles, although Yates suggested that these sites lay within a wider pastoral landscape. This suggests that the Thames Valley may have contained at least two distinct agricultural systems, utilising morphologically similar field systems. The archaeological excavations in the Thames Valley also provided evidence for a variety of boundary types, variously featuring fences, ditches and banks, hedges and hurdles (Yates 1999, 165). The full extent of fields was determined at only a few sites, and in common with many other prehistoric farming landscapes the enclosures were found to be small with the largest parcel being around a hectare in size (Yates 1999, 166).

Yates also noted that while the field systems dated from the Bronze Age, there was no evidence that they all fitted into an overarching plan. Yates concluded that the co-axial systems found in the Thames Valley had originated as individual systems created by the separate communities that lived along the banks of the river (Yates 1999, 158). The sites did not share the same alignment, and the few plans included by Yates indicate that the Bronze Age boundaries were arranged perpendicular to the river, thus repeating the relationship with watercourses seen at Flag Fen and on Dartmoor. In the Thames Valley Yates also found evidence that pre-existing barrows appeared to have been used as sightlines when positioning the boundaries (Yates 1999, 160). A similar arrangement had been observed by Pryor at Flag Fen (Pryor 2013, 412).

As noted previously the regularity of the prehistoric field boundaries led to the conclusion that they originated as planned agricultural landscapes, albeit in most cases on a relatively small scale. The Dartmoor reaves extend over large areas of the moor but in places the surviving prehistoric stone walls are fragmentary with large gaps within the field system. Evidence for other prehistoric field systems is at a much smaller scale than those found on Dartmoor. The animal handing system and causeway at Flag Fen covered less than a square kilometre, and the Thames-side sites were even smaller. The prehistoric fields within were also small, typically covering a hectare or less (Yates 1999, 166).

The major discoveries of the prehistoric fields on Dartmoor were located on marginal land long since abandoned for arable farming, while the paddocks and drove-ways found at Flag Fen had been preserved beneath wetland, another environment with limited agricultural activity. The better soils of lowland England had been farmed for hundreds of years and therefore it was presumed that evidence for earlier field systems had been lost through centuries of cultivation (Rodwell 1978, 90).

The first relict field systems

In the early twentieth century Miller Christy identified a collection of 15 long narrow parishes lying side by side between Dagenham and Downham in Essex, that were cut through by a road of probable Roman origin. In this regular arrangement Christy perceived the fragmentary remains of an early system of landscape organisation. Knowing that Essex was an area of early Roman colonisation, Christy attributed the pattern to the surviving remnants of Centuriation, the regulated division of vast agricultural landscapes seen in other countries occupied by Rome. Christy was further convinced that the only possible source of a regular landscape in Essex must be Roman. He considered that 'any Essex road which runs … quite straight for as much as three miles, especially if accompanied by parish boundaries, was a road of Roman origin' comparing them to the otherwise irregular patterns of boundaries and lanes in the county (Christy 1926, 90).

In the late nineteenth century Flinders Petrie had proposed a method of examining the English countryside by identifying and then comparatively dating its component features. This methodology he called 'Landscape Stratigraphy'. Its development rested on the easy availability of relatively large-scale maps, recently produced by the Ordnance Survey. The 6-inch and 25-inch surveys, in particular, revealed relationships between features that would have been difficult to discern when viewed on the ground. In a muted lowland landscape, in particular, it is difficult to find a viewpoint from which it is possible to see a large area of field boundaries. The influence of the Ordnance Survey maps, if not that of Petrie himself, is clear when reading Christy's work, one article for example describing in detail how two roads that lay 3 miles apart ran parallel for 10 miles (Christy 1926, 97). In the gently undulating countryside of north Essex, this relationship would be extremely difficult to discern without using a map.

To support his argument for Centuriation, Christy highlighted that a Roman road appeared to split into six branches that then fanned out to spread across the Dengie peninsula and which in many cases were subsequently followed by parish boundaries. The straight form of these roads confirmed their Roman origin to Christy, who postulated that they were constructed both to provide access to the wheat producing clay lands and the coastal grazing marshes of the peninsula (Christy 1926, 91).

Little interest in Christy's approach was shown by archaeologists until the later decades of the twentieth century when research once again focused on the county of Essex and revisited some of his findings, utilised his general methodology, and added important new forms of enquiry. In an article published in the late 1970s, Warwick Rodwell noted that a relatively regular layout of fields and local roads found between Braintree and Kelvedon in Essex appeared to be 'slighted' by a Roman road (Rodwell 1978, 93). The Roman road cut obliquely across a landscape of small sub-rectangular fields, dividing the regular parcels into potentially inconvenient enclosures. Rodwell concluded that this relationship was only plausible if the construction of the Roman road post-dated the layout of the fields, as farmers would surely avoid establishing field boundaries that created inconvenient parcels of land (Drury and Rodwell 1980, 62). This 'slighting' of the field system by the Roman road provided the *terminus ante quem*, the last date that the field boundaries could have been laid out before the line of the road could have influenced the arrangement. On this basis Rodwell concluded that the field boundaries had been established 'in or by the late Iron Age' (Drury and Rodwell 1980, 62).

The underlying pattern of field and parish boundaries and roads between Kelvedon and Braintree was morphologically similar to the prehistoric reaves on Dartmoor although they covered a much larger area than any of the individual reaves systems. In Essex groups of rectilinear fields abutted onto long sinuous axial boundaries or roads that ran upslope, resembling individual reaves that had been subdivided to create smaller enclosures. The parish boundaries in the area followed the same co-axial path to the watershed and created the sub-rectangular territories that Christy had identified in the early twentieth century (Rodwell 1978, 97). Rodwell and Drury also concluded that the regularity of the underlying arrangement of long co-axial boundaries was evidence that features of a planned prehistoric agricultural landscape had survived through millennia of farming, becoming what they called a relict field system. They further concluded that although the fields had been abandoned for intensive agricultural production in the fourth century the landscape must have remained open for the boundaries to survive (Drury and Rodwell 1980, 62).

Not all relict landscapes in Essex were, however, of prehistoric date. Decades after Christy first noticed the grid-like layout of fields and lanes, Rodwell also concluded that the rectilinear arrangement of roads and fields in south Essex indicated that elements of an earlier boundary pattern had survived and been fossilised into the modern landscape. The layout of roads and field boundaries on the Dengie peninsula created a 'rough' grid pattern morphologically distinct from the prehistoric fields found on Dartmoor (Williamson 2016, 9). The landscape was divided into sub-square parcels and differed from the characteristic brickwork pattern of narrow sub-rectangular fields found between Braintree and Kelvedon. A similar arrangement of square fields was found around Thurrock to the south. Archaeological excavations within the field systems showed that Roman and early Saxon features appeared to be situated within the framework, leading Rodwell to conclude that the two morphologically similar systems in Dengie and Thurrock must date from the Roman occupation (Rodwell 1978, 64).

Although Rodwell was sure that this landscape pattern was not the result of Centuriation, he concluded that the square fields found in south Essex must have been laid out within imperial Roman estates (Rodwell 1978, 93). Rodwell did not explain why the Romans did not import the system of Centuriation to Britain nor why they chose to invent a separate form of land apportionment for the imperial estates of south Essex. Notably, Oliver Rackham, who did much to promote relict field systems in his book *The History of the Countryside*, suggested that the Romans did not impose Centuriation in Britain because the subdivided agricultural landscape was already in existence before their arrival (Rackham 1986, 160).

Rodwell and Drury's identification of relict field systems in Essex in the late 1970s was eagerly taken up by historians interested in landscape. As noted above perhaps most significantly by Oliver Rackham, whose book *The History of the Countryside* discusses the Essex fields in detail before also moving on to another famous example of a relict field system.

During the 1980s more relict field systems were identified, some in upland regions such as those in Swaledale and on the Isle of Jura, but many more in the lowlands (Fleming 2008, 164). A particularly extensive system of field boundaries, called the Scole–Dickleburgh field system, was found on the boulder clay plateau of south Norfolk. Following systematic landscape regression analysis, Tom Williamson demonstrated that many of the field boundaries and lanes within the area shared a north–south orientation (Williamson 2016, 421). Williamson noted how the pattern of co-axial boundaries appeared to be unconnected to the medieval settlement pattern and crucially the lanes that linked the settlements did not conform to the regular landscape. Furthermore, there was evidence that some medieval features appeared to be located so that they blocked or otherwise diverted the north–south axial boundaries, which was curious in a layout whose regularity otherwise indicated deliberate organisation. Through his analysis Williamson suggested that the arrangement of fields 'did not evolve from the gradual expansion of cultivation from medieval settlements' (Williamson 1987, 421). By comparing his regressed landscape with surviving early maps, Williamson concluded that the underlying landscape framework had survived despite piecemeal alterations over the centuries (Williamson 1987, 425). The extensive organised landscape was 'slighted' by the Roman Pye Road (the modern A140) leading from *Venta Icenorum* to Coddenham. Furthermore, the Scole–Dickleburgh field system contained clear morphological similarities with known prehistoric field systems. The long, sinuous axial boundaries progressing from the Waveney Valley in the south, to the watershed in the north, resembled the layout of the Dartmoor reaves and they also shared a similar relationship to the broad sweeps of the local topography (Williamson 1987, 426).

Several commons within the Scole–Dickleburgh field system appeared to post-date the laying out of the boundaries, as they blocked the axial boundaries and tracks, suggesting that some commons and land use as well as field boundaries were subject to small scale alteration over the centuries. As with other relict field systems in the lowlands the longevity of the boundaries was underlined by their use in forming the divisions between parish territories. The parish boundaries followed lanes and field divisions and by joining, following and then leaving the lane, ditch or hedged field they indicated that the boundary feature preceded the parish territory (Williamson 1986, 245). As limited evidence for Bronze Age settlement had been found on the boulder clay plateau of south Norfolk, this argued against the field system being contemporary with the Dartmoor reaves, despite the morphological similarity. Williamson dated the relict landscape around Scole–Dickleburgh to no later than the late Iron Age due to the relationship of the Roman Pye Road (Williamson 1987, 429).

Lying close to the Scole–Dickleburgh field system in north Suffolk, around South Elmham, is a separate rectilinear field system that Rackham dated to the Bronze Age. His conclusion was based upon the morphological similarity to the Dartmoor reaves, with Reave walls replaced by hedges (Rackham 1986, 156). Rackham considered that the Roman Stane Street had been 'insinuated' into the field system along one of the co-axial boundaries (Rackham 1986, 156).

In 1997 Williamson's interpretation of the Scole–Dickleburgh system was challenged by David Hinton, which prompted Williamson's reconsideration of his relict landscape in south Norfolk (Hinton 1997; Williamson 1998). Instead of a complex arrangement of rectilinear fields arising from a single planning event, Williamson now saw the infilling of minor boundaries between 'sub-parallel lanes' that led from the valley to the watershed (Williamson 1998, 25). These routes were slightly sinuous but followed a predominately direct course. Relating this to Everitt's 'river and wold' model, Williamson proposed that these were originally transhumance tracks leading to wood pasture (Williamson 1998, 26). Moreover, similar patterns of sub-parallel lanes persisted across the lowland woodland region, influencing the form of territorial arrangements and parish boundaries. Williamson further noted that, if apparently co-axial landscapes of parallel boundaries and lanes could have arisen as a series of tracks leading from valley to distant upland resources, this raised doubts about using datable landscape features as evidence for a *terminus post quem*. A Roman road, which may hinder the laying out of fields, is of little concern to a transhumance route (Williamson 1998, 26). In Scole–Dickleburgh while the sub-parallel lanes might overlook an inconvenient Roman road, Williamson noted that the watershed boundaries were often the terminus for the axial boundary. He concluded that this indicated that the Scole–Dickleburgh system responded to possible pre-existing territories in much the same way as prehistoric field systems in Wessex and Dartmoor (Williamson 1998, 26).

Williamson's reassessment of the landscape of south Norfolk led him to propose that the modern field system was the result of a wider landscape framework that had developed organically and was formed by the fossilisation of late prehistoric transhumance routes, which linked the valley communities to distant resources (Williamson 1998, 27). Maintaining his initial conclusion that the basic framework of the landscape was in place by the later Iron Age, Williamson reiterated that the arrangement visible today resulted from centuries of piecemeal alteration, which added, removed and altered boundaries (Williamson 1998, 21). Furthermore, the survival of the wider field pattern until modern times indicates that its form, whether slighted or not, did not render it completely impractical for agricultural use.

The continued utilisation of older features within a relict field system was further illustrated by two investigations in south Hertfordshire. The survival of transhumance routes as roads and field boundaries was a feature of both systems and in both examples the parish boundaries joined and departed from the roads, indicating the track preceded the boundary in the landscape (Williamson 1986, 245). The Hertfordshire relict landscapes were far more compact that the examples previously discussed in Essex, Norfolk and Suffolk. In scale they were closer to the prehistoric reave groups on Dartmoor, although they dwarfed the ancient paddocks and drove-ways of Flag Fen.

The relict landscape preserved in and around a large area of woodland near Wormley – partly as earthworks, partly as modern field boundaries – contained long ditched tracks that ran at right angles to the river Lea up onto the watershed at the western edge of the parish (Bryant *et al.* 2005, 5). These bounded drove-ways had, it was suggested, provided defined routes for moving livestock across unenclosed farmland between the river valley and upland pastures on the watershed (Bryant *et al.* 2005, 6). The field pattern gradually developed over time through piecemeal insertion of boundaries within the framework of drove-ways (Bryant *et al.* 2005, 14). Furthermore, there was evidence that the field system was altered and adapted to the needs of the community. Additional transhumance routes had been inserted into the landscape as well as field boundaries that had been slotted between the framework provided by the drove-ways over time (Bryant *et al.* 2005, 14).

This element of alteration was also evident at Arkley in the Hertfordshire parish of Ridge, investigated around the same time by Jonathan Hunn. Here once again a rectilinear, co-axial field system was laid out around a pattern of parallel tracks that led from the valley of the river Cole to the watershed. But there was an additional axis of equal strength running parallel to the valley following a route close to the 100-m contour (Hunn and Turner 2004, 116). The Arkley relict field system could not be dated using horizontal stratigraphy but the survival of some of the co-axial tracks as parish and hundred boundaries, together with the morphological similarity to both Scole–Dickleburgh and the Dartmoor reaves, led the author to conclude a prehistoric, Bronze or Iron Age origin (Hunn and Turner 2004). The framework of drove-ways and long parish boundaries in Arkley survived and continued to be used through the early medieval period. When farming returned to the area the field pattern developed piecemeal within the sparse landscape grid.

The infilling of an older, sparser pattern of lanes and boundaries was also a feature of the relict field system in the Arrow Valley in Herefordshire. Archaeological excavation of Late Iron Age and Romano-British settlements that lay close to the terraces of the river Arrow provided dating evidence for several apparently contemporary field ditches (White 2003, 44). Paul White noticed that the orientation of the prehistoric ditches, lying perpendicular to the watercourse, was seemingly shared by the modern field surrounding the site. This led White to conclude that the modern boundary pattern provided evidence of a wider relict field system dated to the late Iron Age (White 2003, 46). Conclusive dating evidence for the ditches was elusive, the earliest artefacts found in the main crosswise ditch was late medieval (White 2003, 45). Furthermore, the apparently regular field pattern broke down around areas of ancient woodland (White 2003, 75). No evidence was found for field boundaries within the woods, which indicated that the woodland must predate the development of the field boundaries. White concluded that the results of the excavations indicated that late prehistoric fields were subdivided during the medieval period, as they had been in the relict landscapes of Scole–Dickleburgh and Wormley (White 2003, 45).

Relict fields in the Midlands

During the medieval period, and into the early modern, travellers would have understood that the English Lowlands could be loosely categorised into two general landscape types. On the East and West sides of the country lay 'woodland' countryside, a landscape of scattered farmsteads and hamlets within early enclosed hedged fields which were interspersed with greens, commons and woods. This was the landscape Rackham called 'ancient' as he understood it to result organically from piecemeal enclosure and woodland assarts, and therefore contrasting with the post-medieval planned boundaries in the former open fields. The earliest discoveries of 'relict landscapes' were located within this 'woodland' zone where areas of semi-regular frameworks of lanes and boundaries were particularly visible within the otherwise characteristically irregular field pattern.

The second broad type of medieval countryside, often referred to as 'champion' or 'fielden', was a landscape of large open fields, nucleated villages, with few outlying hamlets and farmsteads and apparently few hedges, woods and commons, although as we shall see in later chapters this is something of a generalisation. The champion belt lay between the two woodland zones and extended diagonally across England from North Yorkshire to the South Downs. The enclosure history of champion countryside was arguably more truncated than woodland countryside: many Midlands parishes were entirely enclosed in the eighteenth and nineteenth centuries by Parliamentary Act. This officially sanctioned enclosure led to the re-planning of the earlier landscape of open field strips and furlongs into the straight sided, thorn hedged fields that are now typical of the Midlands landscape. Rackham called this countryside 'planned' and he presumed that any evidence of relict landscapes must have been destroyed then, if it had not already been swept away during the formation of the open fields (Brown and Foard 1998).

Working in Cambridgeshire in the 1970s, on the eastern fringes of the champion belt, Christopher Taylor and Peter Fowler found evidence that earlier ditches lay beneath some medieval open field headlands (Taylor 1978, 159) but it was not until 2006 that Susan Oosthuizen published the results of her research in the Bourn Valley, west of Cambridge. Oosthuizen had identified what appeared to be a planned relict field system that had survived the introduction of open field farming in the champion region (Oosthuizen 2006, 9). In her book, *Landscapes Decoded*, Oosthuizen persuasively argued that the valley landscape was deliberately laid out in the later Saxon period, but sometime before the tenth century when the field boundaries were used to form the hundred and county boundaries. Oosthuizen suggested that the Saxon relict field system also incorporated elements of a late prehistoric or Romano-British field pattern which lay in the same valley, making it an unusual two-phase field system (Oosthuizen 2006, 4). Oosthuizen described boundaries that formed the basis of the Saxon grid as either 'linear commons' or 'ancient alignments'. The former ran parallel to the river and watershed in much the same way as the terminal reaves in Dartmoor; the ancient alignments were arranged perpendicular to these, following the characteristic route from river to watershed and, Oosthuizen argued, reflected or preserved older boundaries (Oosthuizen 2006, 12). In conjunction the ancient alignments and linear commons formed a rough grid into which fields, furlongs and medieval settlements slotted (Oosthuizen 2006, 60). Oosthuizen's research into the regular landscape of the Bourn Valley was influential in expanding the search for relict field systems into the former champion countryside where it had been presumed little evidence would survive.

There had previously been suggestions that the open fields contained evidence for earlier field patterns although these tended to result from more conventional archaeological approaches. In particular, Stephen Upex investigated the fields within the Northamptonshire parish of Haddon (Upex 2002, 63). Through archaeological fieldwork he identified earlier ditch features under each of the five headlands that were excavated (Upex 2002, 17); the headlands lay near to a high concentration of early medieval pottery scatter (Upex 2002, 86). This he interpreted as evidence that 'the early medieval farmers had simply taken over' the Romano-British fields (Upex 2002, 87). Upex concluded that this cluster of comparatively small fields had continued in use during the early medieval period while the wider landscape was abandoned. Using morphological analysis Upex applied these conclusions to neighbouring parishes with similar clusters of small furlongs and concluded that there was widespread evidence for a level of post-Roman continuity in the area (Upex 2002, 90). A similar approach, combining morphological analysis with fieldwork and excavation, has been adopted on a much wider scale by Stephen Rippon, Chris Smart and Ben Pears in their book *The Fields of Britannia*, published in 2015, which summarised the results of the research project of the same name (Rippon *et al.* 2015, 17). This argued that the medieval landscape evolved within a 'framework inherited from the Romano-British countryside' (Rippon *et al.* 2015, 342). They further argued that the previous evidence for discontinuity between the fourth and sixth centuries has been overstated and life in the countryside continued much as before; and that a review of pollen evidence from a wide range of archaeological sites refuted the idea of widespread woodland regeneration, of any significant duration, in the immediate post-Roman period (Rippon *et al.* 2015, 101).

Of particular relevance to the subject of this discussion, however, was the way the Fields of Britannia project compared the layout of long buried field ditches revealed and dated by archaeological excavations with the neighbouring 'historic landscape', as depicted on the First Edition Ordnance Survey 6-Inch maps (Rippon *et al.* 2015, 100). The relationships between the relative alignments of the two features were classified into one of three groups:

- 'unrelated' where there was no similarity of orientation between the two features;
- 'oriented' where the excavated Romano-British feature shared an alignment with the historic landscape (within 5°), but there was direct correlation between the earliest boundary evidence and the nineteenth-century landscape;
- 'aligned' where the excavated Romano-British ditch shared the same alignment as the historic landscape, forming part of the modern boundary system.

The authors concluded that field systems of different periods that shared either orientation or alignment provided 'possible evidence for continuity', noting that ditches which are abandoned begin to silt up, but as long as the period of abandonment is relatively short, the authors suggest a few decades, the earthwork would remain visible (Rippon *et al.* 2015, 101).

The analysis of the boundaries in the Central Zone, an area which roughly corresponds with the champion belt, led the authors to conclude that '73 per cent of the excavated Romano-British field systems have a common orientation or alignment with historic landscape characteristic of former open fields' (Rippon *et al.* 2015, 330). Given these results it is unsurprising that the authors concluded that Romano-British fields directly influenced the medieval landscape.

Alternative arguments

Nevertheless, the suggestion that the English lowland landscape preserves, in places, Romano-British or prehistoric fields and boundaries has not gone unchallenged. Once again archaeological investigations of known prehistoric field systems have informed the discussion of relict landscapes and, in particular, the underlying presumption that regularity results from planning has been questioned. Prehistoric field systems have been re-examined and archaeological excavations have indicated that the Dartmoor reave walls preserve within them evidence for differing construction techniques along the path of single reaves (Johnston 2005, 8). This would appear to contradict the model of a planned layout as it suggests they developed over time rather than in a single event. Similar research in Ireland questioned the origin of the walls at Céide Fields where instead of the planned regular field boundaries, Molloy and O'Connell argued that the walls resulted from the stacking of stones that had been cleared from the fields (Molloy and O'Connell 1995, 222).

Returning to Dartmoor, the terminal reaves, the transverse walls which formed the upper boundary of the prehistoric field pattern, were found to have had great longevity in the landscape. These boundaries were recognised long before they became fossilised with the construction of the upstanding stone walls (Johnston 2005, 4). Johnston concluded that the Bronze Age terminal reaves formalised pre-existing landscape boundaries that may have formed at any time from the clearance of trees from Dartmoor during the Neolithic (Johnston 2005, 10).

Similar questions have been raised about the lowland relict field systems and in particular whether a regular pattern necessitates planning, or whether aligned boundaries could arise through the efficient utilisation of the local landscape and resources. At approximately the same time that Oosthuizen was writing her study of the Bourn valley, *Landscapes Decoded*, Sarah Harrison was investigating a group of long narrow parishes in south Cambridgeshire, only around 15 km away. Unlike Oosthuizen, Harrison did not interpret the regularity of the boundaries and lanes as proof of planning but instead as reflecting the daily concerns of the early society (Harrison 2002, 40). Tracks leading from the watercourse to watershed developed as 'resource linkage routes' allowing the population to make full use of their varied environmental assets (Harrison 2005, 123). These transhumance tracks both derived from the landscape, through their relationship to the local topography, and also formed the manmade framework into which the later open fields and territories developed.

The central importance of paths linking populations with more distant resources was further highlighted by Mark Gardiner in an analysis of transhumance in medieval England which argued that the practice was altered and adjusted as land use, settlement and farming developed. In particular Gardiner identified that the character of transhumance had transformed over the millennia between the sixth and sixteenth centuries (Gardiner 2018, 109). The earliest phase was characterised by populations utilising distant resources, with seasonally occupied farmsteads within a landscape containing relatively few people, settlements and fixed boundaries. This period also saw the beginning of the gradual shift as the seasonal settlements became permanent (Gardiner 2018, 111). Gardiner dated the commencement of the second phase of English transhumance to 900 CE and he argued that it is this stage that can be most easily traced in the landscape today, noting how early drove-ways have become fossilised as lanes, paths and boundaries (Gardiner 2018, 113). Gardiner further argued that the movement of livestock to areas remote from the vill during the summer months allowed arable cropping to take place in fields without the need for stock proof barriers. The final phase of English medieval transhumance was one of decline as the rights of settlements to access distant resources were restricted and lost in much of lowland England (Gardiner 2018, 115).

The relict field system in Dengie has also been re-examined by Tom Williamson and he re-interpreted the landscape framework as a 'rough grid' formed by the intersection of two sets of tracks linking resources. One axis followed the typical co-axial path as it led from the water course (in this case the estuaries) to the watershed, while the second linear component of the grid followed a path along the peninsula and appeared to be lanes linking inland settlements to seasonal 'wicks' or farmsteads on the salt marshes at the far eastern coast of the promontory (Williamson 2016, 9). Within this organically derived, but somewhat regular grid, field boundaries were added, altered and removed over many centuries (Williamson 2016, 10). Williamson further noted that the grid appeared to disappear as it passed through ancient woodland indicating that the wooded areas predated the boundaries (Williamson 2016, 7).

As touched upon previously in 1997 David Hinton re-examined the Scole–Dickleburgh landscape. This resulted in Hinton challenging two underlying tenets of relict field systems; namely that landscape stratigraphy can be used to date the boundaries, and that the survival of the field pattern provides evidence for continuous agricultural exploitation (Hinton 1997). Hinton's rejection of a prehistoric origin prompted Williamson's own reassessment of the field pattern discussed above.

Also working in East Anglia, Martin and Satchell suggested that many of the region's so-called relict field systems were not survivals of prehistoric features but associated with early medieval agriculture. They noted that Williamson had suggested the field system in the Elmhams was likely to have originated before the breakdown of the multiple estate in the early medieval period, far later than the Bronze Age date proposed by Rackham (Williamson 1987, 158). Martin and Satchell concluded that the vast Scole–Dickleburgh field system was not a single planned unit as Williamson had originally suggested, but a conglomeration of numerous smaller individual patterns which all shared a similar alignment based upon the local drainage patterns (Martin and Satchell 2008, 216). This corresponded to Williamson's reassessment of his earlier interpretation discussed previously, which concluded that the field boundaries developed within a framework of earlier transhumance tracks. Turning their attention to Essex, Martin and Satchell further noted that where ditches had been excavated in the supposedly Romano-British field system around Thurrock in Essex, the pottery finds dated to the twelfth and thirteenth centuries (Martin and Satchell 2008, 215).

The challenges of dating relict landscapes had been noted by Williamson, who disagreed with Rackham's conclusion that field pattern in the Elmhams was of Bronze Age origin. Williamson used landscape stratigraphy to conclude that the system must postdate the construction of the Roman road, upon which it neatly aligns (Williamson 1986, 245). The problem of dating based upon a combination of morphology and landscape stratigraphy is highlighted by research into the Stonehenge landscape. In this area several prehistoric field systems that appear to be contemporary are found to variously respect, overlie, and occasionally both respect and overlie, the earlier linear features (Spratt 1991, 453).

While proponents of relict field systems have generally assumed that they indicate the continuous agricultural usage of the areas in question, in 2003 John Hunter suggested a strikingly alternative explanation. Reconsidering the relict landscape that lies between Braintree and Kelvedon in Essex, previously examined by Rodwell and Drury, Hunter noted that documentary sources indicated that the manor of Cressing Temple had, in fact, been carved out of unenclosed 'waste' from the mid-twelfth century following the grant of land to the Knights Templar in 1137 (Hunter 2003, 15). Hunter concluded that, if the long boundaries that formed the main elements of this relict landscape were indeed of pre-medieval origin, they must have survived as earthworks under the rough grazing and wood pasture while the land was 'waste', and then been re-used. Hunter argued that 'old boundaries filled with silt and leaf mould would be easier to re-establish than digging out new ones' and so the ancient ditches were reinstated to form the boundaries of the new intakes of land from the waste (Hunter 2003, 17). Hunter's conclusion directly questioned the general assumption that the survival of a relict field system is evidence of continuity of population. The supposed reuse of the prehistoric field boundaries in Cressing was not evidence of continuity of settlement but that the form and function of the older boundaries were both recognisable and perhaps more importantly, useful to the later farmers clearing the waste and establishing new fields (Hunter 2003, 7).

Conclusion

This chapter began with a brief discussion of prehistoric field systems surviving in 'archaeological' form, for their character has had a direct influence on how relict field systems have been identified and interpreted. In both cases, there has been a tendency to assume that regular boundary patterns could only arise as a result of large-scale landscape planning. Similarities of morphology have, moreover, been interpreted in chronological terms, with many of the early proponents of relict landscapes tending to date particular examples to the Bronze or Iron Ages. But the true extent of this morphological similarity has at times been somewhat superficial, for example there is little discussion about the relevance of scale. A key argument for giving certain relict field systems a prehistoric origin is that the regular field pattern extends across several parishes and, in some cases, into more than 100. Therefore, whoever planned and laid it out must have done so before these territorial units came into being. However, with the notable exception of the Dartmoor reaves, organised prehistoric field systems cover smaller areas, just a few hundred hectares, and not the many square kilometres covered by relict field systems. Furthermore, the individual enclosed parcels that made up the prehistoric field patterns tend to be much smaller than those commonly found in relict field systems.

The analysis of Gardiner, Williamson and Harrison in particular suggests an alternative origin for the somewhat regular pattern of boundaries occasionally visible on the First Edition Ordnance Survey 6-Inch maps. Instead of a deliberately planned landscape they argue that drove-ways linking settlements to distant resources established a sparse network of lanes or routes (Williamson 2016, 10; Gardiner 2018, 113). Their analysis suggests the regular field patterns developed organically through a combination of transhumance and piecemeal enclosure.

This interpretation has not, however, been regularly tested and in many contexts does not explain or provide a satisfactory justification of why certain landscapes contain an unusual regularity of long boundaries especially where they have an unconformable relationship with features such as Roman roads.

In the following chapters a number of the relict field systems discussed previously will be re-analysed using GIS mapping to place them within their topographic and environmental context, as well as incorporating recent archaeological fieldwork where available and the wider landscape. The techniques used to identify and date so-called relict landscapes will be examined, and how the debate has contributed to the understanding of the development of English lowland landscape. Consideration will also be given to the apparent longevity of the co-axial arrangement; the Dartmoor reaves system and co-axial fields of Co. Mayo are separated by two millennia. When this is further extrapolated into the world of relict landscapes, this extends the date into the Late Iron Age. What could have led to the creation of morphologically similar prehistoric field systems over such a long period of time?

CHAPTER TWO

The relict field systems in west Cambridgeshire

The previous chapter has illustrated how the identification and interpretation of relict landscapes in lowland England has, over the last 40 years, become hugely influential in understanding the history of the English countryside. More recently the Fields of Britannia project suggested that up to 70 per cent of post-medieval field boundaries across large swaths of lowland England were inherited from Romano-British field systems, evidence which contributes to debates around continuity of population and impact of migration to England following the withdrawal of the Roman Legions (Rippon *et al.* 2015).

This chapter addresses issues of how so-called relict landscapes are recognised, analysis of their construction or design and how they are dated, through a detailed study of a small area. The use of a case study provides an opportunity to address some of the broader questions relating to the morphology of historic landscapes and apply established methodologies such as 'landscape stratigraphy' in conjunction with modern techniques, particularly GIS mapping technology, utilising geological, topographic and LiDAR data and how this contributes to our understanding of how and why the pattern of fields, lanes and villages developed.

As mentioned in the previous chapter, Susan Oosthuizen's *Landscapes Decoded* has been influential particularly in highlighting the survival of relict landscapes in former champion areas, characterised by extensive open fields. Oosthuizen carried out a detailed analysis of a regular landscape pattern in the Bourn Valley in western Cambridgeshire, and through her interpretation of the boundaries and lanes concluded that the valley contained evidence for two planned landscapes, one of probable Late Iron Age origin, and the other laid out in the early medieval centuries.

Although not available to Oosthuizen during her research, the first decades of the twenty-first century saw a large-scale residential development of a new town located within the Bourn Valley. This provides an unusual opportunity to assess the archaeological evidence for planned landscapes over a large area of a well-known and important relict field system. Although the discussion of many relict field systems includes archaeological fieldwork, in most cases this evidence comes from small sites containing just a few trenches, rather than the large-scale rescue excavations that extended across the Cambourne new town Development Area.

Despite Oosthuizen's detailed description of the Bourn Valley field pattern, her analysis touched only briefly on environmental factors. These would have undoubtedly been of critical importance to any early farmers who lived in the valley and therefore this discussion will begin with an examination of the natural landscape, including the climate, topography and soil type before moving onto the archaeology.

Lying just to the west of the city of Cambridge is a roughly triangular area of higher ground (Figure 2.1). Cambridge lies at the easternmost point with the other two corners at Sandy in Bedfordshire in the southwest, and Godmanchester to the northwest. To the north and east the plateau is bounded by fenlands, and on the south and west by wide valleys of lowland rivers; on these three sides the contrast with the low-lying surrounds contributes to the sense of a distinct landscape even today, despite the elevation of the clay plateau reaching just 80 m OD at the highest point, barely a hillock in national terms. The plateau covers an area of approximately 260 square km and lies within the southeast Midlands, a region typically categorised as a landscape of open fields and nucleated villages. However, the area has a distinct character of its own, containing a mix of elements characteristic of both 'woodland' and 'champion' countryside. The triangular clay plateau is a visible island of higher ground within a predominately flat landscape; but if it once had a singular place-name of its own it has been lost. In *The Cambridgeshire Landscape*, Christopher Taylor

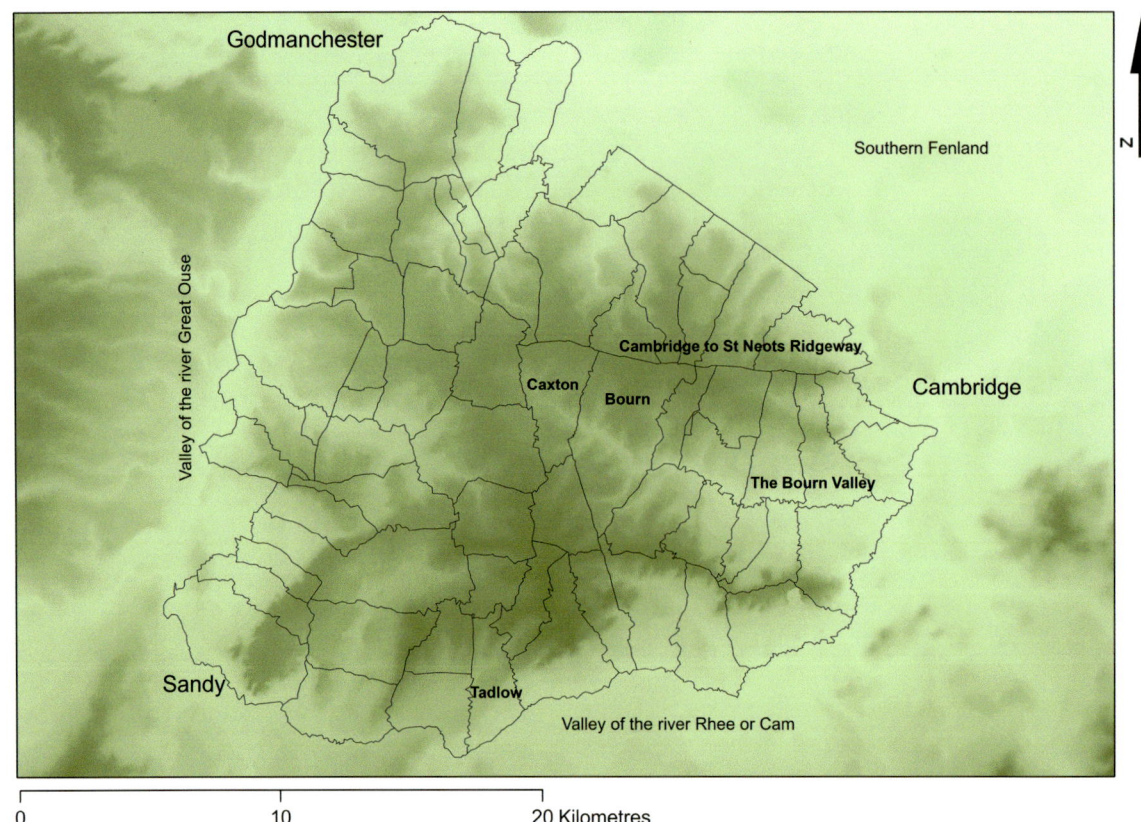

FIGURE 2.1. The topography and parishes of the West Cambridgeshire Clay Plateau Environment.

referred to that portion of the area lying within the county as the Western Clay Plateau (Taylor 1973, 24). Until the alteration of the English Counties in the 1970s the plateau was divided between three counties, Bedfordshire, Cambridgeshire and Huntingdonshire, with the majority of the land held within the latter two counties. The plateau is bounded by the river Great Ouse and two of its tributaries, the Ivel on the west and the river Rhee or Cam, sometimes Granta along the south. After leaving the Western Clay Plateau the river Great Ouse flows northeast into The Fens. The wide shallow valley of the river Rhee is formed by the clay plateau on the north and the chalk foothills of the East Anglian Heights to the south.

The principal soil type found on the plateau was formed from a surface deposit of boulder clay made at the end of the last glaciation, 10,000–12,000 years ago. This ubiquitous clay layer overlies and obscures a much more complicated solid geology, made up of three principal components that lie in bands of uneven widths with an approximately northeast–southwest orientation. Underlying the northwestern portion of the area and lying adjacent to the rivers Great Ouse and Ivel is the Kellaways formation, a mostly impermeable mix of siltstone, mudstone and sandstone bedrock that was laid down during the mid-Jurassic. Lying immediately to the south of the Kellaways formation is a zone of undifferentiated but predominately impermeable bedrock which dates from the mid to late Jurassic period, which includes the West Walton formation, Ampthill Clay formation, and Kimmeridge Clay formation (Landis 2020). Dividing the plateau into two unequal parts is the narrow band of Lower Greensand. This acidic bedrock takes a meandering route from Lolworth in the northeast, through Bourn and Great Gransden before outcropping in Gamlingay Heath and forming the Sand Hills in Sandy where it meets the river Ivel. The permeable Lower Greensand bedrock was laid down in the Cretaceous period and is made up of sand and sandstone; springs frequently arise where the permeable sands meet impermeable bedrocks, and in places this has also led to small areas of peat soils more typical of wetter environments.

Lying to the south of the Lower Greensand is a zone of the undifferentiated permeable and impermeable bedrocks of the Upper Greensand and Gault Clay. To make this area even more complex, there are also outcrops of alkaline Grey Chalk, another example of a permeable bedrock. The largest chalk outcrop forms the ridge between Haslingfield and Croydon, but there are other smaller outcrops to be found in the parishes lying closest to the city of Cambridge. In summary, the plateau bedrock is divided roughly in half, with impermeable clay bedrocks tending to lie to the north and west and more permeable bedrock underlying the land to the south and east.

As previously touched upon, the complexity of the bedrock underlying the plateau is in marked contrast to the simplicity of the surface geology, and by extension, soils. By far the most widespread soil type found upon the plateau is the Hanslope Association. This fertile clay tends to be located upon the higher ground and ridgetops and these sloping sites benefit from natural surface drainage. While in some areas of the country Hanslope soils can only be drilled in the autumn, the area between Cambridge and Bedford has the most continental climate in Britain, which, in addition to exposing it to extremes of temperature, makes it a very dry zone, drier even than parts of East Anglia, meaning spring cultivations are generally successful (Hodge 1984, 209).

The second principal Soil Association found within the area of the plateau is Evesham 3, and this is typically located in the valleys. The Evesham soils are rarely available for spring cropping even in this dry district. The clay land in the valleys reaches soil water capacity in the autumn and typically remains waterlogged until March or even April, too late for spring planting. Evesham soils can be successfully cultivated in the autumn but even in these months the field work window is much shorter than on the neighbouring Hanslope soils (Hodge 1984, 191).

The Hanslope and Evesham Associations cover the greater part of the plateau but on the chalk outcrop a thin band of fertile and easily worked, well drained loam of the Wantage Association (Hodge 1984, 342) lies between the Hanslope soils of the upper slopes and Evesham clays in the valley bottom. In the southwest of the plateau, the parishes closest to the Lower Greensand outcrop also contain loam soil types including Frilford and Bearstead 1 Associations, although all these light soils are particularly prone to summer doughtiness due to the dry climate (Hodge 1984, 199 and 115). The narrow strip of loams and gravels on the banks of the rivers Ivel and Great Ouse from Sandy to Hemmingford Grey have, in places, been used for market gardening from at least the seventeenth century.

The easily worked and fertile soils lying in the valleys of the rivers Great Ouse and Ivel, along the western and northern sides of the clay plateau, have long been attractive for human settlement. They also contain a concentration of ritual sites including several Neolithic cursus monuments as well as henges and the Sand Hills contain the earthwork remains of three Iron Age hill forts (Lock and Ralston 2017). Evidence for Roman settlement is also found along the banks of the rivers Ivel and Great Ouse. On the eastern side of the clay plateau there was evidence for a Roman fort at Grantchester, but with the notable exception of the Roman roads, particularly Ermine Street, and several potentially ancient roads identified by the Viatores there was, until recently, comparatively little evidence for prehistoric and Romano-British activity upon the clay plateau (Margary 1964, 264).

Archaeological fieldwork carried out over the last 20 years, principally on the long watershed that lies in the northern half of the Western Clay Plateau, between Cambridge and St Neots, has however found evidence for early farming, tracks and settlement. This extensive fieldwork was undertaken in advance of the building of new towns and roads and has shown that, despite a lack of visible evidence in the form of crop marks or surviving earthworks, the upper slopes of the clay valleys were being utilised and even settled from the Bronze Age into the Romano-British period (Wright *et al.* 2009, 65). Much of this information comes from the extensive archaeological investigations carried out prior to the building of the new town of Cambourne, located high on the southern side of the clay watershed that lies between Cambridge and St Neots mentioned previously and which was formed by the valleys of the Bourn brook and the river Great Ouse.

Archaeological excavations confirmed that the Ridgeway track that runs along the top of the watershed between Cambridge and St Neots, which has long been supposed to be ancient in origin, was indeed in use by the Bronze Age if not before (Wright *et al.* 2009, 65). Furthermore, farmsteads with occupation dates ranging from the Bronze Age to the late Romano-British period lay alongside the track, although the prehistoric houses were probably only inhabited seasonally (Albion Archaeology 2005, 26). The archaeological fieldwork has provided a clearer understanding of the occupation phases on the clay plateau and has in particular revealed that prehistoric and Romano-British settlement had not been limited to the river valleys as previously supposed but had extended onto the clay slopes.

The archaeological excavations on the upper slopes, close to the watershed, found that in the Bourn Valley the pattern of continuous habitation was disrupted at the end of the Romano-British period, and this is typical of the situation on the more challenging soils in England (Wright *et al.* 2009, 115). Archaeobotanical analysis of pollen grains and faunal remains found in wet or waterlogged conditions in former ditches suggested that the local vegetation changed towards the end of the Romano-British period with more grass species present and increased evidence for flora and fauna that favour damper environments, possibly implying that the local climate had become wetter (Wright *et al.* 2009, 115). Further evidence for a changing environment came from remains of hydrophilic snail species found within contemporary ditch deposits (Wright *et al.* 2009, 115). The environmental analysis found little evidence to indicate widespread woodland regeneration but there was an increase in the frequency of alder and hazel pollen, which points to an increase in the presence of woody shrubs on the slopes.

Relict field systems in the Bourn Valley

Lying immediately below the Ridgeway is the Bourn Valley, the area occupied by Susan Oosthuizen's relict field system. The brook or 'bourn' from which the valley gets its name travels roughly west to east for 26 km from Caxton to join the river Cam at Grantchester. On the north side of the brook the slope leads up to the area subject to many of the rescue excavations previously discussed and carried out prior to the building of Cambourne. On the south the valley side is formed from the curving outcrop of chalk, the surface geology changes from Hanslope Association soils on the hill-top and slopes to Evesham Association soils in the valley, although on the south there is the thin band of Wantage soils as previously discussed.

Oosthuizen's 2006 publication *Landscapes Decoded* remains one of the most detailed descriptions of a relict field system, its origins and its subsequent effect on the medieval farming systems and settlements. Oosthuizen's work has been particularly influential in highlighting that evidence of relict field systems can be found in former champion land – in the layout of furlongs – as well as by questioning whether the introduction of open field farming led to widespread re-planning of the countryside (Brown and Foard 1998). In addition to being a supporting cornerstone of debates around planned landscapes, Oosthuizen's dissection of the development of the Bourn Valley landscape has influenced interpretations of archaeological fieldwork, both locally and nationally. Oosthuizen's relict landscape is also unusual in that it contains elements from several periods, one of which is post-Roman (Oosthuizen 2006, 99).

Within the Bourn Valley, Oosthuizen noted the presence of numerous sub-linear tracks and boundaries that traversed the slopes between the brook and the watershed and appeared to lie roughly parallel to one another, following a rough north–south orientation (Oosthuizen 2006, 70–1). In particular she noted their morphological similarity with the pattern of upstanding prehistoric co-axial stone walls of the Bronze Age Dartmoor reaves, discussed previously (Oosthuizen 2006, 87). In West Cambridgeshire Oosthuizen interpreted this pattern of linear boundaries and tracks as the visible remnants of an Iron Age field system (Oosthuizen 2006, 87). The arrangement of north–south boundaries, which she variously termed either 'ancient alignments' or 'cross valley alignments' was, Oosthuizen suggested, originally based upon farmsteads spaced between 300 m and 1 km apart along the Bourn Valley (Oosthuizen 2006, 88). Oosthuizen concluded that the survival of these prehistoric divisions indicated that during the Romano-British period farming continued to be organised within the prehistoric field pattern, despite the increase in population and demand for greater agricultural production (Oosthuizen 2006, 88).

Oosthuizen concluded that the cross valley alignments that formed part of the Iron Age co-axial field system survived long enough to be incorporated into the Saxon proto-common field (Oosthuizen 2006, 93). This second planned farming landscape in the Bourn Valley was dated by Oosthuizen to have been laid out during the early medieval period. It comprised a system of long east–west narrow commons, that lay parallel to the watershed and incorporated the previously mentioned and north–south aligned ancient alignments as sub-divisions in the proto-common field. Taken together this creates the perpendicular arrangement of boundaries that formed a grid like landscape, a feature that is particularly noticeable on the lower valley slopes in Figure 2.2 (Oosthuizen 2006, 87). The 'linear commons' were fossilised in the long east–west boundary features, visible on the First Edition Ordnance Survey 6-Inch map and they met the cross valley alignments at approximately 90° as can be seen in Figure 2.2. An examination of several village plans that lay within the study area indicated that several small settlements appear to have developed or expanded along junctions of these north–south and east–west boundaries, creating a regular grid-like pattern of village lanes (Oosthuizen 2006, 60).

2. *The relict field systems in west Cambridgeshire* 29

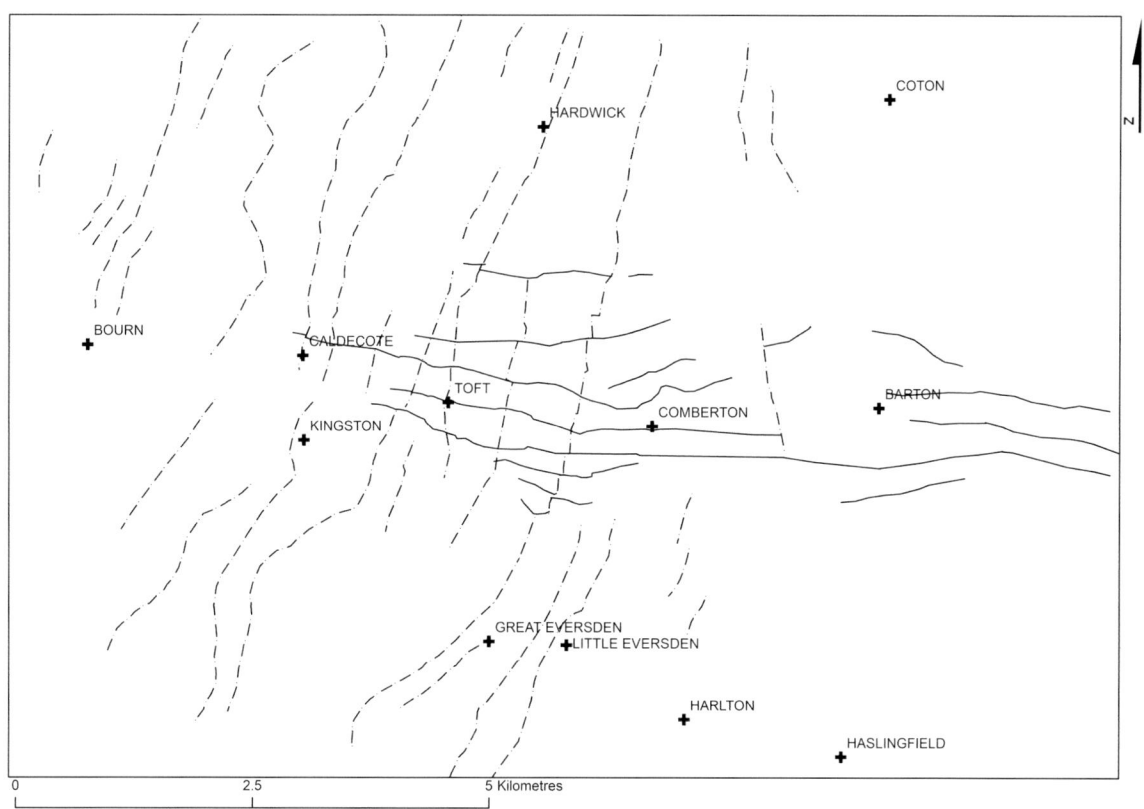

FIGURE 2.2. The 'ancient alignments' (north–south) and 'proto-common field' commons (east–west) in the Bourn Valley (after Oosthuizen 2006).

Oosthuizen concluded the east–west aligned linear commons were laid out as divisions between the fields in her putative early medieval proto-common field system (Oosthuizen 2006, 96). Oosthuizen argued that the long narrow greens had originally extended over 8 km and appeared to be deliberately spaced around 200 m apart (Oosthuizen 2006, 107). The scale of this arrangement indicated to Oosthuizen that the landscape must have been laid out in a single planned event (Oosthuizen 2006, 98). The intention of the layout, Oosthuizen concluded, was to allow intensive arable cultivation of the intervening fields, with the linear greens acting as drove-ways to allow regular movement of the livestock through the arable lands, and therefore encouraging manuring (Oosthuizen 2006, 108).

By considering local hundredal boundaries and more general histories of the Bourn Valley Oosthuizen concluded that the proto-common field system must have been established by the mid-ninth century at the latest. This was the last date when the valley was likely to be under single control, when it was held by the *Haeslinga* people, and the vestigial remains of their former large estate is still visible in the place-names of Haslingfield, Harlton, Hauxton and Harston (Oosthuizen 2006, 107). These early dates indicated that the field pattern was presumably preserved or at least undisturbed by the Danes during the occupation and turmoil of the following century (Oosthuizen 2006, 100). Oosthuizen also noted that the hundredal boundaries appeared, in places, to step around the field pattern, and so concluded that the planned fields had expanded over the entire valley before these territorial divisions became fixed, which she dated to the tenth century (Oosthuizen 2006, 100).

Oosthuizen argued that the proto-common field was part of a wider organisation of resources. Lying in the base of the valley was a large area of open common, called the Ofal or 'old field' (Oosthuizen 2006, 52). The unsettled expanse of the former common 'waste' is visible from the distribution of church sites in Figure 2.3, which indicates that most of the early settlements appear to have actively avoided building on the seasonally waterlogged Evesham soils. In Oosthuizen's model, in addition to the extensive wet grassland of the Ofal, the inhabitants of the valley settlements also had access to the watershed commons on the surrounding hillslopes providing them with large amounts of grassland resources.

The proto-common field system Oosthuizen identified in the Bourn Valley raises a number of questions, not least that the valley appears to contain two deliberately planned agricultural landscapes that were laid out around a millennium apart. And despite changes in farming technology over the centuries substantial parts of the prehistoric system were apparently incorporated into

FIGURE 2.3. Soil type and churches in the southeastern Bourn Valley.

an early medieval layout. When the early medieval population went to the trouble of reorganising their fields and greens, why did they utilise the Iron Age boundaries when they could easily have swept away the earlier divisions? What was it about the Iron Age field boundaries that continued to be useful to the early medieval farmers? Or could there be other reasons why the regular pattern of lanes and boundaries arose in the Bourn Valley? In order to begin to answer some of these questions, we should begin by looking at the Iron Age relict field system, and in particular the archaeological excavations carried out prior to the building of Cambourne new town.

As previously mentioned there has been extensive archaeological exploration in the Cambourne Development Area, which lies within the expanse covered by Oosthuizen's relict field system. In particular the area around Cambourne contained a number of the prehistoric ancient alignments or co-axial boundaries that she identified. The development area was evaluated using numerous trial trenches, and those found to contain evidence for groupings of ditches and/or post holes were chosen for further investigation and excavation (Wright *et al.* 2009, 6). Figure 2.4 shows the distribution of the 12 named excavation sites within the development area and the ancient alignments identified by Oosthuizen.

As already noted, most of these sites represent prehistoric and Romano-British farmsteads strung along the Ridgeway (Albion Archaeology 2005, 26). Although the farmsteads may have only been inhabited seasonally, they were accompanied by a settlement infrastructure of ponds and ditches and trackways (Albion Archaeology 2005, 25). Beginning in the Middle Iron Age, settlement expanded from the watershed onto the upper slopes of the Bourn Valley,

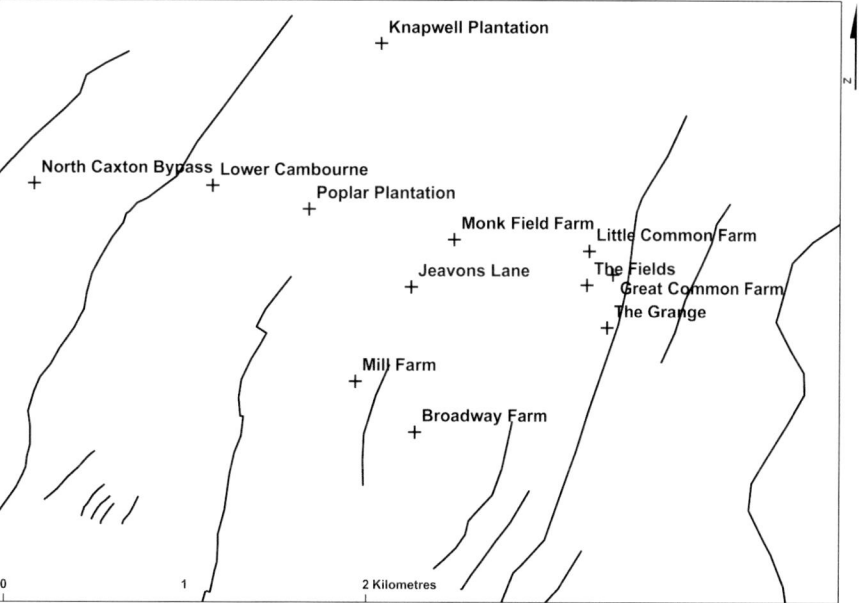

FIGURE 2.4. The distribution of the named sites within the Cambourne Development Area. Oosthuizen's 'ancient alignments' shown as black lines.

and this colonisation phase was notable for the building of unenclosed roundhouses (Wright *et al.* 2009, 73). The excavators noted the location of a farmstead grouping at the head of each of the small spur valleys, something they interpreted as an organic response to environmental influences rather than as a consequence of centralised planning (Wright *et al.* 2009, 73). Little evidence for field boundaries was found in association with the earliest of these sites, although it was presumed by the archaeologists that the inhabitants would have cultivated land on the valley slopes. In the Late Iron Age the farmsteads were enclosed with newly dug ditches, which would have almost certainly improved the conditions in the farmyards through drainage (Wright *et al.* 2009, 73). Even then, however, there was relatively little evidence for contemporary field divisions in the wider landscape, which suggested that the valley slopes were home to a primarily pastoral farming system, although it was also thought possible that evidence for enclosures could have remained undiscovered beyond the excavation areas (Wright *et al.* 2009, 73). Several of the farmsteads had small enclosures or paddocks lying immediately adjacent to the farmyard and these were bounded by field ditches. A good example is the Iron Age farmstead discovered at the Little Common Farm [NGR533140,259180], which included five small enclosures radiating out from the farmyard and in morphology resembled a typical aggregate field pattern (Wright *et al.* 2009, 56). The farmstead at the Jeavons Lane site [NGR533230,259040] was also accompanied by three tiny, ditched paddocks or pens that lay close to the farmyard but, unlike those at Little Common Farm, these were arranged in a cohesive pattern (Wright *et al.* 2009, 45). Overall, however, the archaeological evidence from the Cambourne Development Area suggests the Iron Age landscape on the northern slopes of the Bourn Valley was predominately unenclosed (Wright *et al.* 2009, 73).

A number of the Iron Age farmsteads investigated in the development area appeared to have been abandoned either before or around the time of the Roman Invasion, and only two settlement sites, Lower Cambourne [NGR531080,259460] and Knapwell Plantation [NGR532100,260225], contained material evidence that suggested they remained in occupation into the Roman period (Wright *et al.* 2009, 71). Several of the deserted Iron Age farmstead sites were subsequently resettled from the mid-Romano-British period, but the reoccupation of the sites led to significant changes (Wright *et al.* 2009, 87).

The resettled farms were completely redesigned and surrounded by newly constructed ditched outer enclosures (Wright *et al.* 2009, 88). Within the settlement site at Lower Cambourne the extent of the reorganisation was so complete, as illustrated by Figure 2.5, that it is unclear precisely how much of the earlier arrangement of ditches and gullies was visible at the time of the re-colonisation. Certainly, there is little sign of the reuse of existing features and in some cases entirely new drove-ways and entrances were created. Even the two sites where settlement appears not to have been interrupted in the Late Iron Age and Early Romano-British period contained evidence of major reorganisation. Many of these changes appear to have 'improved' the farmsteads, a good example from

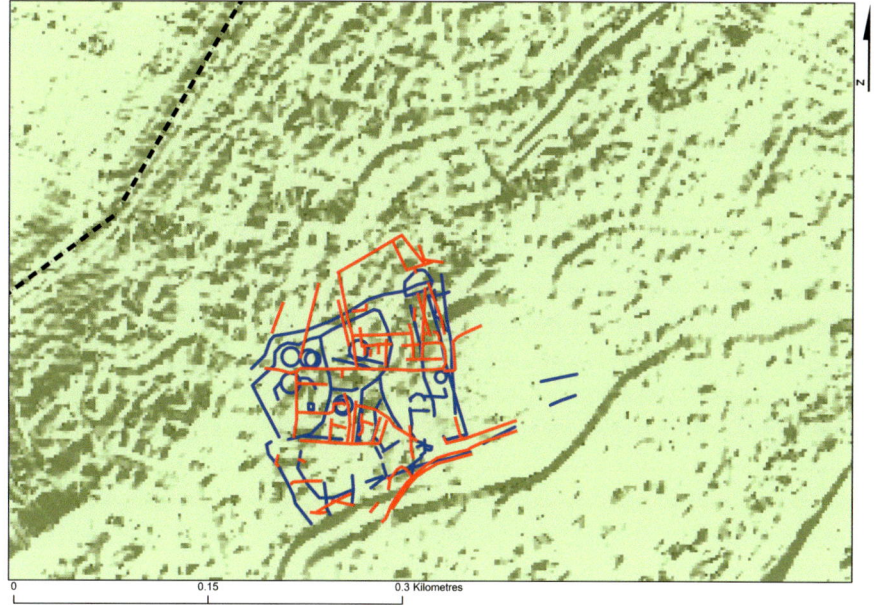

FIGURE 2.5. Phases of the Lower Cambourne site (after Wright *et al.* 2009, 15; Ousthuizen 2006, 154–5). The Iron Age farmstead is shown in blue and the mid-Romano-British farm is shown in red. One of Oosthuizen's ancient alignments is plotted as a dotted line running to the northwest of the settlement site, along a minor watershed. It is apparently unrelated to either occupation phase.

the Lower Cambourne site was that the new enclosure ditches were arranged to drain into a deliberately constructed pond with a cobbled base (Wright *et al.* 2009, 22).

The middle of the Romano-British period was also the first period where archaeological evidence for enclosed fields was found adjacent to the farmyards. Unfortunately, few examples of the probable field boundary ditches were fully excavated and sometimes only one or two features lying close to the farmsteads were uncovered and even then, only a few metres of the ditch would be excavated (Wright *et al.* 2009, 87). But two sites, both located at the extremities of the new town development area, produced more extensive evidence. The western site, which lay close to the North Caxton Bypass [NGR 530050,259450], was an irregular shape and incorporated a long pan-handle like extension aligned roughly west–east. Within the narrow zone 17 shallow ditches were identified and interpreted as boundaries of Romano-British fields.

The aligned enclosures ranged from 18 to 25 m in width; at the western end the field ditches followed a north-northwest to south-southeast orientation, possibly influenced by the adjacent Roman road, Ermine Street to which they ran roughly parallel (Wright *et al.* 2009, 10).

Moving east across the site the orientations of the boundary ditches shifted gradually but significantly until they achieved a north-northeast to south-southwest alignment, following the direction of the slope. The changing orientation across the site was thus almost certainly due to the competing influences of very local factors – Ermine Street in the west, and the natural topography in the east (Wright *et al.* 2009, 10).

The second site, called The Fields [NGR 533140,258980], lay just to the south of the Little Common Farm site discussed previously (Figure 2.6). Unlike most of the other sites this produced no evidence for settlement but contained a series of small rectangular fields separated by shallow ditches, with the entire area covering little more than a third of a hectare. Analysis of the ditches suggested the presence of two distinct field systems, each made up of rectangular parcels (Wright *et al.* 2009, 57). Although both sets of ditches were dated to the mid to late Romano-British period, they were clearly created in two unrelated phases. The first was laid out on a rough north–south and east–west grid, with a drove-way forming its western edge. The latter cut through an Iron Age ditch at the north end of the excavation; a feature the archaeologists thought was likely to be associated with the Little Common Farm site which lay immediately to the north (Wright *et al.* 2009, 57). The second field group was made up of morphologically similar fields, once again defined by shallow ditches but this time the boundaries were oriented slightly north-northwest to south-southeast with the perpendicular ditches following a west-southwest to east-southeast alignment, as illustrated in Figure 2.7. The ditches of this second field pattern cut into the earlier drove-way and through the fields and ditches of the earlier system (Wright *et al.* 2009, 57).

The apparent reorganisation is particularly curious given that the size and shape of the enclosed parcels in both systems appear similar, giving little indication as to what led to the rearrangement and the hours of labour in digging the new ditches it required. Interestingly, the medieval ridge and furrow on the same site followed yet another alignment, this time to the northwest, as can be seen in Figure 2.8 (Wright *et al.* 2009, 58). The answers may lie in the location

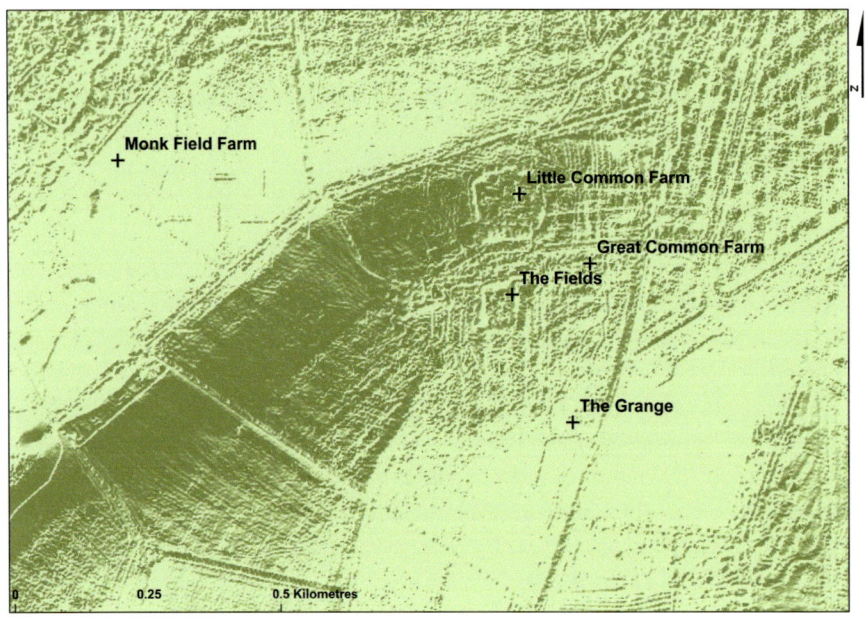

FIGURE 2.6. Illustrating the location of The Fields site at the head of a dry valley (LiDAR Composite Digital Terrain Model (DTM) 1 m) (Wright *et al.* 2009, 71).

FIGURE 2.7. The field ditches excavated at The Fields, with the two phases identified by the archaeologists (after Wright *et al.* 2009, 58).

of the site at the head of the dry valley and close to a small curve in the minor watershed as can be seen in Figure 2.9. If topography, and therefore drainage, was the main influence on the orientation of the ditches then in this case the size of the enclosure would determine the precise orientation. For example, a small group of enclosures that covered less than half a hectare would reflect the landform in the immediate proximity, in this case the small curve in the

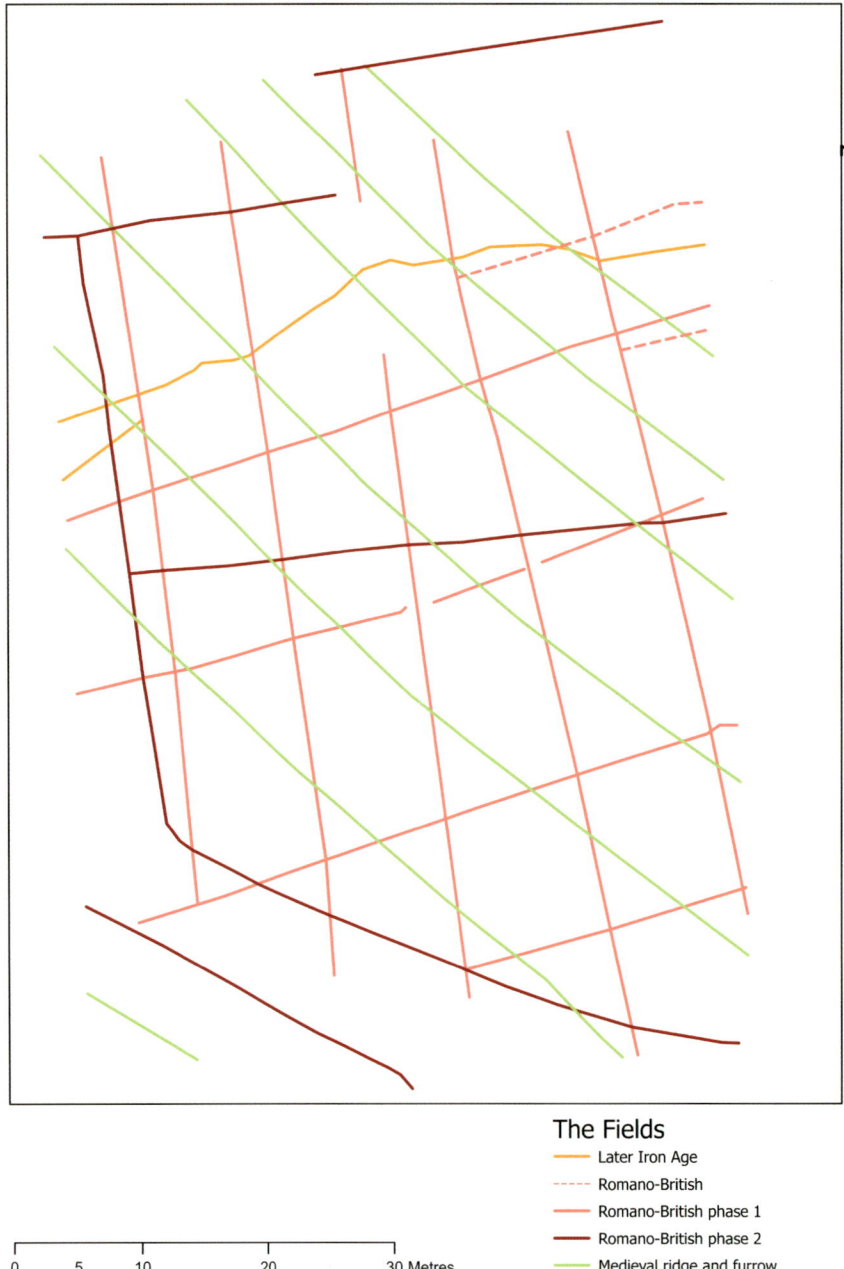

FIGURE 2.8. The field ditches excavated at The Fields, overlain with the medieval ridge and furrow identified by the archaeologists (after Wright *et al.* 2009, 58).

ridge which provided several possibilities for the Romano-British ditches to be arranged perpendicular to the watershed.

By contrast, when the cultivated area was larger, for example when the small area was incorporated into the medieval furlong covering many thousands of square metres, the strip alignment would need to respect the same landforms but on a larger or furlong scale. As a result, the medieval furrows were arranged

FIGURE 2.9. The features excavated at The Fields (after Wright *et al.* 2009, 58), overlaid on LiDAR Composite DTM 1 m, showing the curving watershed.

to reflect the overall perpendicular relationship with the general slope of all the land, visible in Figure 2.6, contained within the furlong. They therefore overlooked the influence of the small watershed curve, which would only add unnecessary complexity to the strip arrangement.

Proponents of relict field systems still might consider the sites discussed in the previous paragraphs as evidence of a repeated alignment of field boundaries across the Cambourne Development Area. The field boundaries closest to

Ermine Street were oriented in the same approximate direction as the second set of ditches found in The Fields which lay around 3 km to the east; but the evidence gathered from excavated sites lying between these two extremities suggests the pattern was more complex. Not all of the sites excavated contained evidence for surrounding field patterns, but in those that did the field ditches did not conform to a single shared alignment. The lack of a consistent orientation provides no support for the idea that a single, cohesive, prehistoric or Romano-British relict field system extended across the whole of the Cambourne Development Area.

To summarise, the archaeological fieldwork indicates that from the Middle to Late Iron Age farmsteads were constructed and farmed within a predominately open landscape with few permanent boundaries and were probably concerned primarily with grazing livestock. From the middle of the Romano-British period Iron Age farmsteads were resettled, redesigned and possibly 'improved' and some of the farms appear to have been accompanied by new field boundary ditches. In sites where evidence for field boundaries was found there was a tendency for the ditch divisions to follow the natural slope and therefore improve the land through surface drainage. As with the locations of the Iron Age farmsteads at the heads of the minor valleys the greatest influence upon the direction of the Romano-British field ditches appears to have been the local landform. In common with other examples of prehistoric fields the Cambourne examples were small in size and covered only limited areas. As previously mentioned, the study area lies on the south facing slopes of the watershed between the river Great Ouse and Bourn brook. The landscape contains numerous minor hill spurs and dry valleys, many of which have a rough northeasterly orientation,

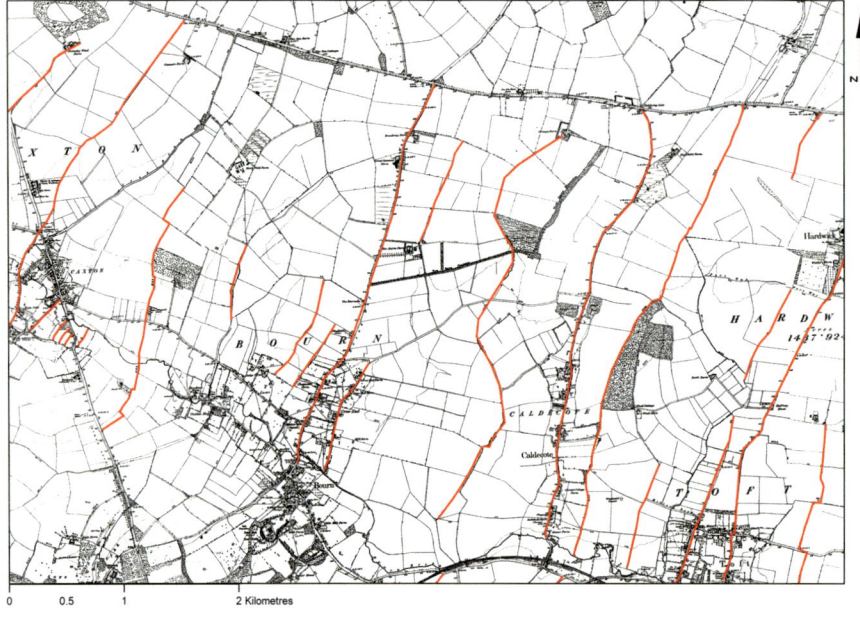

FIGURE 2.10. The First Edition Ordnance Survey 6-Inch map covering the northwestern Bourn Valley with Oosthuizen's ancient alignments (in red) (Oosthuizen 2006, 154–5).

leading to the frequency, but crucially not the ubiquity, of boundary ditches with directions falling between the north and west occidental points.

Within this landscape of small farmsteads each with their own discrete field systems, what could have led to the creation of the cross valley alignments identified by Susan Oosthuizen as fossilised features of an Iron Age field system? In common with many landscape historians interested in relict field systems, Oosthuizen utilised the First Edition Ordnance Survey 6-Inch maps to identify patterns of long uninterrupted field and parish boundaries, paths and roads lying parallel to each other within the Bourn Valley, illustrated in Figure 2.10. As discussed in the previous chapter the presence of these parallel boundaries is typically considered characteristic of planned subdivision at a parish, township, farm and field level.

In the Bourn Valley the long boundaries do appear to conform to a repetitive landscape arrangement, and it is very easy to see how this could be interpreted as evidence for a large-scale planned field system. Although not particularly consistent in spacing they all share a similar general orientation. In order to allow a clearer analysis of their relationship with the natural topography the detail of the Ordnance Survey 6-Inch maps have been removed in Figure 2.11, which shows the ancient alignments over a LiDAR plot of the same area.

The correlation between the long boundaries and the natural topography is immediately apparent and the pattern continues further east in the parishes of Hardwick and Toft. Toward the eastern end of the valley the ancient alignments gradually peter out as the topography becomes more muted, as it approaches the level land around Cambridge. The roads, tracks, parish and field boundaries all appear to either reflect or respect the landforms, following the watersheds, ridges and dry valleys.

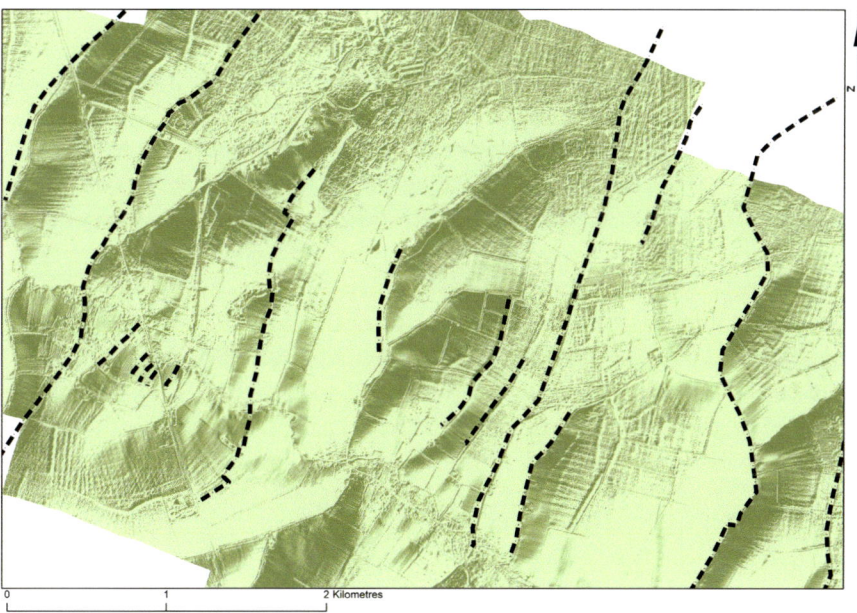

FIGURE 2.11. LiDAR plot of the northwestern Bourn Valley. Ancient alignments after Oosthuizen (2006).

By including topography in the landscape analysis, it becomes clear that the pattern of parallel features which appeared so artificial in fact results from entirely natural influences; or, perhaps more accurately, the influence of local landforms and land-use systems engendered by wider environmental patterns. In the Bourn Valley many of the parish boundaries followed 'Mare Ways', lanes or paths which led from the floor of the valley to the watershed. These lanes were likely to have arisen as 'resource linkage routes' between the settlements, the watershed and the Bourn itself (Harrison 2002, 45; 2005, 159). There is no conflict with the routes being located upon the minor hill spurs, a correlation between watersheds and ancient paths is well known if not fully understood. The origin date for these lanes is unknown, not least because the route would have been useful to an inhabitant of any period who wished to access the watershed resources, and while several may have prehistoric origins the continued importance of local transhumance into the medieval period means they could be of much more recent origin (Gardiner 2018, 113).

Roman roads and slighted field boundaries

When writing *Landscapes Decoded* Oosthuizen had little archaeological fieldwork available to support her argument for the dating of the various long boundaries in the Bourn Valley. At the time a single Late Iron Age coin had been found close to the junction of one of the co-axial lanes with the Cambridge–St Neots Ridgeway, and as a result Oosthuizen based her dating hypothesis upon a combination of morphological analysis, principally comparison with the Dartmoor reaves, and landscape stratigraphy. Applying these methods, Oosthuizen was able to propose origin dates for the different elements in the Bourn Valley.

The relationship between features of a known date and the supposed relict features to be dated is fundamental to the process of landscape stratigraphy. As discussed previously, Flinders Petrie devised the method of using large-scale maps to view the relationship of known Roman roads with fields, lanes and settlements. A modified version of this methodology was used by Rodwell and Drury in their analysis of field systems in Essex and this will be discussed in more detail in the following chapter. In summary, where the Roman roads cut obliquely through or 'slighted' the fields, then the landscape was interpreted by Rodwell and Drury as pre-Roman, conversely where the road and fields were conformable they must be contemporary. Happily, for the purposes of this case study the West Cambridgeshire Clay Plateau contains several major Roman roads including Ermine Street – the line of which formed part of the boundary of the parish of Bourn.

Lying immediately to the west of Bourn lies the parish of Caxton, within which Oosthuizen identified a number of field boundaries visible on the First Edition Ordnance Survey 6-Inch map that the Roman road appeared to 'slight', leading to triangular shaped enclosures. Several of the boundaries were very long and shared by multiple fields, which suggested to Oosthuizen that Ermine Street had been imposed upon an earlier landscape of regularly arranged fields. In isolation this argument is persuasive, but as we have seen previously in this chapter, more recent archaeological fieldwork has shown that there was no large-scale field system in the Bourn Valley in the Late Iron Age. Furthermore, where evidence for Romano-British fields has been found these have been small groupings arranged to utilise the immediate environmental conditions, and not part of an extensive planned landscape. In the absence of a relict landscape what could have led to the disharmonious relationship between the Roman road and field pattern? At this point it is perhaps worth mentioning that the landscape of small fields shown on Figure 2.12 emerged in the post-medieval period: the fields around Caxton were enclosed before 1750 from open fields, and both the shape of individual boundaries, and their relationship with the ridge and furrow shown on twentieth-century aerial photographs shows that this took place in a 'piecemeal' fashion, with the new boundaries following the lines of the earlier strips (RCHM 1968, 44).

As Figure 2.12 illustrates several of the long boundaries were actually lanes and these led to medieval sites, namely the isolated parish church, a moated medieval settlement and Bourn village. A curious characteristic of the rough grid that was formed by the boundaries is that the orientation slightly alters on either side of the Roman road. This is noticeable in relation to the southwest to northeast boundaries but the discord between the west–east boundaries that lie on either side of Ermine Street is even more convincing. The Roman road clearly cuts across this pattern of field boundaries and local lanes at an oblique angle, but could it be significant that Ermine Street 'slights' the Bourn brook as well as the rough grid?

As earlier discussions in this chapter have argued, the local environment is a significant influence on the eventual pattern of fields, lanes, furlongs and

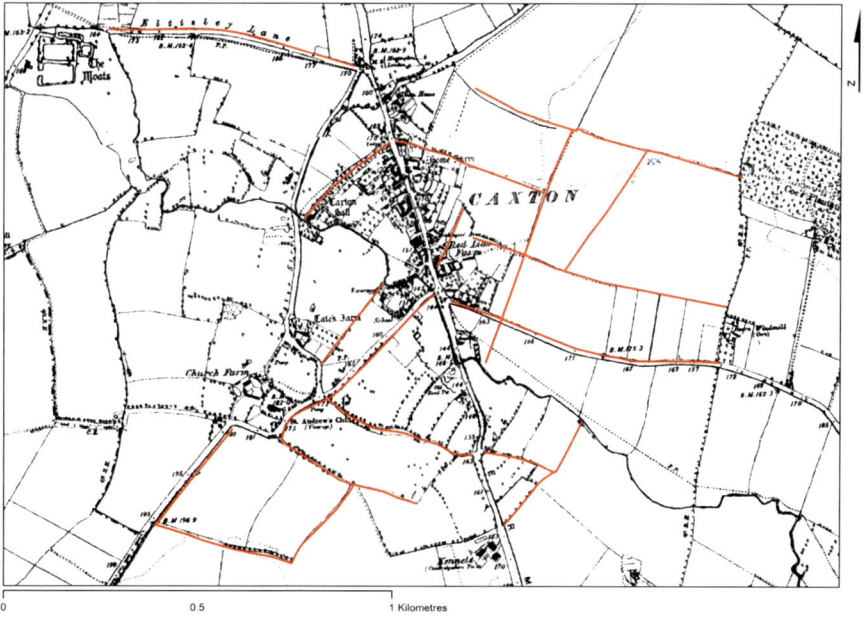

FIGURE 2.12. The pre-Roman boundaries identified by Oosthuizen (2006). Oosthuizen's prehistoric field system is plotted in red, overlaid on the First Edition Ordnance Survey 6-Inch map.

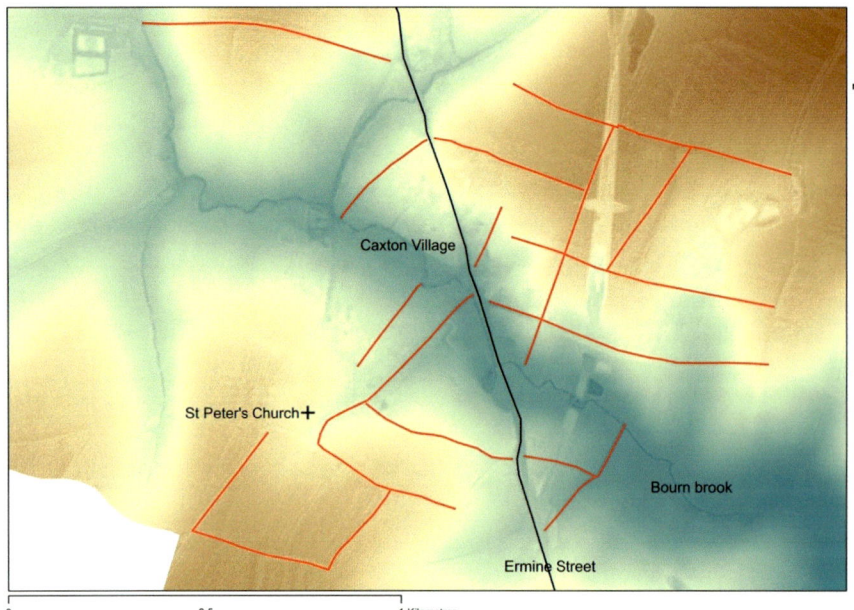

FIGURE 2.13. The pre-Roman boundaries identified by Oosthuizen, overlaid on LiDAR Composite DTM 2 m.

boundaries. Figure 2.13 shows the same 'prehistoric field' boundaries identified by Oosthuizen but this time overlaying a modern LiDAR plot. By removing all but Oosthuizen's 'prehistoric' land divisions it is clear that the former furlong boundaries are strongly related to the land height changes associated with the valley of the Bourn brook. The grid pattern would appear to relate directly to the watercourse; on the whole the boundaries are arranged to be perpendicular to the general course of the brook.

This arrangement appears to be primarily a response to local environmental conditions and almost certainly reflects the tendency of open field strips on heavy land and moderate slopes to be laid out at right angles to the contours, to facilitate surface drainage. The importance of utilising the local topography to optimise surface drainage, and thereby increase the chance of a safe harvest, was of greater significance to farmers of any subsequent period than the difficulty of cultivating an awkwardly shaped field, furlong or strip created by the immediate proximity of a major road that followed a different alignment.

The presence of the triangular fields frequently found alongside Roman roads is usually given as one of the reasons that the field pattern must predate the road, on the basis that no one would deliberately create such an inconvenient field shape; however modern views of the difficulty of farming triangular fields is perhaps overstated, particularly as the imposition of the road on the landscape is almost certainly more noticeable on a map, than it is when working in an individual strip or furlong.

At its most fundamental level the interpretation of landscape disruption and 'slighting' tends to imply that the majority of fields and furlongs were

FIGURE 2.14. Plan of the ridge and furrow in Caxton (after RCHM 1968), and 'pre-Roman boundaries' (after Oosthuizen 2006).

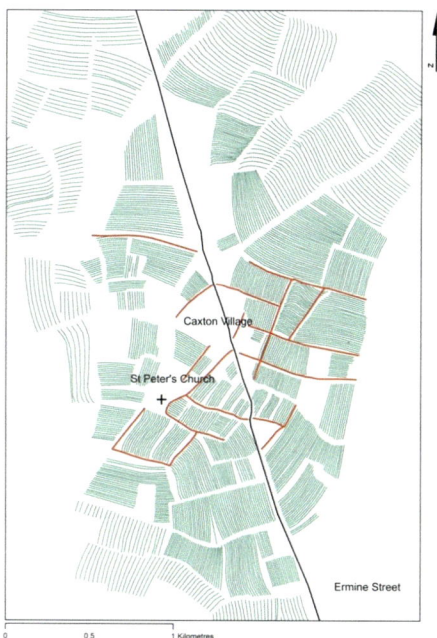

more or less regular in shape, but was this true? Fortunately for answering this question Caxton is one of the relatively few parishes within the West Cambridgeshire Clay Plateau where ridge and furrow survived as earthworks into the mid-twentieth century and were photographed. The RCHM volume for West Cambridgeshire contains a plan of the former furlongs including the individual lands. This earthwork plan indicates that the furlongs within Caxton are varied in both size and shape; there appears to be a general tendency for trapezoid shaped furlongs with many containing selions of unequal lengths. There are even several sub-triangular shaped furlongs although, notably, none in proximity to the Roman road and one of these is visible to the northwest of the parish church in Figure 2.14.

The wider earthwork plan illustrates just how small an area within Caxton parish was covered by the boundaries that Oosthuizen interpreted as pre-Roman. It also indicates how swiftly the loose grid petered out as the furlongs extended away from the settlement and onto the more complex local topography of hill spurs and dry valleys. Once again, the strips and boundaries were generally arranged to optimise surface drainage of the clay soils as can be seen in Figure 2.15.

Overlaying the post-medieval earthwork plan of Caxton on to the modern LiDAR terrain allows for greater analysis of the relationship between the fields, furlongs and boundaries and the local environment. This indicates that the apparent 'slighting' of the field pattern that lay close to the settlement in Caxton did not originate because the Roman road cut through an existing field system, but because it crossed the valley of the Bourn brook at an oblique angle. The Roman road builders surveying and constructing a direct route from London to Godmanchester, and beyond, were unconcerned by such small-scale changes in topography.

Although they also functioned as boundaries, field ditches were primarily dug as a response to draining land; there were after all much less labour-intensive alternative options available to mark divisions including fences, hedges or even posts, particularly as on their own ditches are relatively poor barriers to livestock. A field ditch is a boundary that is also concerned with improving the land and as such its course will always need to respond to the local topography and that remains true whether the ditch was dug in the Bronze Age or last month. The importance of surface drainage to improve the soil and by so doing increase the likelihood of a good harvest, far outweighs the inconvenience of a boundary set at an odd angle.

The process of dating an agricultural landscape through its relationship with a Roman road is therefore potentially problematic; any landscape that could benefit from surface drainage will contain field ditches that will relate to the natural topography and as such could have been constructed by people at any point in history. The fact that a Roman road appears to 'slight' such a field pattern does not necessarily indicate that the boundaries pre-date the road, but simply reflects the continued importance of optimising the land for farming as well as the different priorities of the Roman road builders.

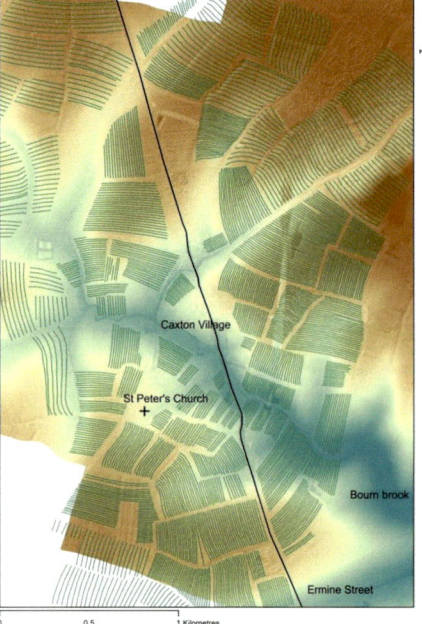

FIGURE 2.15. Caxton ridge and furrow plan (after RCHM 1968), overlaid on LiDAR Composite DTM 2 m.

The Saxon proto-common field

Oosthuizen concluded, from research into the pre-enclosure landscape of the Bourn Valley, that the long east–west boundaries visible on the First Edition Ordnance Survey 6-Inch map related to a planned common field arrangement of cultivated fields separated by long narrow greens, which she concluded had been laid out in the mid-Saxon period (Oosthuizen 2006, 107). Oosthuizen argued that the linear commons were created to allow the Bourn Valley farmers to keep more livestock locally rather than on the shared watershed commons. This was in order that the arable fields could be cropped intensively and without a fallow period; by folding livestock on the stubbles or overnight additional nutrients could be transferred to the soil through animal manure (Oosthuizen 2006, 108). Oosthuizen called this arrangement the 'proto-common field'. In places she noted how the boundaries from what she had concluded was the Iron Age field system were incorporated into the new arrangement, but if the supposedly 'ancient alignments' actually resulted from the landform, rather than prehistoric planning, what does this mean for Oosthuizen's narrow greens, or 'linear commons' as she called them? Are these first millennium features the result of landscape planning or, do they also reflect some aspect of the local environment?

In *Landscapes Decoded* Oosthuizen considered the possibility that the linear commons that run roughly parallel to the brook could have been 'laid out as drove-ways' but she dismissed this explanation on the basis that they did not lead directly to either Cambridge or Haslingfield, the assumed early estate centre for which this new landscape was planned, as can be seen in Figure 2.2 (Oosthuizen 2006, 107). Oosthuizen further argued that there would be no need for droves to access shared resources, given that the early commons were located upon the watersheds, well above the linear commons (Oosthuizen 2006, 108).

As noted previously, Oosthuizen supposed that the planned landscape was created by the Haeslinga tribe whose principal settlement, Haslingfield, was on the other side of the Bourn brook and at the east end of the valley, as can be seen in Figure 2.2. Given that the function of the linear commons was to provide access to the newly created fields, it is curious that they were not oriented upon the tribal centre, something Oosthuizen notes, and which led her to conclude that they did not function as drove-ways (Oosthuizen 2006, 107). It would seem curious that the proto-common field system would be created only on one side of the valley, and on land located farthest from the tribal centre at Haslingfield.

In this context, it is worth noting that the settlement pattern differs noticeably on either side of the Bourn brook. Haslingfield formerly had a large green, which is fossilised in the modern road and settlement pattern (Oosthuizen 2006, 53). Harlton contained a small green lying to the south of the church, and the road pattern suggests this also might have been larger in the past (Oosthuizen 2006, 55). In contrast the settlements found on the northern side of the Bourn brook, where the linear commons are found, tend to display a rough grid form, as Oosthuizen noted they appear to be influenced by the field boundary pattern as if the settlements had extended over the former open field strips (Oosthuizen 2006, 60–1).

As can be seen in Figure 2.2, the surviving linear commons of the Saxon proto-common field covered only a small part of the area that contained the supposed Iron Age boundaries. Most examples occur further to the east, between the settlements of Comberton and Caldecote, with a second semi-connected grouping between Barton and Grantchester. The spacing of the linear commons varies substantially, as can be seen in Figure 2.16. In the area lying immediately to the west of Comberton church, for example, the distance between the linear commons superficially appears relatively consistent but closer analysis indicates the spacing between them varies markedly, with 190 m separating Tid Brook Common and Millway, 250 m between the Millway and Broadway, with 180 m between Broadway and the next linear common. These differences may seem minor, but when considered in the context of a strip or field they would quickly become significant. The paths the long greens followed were not truly parallel, moreover: by the time the same linear commons met the Toft–Comberton parish boundary the distances between them had altered to 367 m, 230 m and 220 m respectively, and the section just described is arguably the most uniform part of the whole arrangement. The inconsistent spacing must have caused the strips in the furlongs abutting the greens to vary in length and therefore complicated apportioning shares of land. This appears discordant with the intention of a deliberately planned landscape.

It is also noteworthy that several of the linear commons indicated in Figure 2.16 as dashed lines, appear to correlate to natural features. Tid Brook Common is perhaps the most obvious example of this, following the curving line of the watercourse of the same name, while Millway common appears to follow a minor watershed to the west of Comberton church. Surviving pre-enclosure maps indicate that most of the linear greens had names that indicated some form of route or transit, with examples including Broadway, Millway, Holders Lane and Cambridge Way.

Although the changes in elevation on the lower valley slopes are much more muted than those close to the watershed, LiDAR technology does allow even these small rises to be visible. This is even the case for the gentle undulations in the land close to the village of Comberton, which can be seen in Figure 2.16. The relationship between the local topography and the putative Iron Age boundaries can be seen, the black lines passing north to south continue to correlate strongly with topography even in the valley where landfall is minimal. Similarly, laying the linear commons over the modern LiDAR plot (DTM 1 m) indicates how the long boundaries corresponded to the natural landscape; in this example the muted local topography or a feature such as Tid Brook.

Oosthuizen did not consider the function of the linear commons as part of the local route network, but that was evidently one role that they played in the medieval and early modern landscape, with their precise route strongly influenced by the details of the local topography, as with the north–south cross valley alignments. The broadly parallel layout of the linear commons suggests that they may originally have served more than local needs and, like their

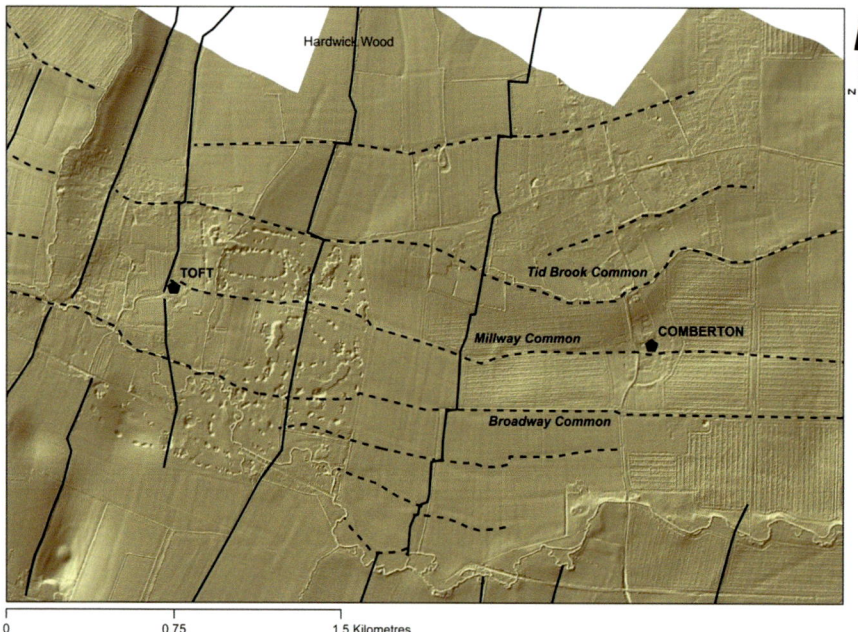

FIGURE 2.16. Elements of Oosthuizen's Bourn Valley relict field system over LiDAR. Ancient alignments (solid lines) and linear commons (dashed lines) after Oosthuizen (2006).

FIGURE 2.17. Three of the linear commons west of Toft (K124/P/80).

north–south counterparts, originated as transhumance tracks, providing access to resources located further up the valley (Compton 2014, 51). By the eleventh century much of the Bourn Valley and the settlements to the east around Cambridge were largely devoid of woodland resources. This was not the case further west, where place-name evidence and resources listed in Domesday Book indicate that significant areas of woodland resources remained. The east–west greens could have originated as a general direction of transit linking the area around Cambridge and settlements located on the edge of the fens to woodland resources on the Western Clay Plateau.

The neat parallel arrangement of the linear commons it should also be noted, has been enhanced (as so often in studies of relict field systems) by a degree of selective removal. The early nineteenth-century Draft Inclosure map for the parish of Toft, for example, shows that there were many more linear commons in the parish than highlighted by Oosthuizen in her analysis. When examined closely many of those that were included do not neatly meet the description of parallel east–west greens as can be seen in Figure 2.17. The narrow commons that lay to the west of the village can only loosely be described as parallel, and their paths diverge from the greens that lay to the east of the settlement. All three linear commons take an irregular route, which when compared to the modern LiDAR plot appears to correlate with the slight undulations in the local landscape. The place-names of each green include '-way' and by the nineteenth century at least an important function was to provide access to local resources. In fact, only the three linear commons that lay to the west of the village of Toft, along with the continuation of the same features to the east of the settlement, were included in Oosthuizen's proto-common field model; and as illustrated

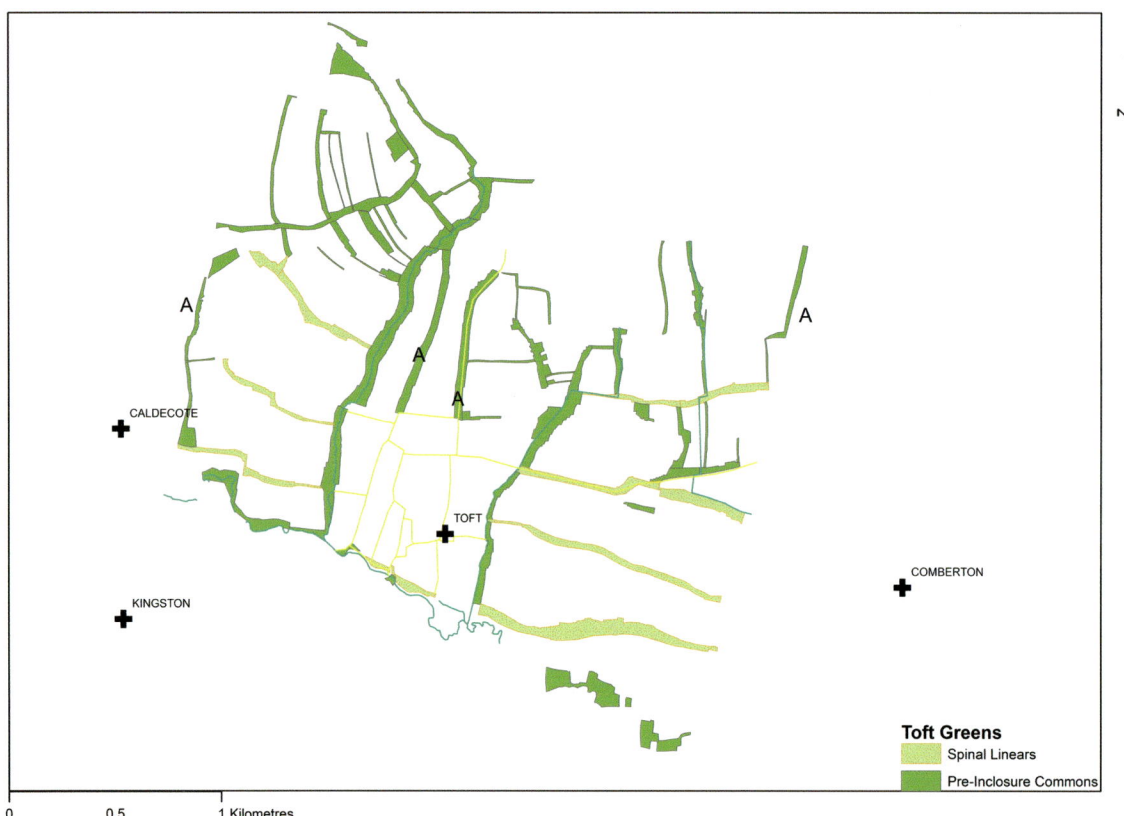

FIGURE 2.18. Pre-Inclosure Commons in Toft (K124/P/80).

in Figure 2.18, these made up only a small proportion of the narrow commons within the open fields of the parish.

Further examination of the Toft greens recorded on the Draft Inclosure Map with the linear commons discussed by Oosthuizen highlights further irregularities. On the enclosure map the long narrow common, then called Holders Way Lot Grass, appeared to terminate at a north–south green, marked by point 'B' on Figure 2.19. There was then a large gap between it and its presumed continuation as Wood Way, which lay almost a kilometre to the west. There was nothing in the nineteenth-century furlong pattern that would indicate that the linear common had ever continued west beyond point B, nor indeed that Wood Way had originally extended east from where it ended upon another north–south linear green. Notably neither of the north–south linear greens were included in Oosthuizen's discussion. Non-conforming features within the east–west commons were similarly excluded, an example can be seen near 'C' in Figure 2.19, the southern route is classified as a spinal linear, but despite the apparently identical morphology the northern section of the linear green was excluded.

The early nineteenth-century map of Toft records a village surrounded by open fields and linear greens and the parish divisions ran through narrow commons. Several linear greens petered out in the midst of furlongs, possibly fossilising routes to lost areas of common grazing but they also provided access

FIGURE 2.19. Pre-Inclosure Commons in Toft (K124/P/80) and Oosthuizen's (2006) proto-common field.

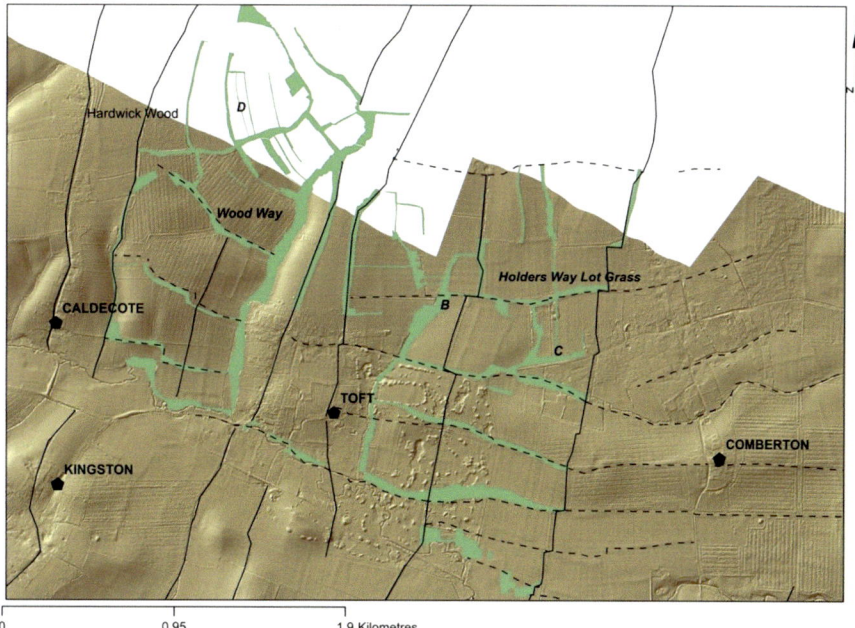

to open field furlongs, strips and the heads of winterbournes. Overall, the Toft map depicts a complex landscape pattern that developed through empirical knowledge of how best to utilise the local soils, resources and topography and which owed its apparent regularity to the combined influences of resource linkage routes with topography and environment.

Close comparison of the Toft Draft Inclosure Map with Oosthuizen's proto-common field described in *Landscapes Decoded* highlights, with particular clarity, the risk of confirmation bias when determining the importance of features in a landscape, particularly from maps. Selecting features that appear to support the hypothesis while simultaneously discounting those that do not is an accepted methodology in the process of identifying relict field systems. In *Landscapes Decoded* Oosthuizen discussed various methods of retrogressive analysis, which evolved from the concept of landscape stratigraphy. Retrogressive analysis has been an accepted methodology where 'later' boundaries, in particular medieval and post-medieval field divisions are removed in order to illuminate the earlier field pattern. There are several methods of determining which boundaries to remove, documentary or place-name evidence can be used to indicate the probable age of a boundary before removal, but in many situations the decisions are based upon morphological comparison and landscape stratigraphy. As Oosthuizen notes, this 'gives rise to some uncertainties about [the method's] objectivity' (Oosthuizen 2006, 77). This is particularly true for two of the methods Oosthuizen discussed, firstly that a 'major element' in the landscape, for example a boundary that continues for three or more fields or furlongs, is likely to be an early feature, and secondly that only those field or furlong boundaries that conform to the general landscape framework should be retained. Oosthuizen acknowledges the

50 *How the Land Lies*

potential for subjective selection, but notes Stephen Rippon's comments, that the morphological regularity of landscapes containing relict field systems is 'really self-evident' (Rippon 1991, 46; Oosthuizen 2006, 78).

A Bronze Age field system in Tadlow

A second method of ascribing a date to relict field systems uses parish boundaries as evidence of antiquity, arguing that as parish boundaries become fixed around the eleventh century, they can fossilise elements of earlier landscapes. Just a few miles west of Bourn lies another so called relict field system, but as the parish did not contain a Roman road, the evidence for dating the enclosures came from the unusual pattern of the county and parish boundaries. Tadlow is one of three small parishes lying on the north bank of the river Cam or Rhee, the others are Croydon cum Clopton and Arrington. All three parishes share the characteristic long narrow form that has been associated with a planned allocation of resources and landscapes (Harrison 2002, 38). Oliver Rackham's interest was drawn by the curiously stepped appearance of the county boundary with Bedfordshire, which is also found in the parish divisions. The boundaries appear to pick their way around small square fields and in *The History of the Countryside* Rackham briefly discussed Tadlow's regular field pattern:

> At Tadlow (Cambs) the whole parish – fields, the nearly deserted village, even the orientation of the church – obeys a semi-regular grid of either Bronze Age or Iron Age type. This grid is certainly older than the parish and county boundaries, both of which zigzag in obedience to it; its extensions into neighbouring parishes did not survive the unmaking of their open fields (Rackham 1986, 176).

The potential survival of a relict field system was of particular interest as the parish was subject to regular open-field farming, and at the time of Rackham's discovery, relict field systems were typically only found in old or early enclosed landscapes.

The 'semi-regular grid' and the stepped county and parish boundaries that initially caught Rackham's attention are clearly visible on the First Edition Ordnance Survey 6-Inch map, which is reproduced in Figure 2.20. Stepped boundaries occur between the river Rhee or Cam and the 80-m contour on the east of the parish, highlighted by 'B' in Figure 2.20

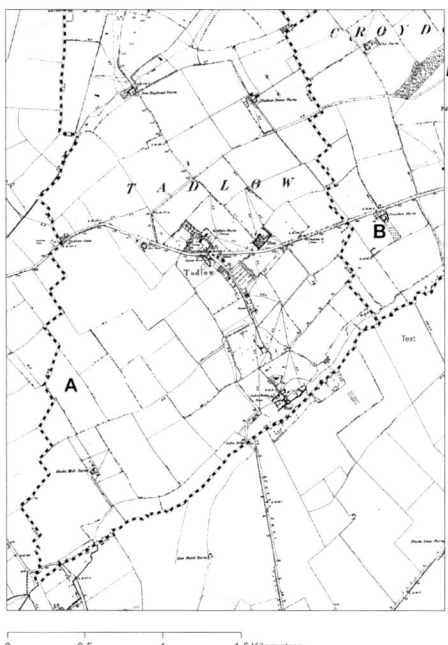

FIGURE 2.20. The stepped parish boundaries in Tadlow (after Rackham 1986).

and between 50 m and the river on the west near point 'A', which is the county division with Bedfordshire.

The county boundary follows a zig-zag pattern in the south of the parish, but to the north it straightened as it followed the path of a long since lost route, called Bar Lane. The road led from Ashwell, which lies south of Tadlow, to St Ives and The Fens and its onward route is preserved in the boundaries of several parishes that lie to the north (RCHM 1968, 145). It was the stepped appearance of the county boundary that in part persuaded Rackham of the antiquity of the arrangement as he argued that the field pattern must predate the formation of the shires.

An alternative argument is that Tadlow's regular field pattern developed within a sparse landscape grid. The parcel boundaries followed two principal alignments; one that took the typical co-axial path up the slope from the river to the watershed whilst the other axis ran roughly parallel to the river and watershed passing from east to west, the pattern resembling those found elsewhere in the Western Clay Plateau, including the Bourn Valley. All but one of the long co-axial boundaries in Tadlow ended before the watershed, terminating on the east–west track called the Ridgeway that passed along a false crest close to the 50 m contour and linked the medieval settlements to the east and west (Compton 2018, 123). Although 'resource linkage routes' typically terminate at the watershed, in regions with large areas of shared common, they more frequently end close to the edge of the 'waste' (Fleming 2010, 65). A kilometre south of the Ridgeway and running approximately parallel was another route called the 'Portway'. The form and function of the two east–west lanes were not dissimilar to the linear commons discussed previously in the analysis of Toft's common droves.

As in the Bourn Valley, the apparently regular field grid in Tadlow does not appear to have originated as a single planned field system but developed organically through the conjunction of resource linkage routes that led up the slope from river to the 'waste', with lanes that passed along the watershed and contours of the low-lying ridge. Later adjustments to field boundaries and farms respected the grain of this landscape and contributed to the small-scale detail of the field pattern (Williamson 1998, 420). Minor alterations to the Tadlow field pattern, including the insertion, removal and alteration of boundaries continued well into the nineteenth century, a reminder that fields have not remained unchanged for centuries (Williamson 1998, 420). But can this explain the stepped form of the county and parish boundaries?

In Tadlow the gradual expansion of farmland eventually led to the arable cropping extending onto the former path of Bar Lane. This could only have occurred after the route was abandoned as it is inconceivable that a route that was important enough to form the boundaries of several parishes would have diverted around individual fields in Tadlow. The county system was in place by the ninth or tenth centuries, but this does not preclude that the small detail of boundaries could be defined or perhaps redefined as the cultivated land extended. A similar argument can be made for the parish boundaries, while the territories are believed to have become fixed during the eleventh century (Blair 2005, 426). This suggests that while the general north–south direction of Tadlow's county and parish boundaries may be early medieval, the stepped path around the furlongs can only have been fixed after the lane fell out of use (Compton 2018, 123).

Conclusion

In this chapter I have looked at one of the most quoted relict field systems in Lowland England. By considering it in conjunction with the local environment, specifically soil type and climate, and the archaeology it is clear that the regular landscape of the Bourn Valley could not have resulted from planning either in the prehistoric or early medieval period. The illusion of a sparse grid in the valley derives in part from the conjunction of two sets of resource linkage routes – one running up the sides of the valley, and one along it, and partly from the interpretation of the apparent regularity of this pattern by Oosthuizen. At a more local level the crucial importance of drainage to successfully farming the heavy clay soils influenced the layout of field boundaries and served to create an illusion of superimposition where the field pattern met a major Roman road. These two themes – namely the regularity created by resource-linkage routes in areas of relatively simple or planar topography, and apparent 'slighting' of field patterns created by the requirements of local drainage – will be explored in the contexts of other relict field systems in the course of the following chapter.

CHAPTER THREE

Revisiting some famous relict field systems

In the previous chapter we saw how a semi-regular landscape pattern can develop organically through the interaction of people with their local environment; and how over time, this can lead to the establishment of regular patterns of lanes and field boundaries that share the same approximate alignment over large areas as they respond to both major and minor topography. As touched upon in the discussion of the previous case studies, there is a tendency for historians to interpret apparently regular patterns of boundaries that cover a parish or more, as the result of a deliberately planned landscape, a so-called relict field system. The most compelling of these arguments have tended to focus upon areas where a seemingly orderly field pattern is visually disharmonious with a terrain-oblivious man-made feature, a Roman road being the most common example. This chapter will briefly consider several well-known relict landscapes and will demonstrate how the local environment has engendered the apparent regularity of lanes and boundaries, as well as their apparent slighting by Roman roads and analogous linear features.

The beginning: relict landscapes in southeast Essex

Given that the earliest discoveries of so-called relict landscapes were in south Essex, and identified by Rodwell and Drury, it would seem appropriate to begin with one of these original examples and apply to it the methodology used in the previous chapter. As discussed in Chapter 1, in the 1970s Rodwell and Drury identified several distinct areas containing regular patterns of boundaries and lanes that were interpreted as the remains of early planned landscapes (Rodwell 1978; summarised in Rackham 1986, 60). One of the more famous of these, identified by Drury (1978) and discussed in depth by Rodwell (1978) and Rackham (1986, 60), is the supposed pre-Roman field pattern around Little Waltham, where small square-ish fields are convincingly slighted by the Roman road that now leads towards Braintree, and to which he ascribed a first century CE construction date.

According to the principles of landscape stratigraphy this meant that the fields unequally split by the Roman road must have originated in the first century CE or earlier, and as they formed part of a larger planned landscape, the entirety of the Little Waltham field system must also predate the construction of the Roman road (Drury and Rodwell 1980, 95).

Although Figure 3.1 does illustrate that the route of the Roman road (shown in red) appears to be broadly unconformable with the surrounding field boundaries, it is perhaps not quite as compelling as Drury's version. In part this is

FIGURE 3.1. Pre-Roman field boundaries near Little Waltham, Essex (after Drury 1978, 134; Rodwell 1978, 95).

because Drury had identified what he concluded was a late prehistoric lane that lay on the western side of the valley and is visible as a double dashed line to the west of Little Waltham in Figure 3.1. Using the this as a guide Drury selected only those portions of tracks and boundaries that lay parallel or perpendicular to the lane, excluding all others (Drury 1978, 134). In his analysis of the same landscape Rodwell linked the resulting disjointed sections with dotted lines to indicate the path of the 'lost' sections but he did not describe Drury's selection methodology (Rodwell 1978, 95). Rodwell's modification gave rise to a denser field pattern and provided more dramatic evidence for the slighting of the landscape by the Roman road.

In places Drury's methodology appears to lead to direct conflict with the technique of landscape regression and in particular the concept that if a feature forms the boundary of more than one field it must predate any boundaries that appear to terminate upon it. There are numerous examples within Drury's original landscape plan where supposedly ancient field divisions end at long boundaries that have not been included in his relict landscape, because the long feature did not align neatly within the identified field pattern; points A, B and C in Figure 3.2 highlight particularly clear examples of this. The long sinuous boundary at point A stretches almost 2 km from the banks of the river Chelmer to end on a minor lane. Drury included approximately 700 m of this feature in his plan, in three discontinuous sections (Drury 1978, 134). The remainder of the feature was excluded from the field plan, despite being the terminus for 15 field boundaries, a number far higher than any of the supposedly ancient field divisions selected by Drury.

FIGURE 3.2. Supposed pre-Roman field boundaries near Little Waltham, Essex (after Drury 1978; Rodwell 1978 in black, other field boundaries in green).

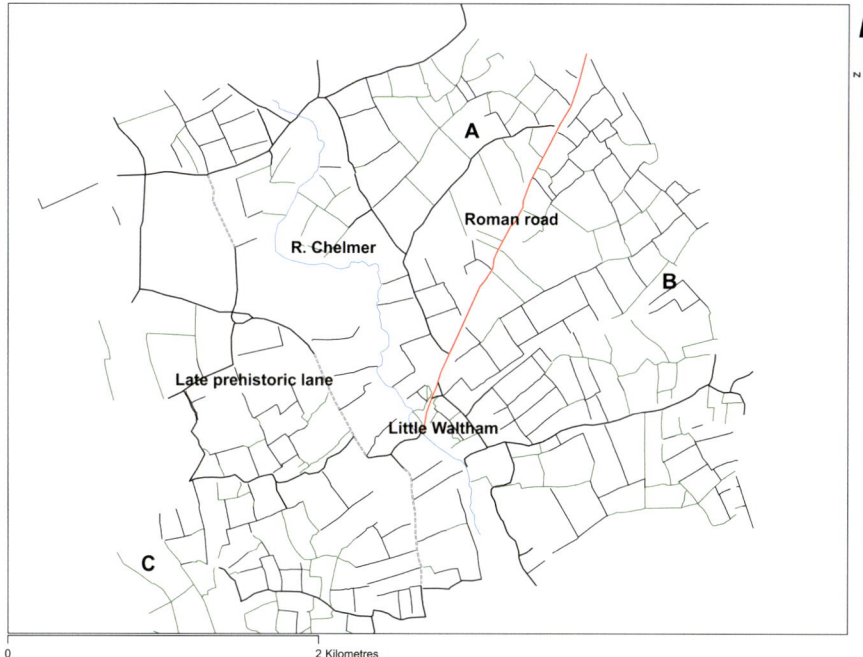

The focus of Drury's analysis is on the Roman road and related field pattern, and he does not comment on how his particular methodology appears to overlook the more typical processes of regression analysis and landscape stratigraphy, both described in previous chapters. Applying these techniques to the Little Waltham landscape provides little evidence to support Drury's presumed supposition that the long features were later additions that did not respect the 'existing' regular field alignments. If it were so then it should also follow that these lengthy inserted features should disrupt the adjacent field pattern or at least cut through it, but there is no evidence for this. Where the 'ancient fields' are found on either side of one of the long features, the field boundaries do not cross it, as would be expected if the parcel divisions had once continued seamlessly across the landscape, before they were interrupted by the insertion of the new feature. Instead, the divisions are staggered or offset and notably the same discontinuous relationship is found between field boundaries on either side of the Roman road that led to Braintree.

While when viewed on a large-scale map the disruption caused by the Roman road in the landscape appears to be clear, with numerous fields on each side that end in oblique edges, closer inspection of the First Edition Ordnance Survey 6-Inch map reveals that there are in fact no examples where the supposedly ancient field boundary is shown to continue across the road. Even those examples that appear to match up on Drury's plan, when checked closely, are actually misaligned by between 10 and 20 m. Closer analysis of the regular field pattern indicates that it is made up of numerous individual small groups of field boundaries and while they initially appear to create a regular grid they are in fact discontinuous smaller groupings. This suggests the landscape around Little Waltham did not originate as a single planned landscape containing tracks, roads and fields, but instead new fields were fitted into the loose framework of existing lanes and boundaries.

The selection methodology used by Drury and in particular the technique of including only those parts of longer features that matched his chosen alignments was frequently utilised in choosing which field boundaries were included within the relict field plan, as Figure 3.2 illustrates. Adding in the nonconforming boundaries reveals how the field boundaries that have supposedly survived from Drury's relict field system fit within a wider pattern that contains both roughly rectilinear and decidedly irregular field shapes. Notably there are frequent examples where Drury's nominated 'prehistoric' field boundaries continue far beyond the length he selected for inclusion in his field system.

In the previous chapter we saw that fields lying close to Ermine Street in Caxton in Cambridgeshire appeared to be slighted by the Roman road because it crossed the minor valley at an oblique angle. On the clay wold in Cambridgeshire the importance of arranging strips and furlongs to optimise surface drainage must have exceeded the inconvenience of ploughing into an awkward corner, and an analogous pattern is visible in the closes of Little Waltham. This similarity is perhaps unsurprising given that the local environments of the two locations are comparable. The same fertile Hanslope clay soils discussed in Cambridgeshire are located upon the valley slopes and higher ground that lies to the north and west of Little Waltham. The soil on the slopes and plateau to the south is of the Streatham type, which is very similar to the Hanslope soils

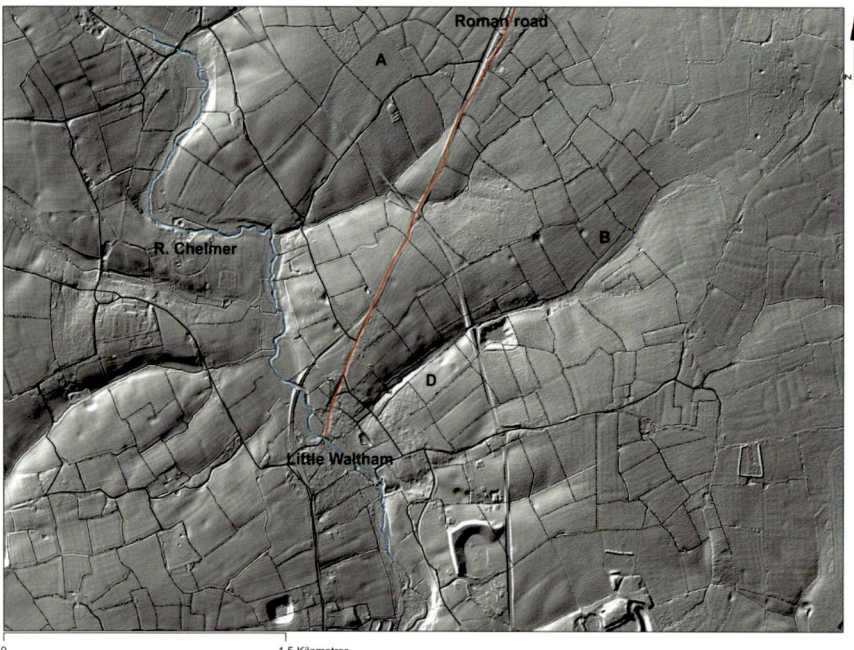

FIGURE 3.3. The nineteenth-century field pattern around Little Waltham, Essex (First Edition Ordnance Survey 6-Inch map, overlaid on LiDAR Composite DTM 2 m.

discussed previously; the principal difference being that the period of waterlogging after the winter rains is marginally shorter for the Streatham soils (Hodge 1984, 313). The soils that lay closest to the river Chelmer belong to the Ludford Association and are free draining sandy loams that are easily workable, but the area is prone to seasonal flooding (Soil Survey 1983, Sheet 4; Hodge 1984, 237). Most of the surviving boundaries in the valley tend to outfall directly into the river, with few ditches that run parallel to the watercourse. Unlike many later writers on the subject of relict landscapes Drury briefly acknowledged the local topography could cause adjustments to the field boundaries (Drury 1978, 134). Rodwell also noted how the 'Iron Age' fields and the accompanying lanes 'were laid out on the valley slopes' (Rodwell 1978, 95). But neither showed an awareness of just how important drainage and topography had been in generating the observed pattern.

As Figure 3.3 illustrates, there was in fact a very close relationship between the field pattern and the local terrain, indeed the importance of topography in influencing the landscape highlights some of the potential biases associated with selection. For example, the LiDAR plot in Figure 3.3 clearly indicates that points D and B lie along the same minor valley. The field boundaries near D, and a section of the long feature itself were incorporated into Drury's relict field pattern, but the morphologically identical boundaries at Point B were not included. Furthermore, the continuation of the long boundary was excluded from Drury's field pattern because it did not conform to the 'correct' orientations.

The importance of several of the minor tributary valleys in determining the regular-ish landscape pattern around Little Waltham is particularly noticeable in the area to the north of the settlement; both the valley close to D on Figure 3.3 and the somewhat parallel valley approximately 750 m further north contain some boundaries selected by Drury for his relict field system. The slight difference in orientation of the two individual valleys almost certainly explains why the field boundaries close to the Roman road are slightly misaligned. The faint disruption to the boundary pattern around the Roman road and watershed suggests that field boundaries in each of the valleys originated in isolation, with the divisions respecting the local terrain, before eventually meeting in former 'waste' as the farmed area expanded.

The LiDAR plot also illustrates with particular clarity how in Little Waltham, as in Caxton, the slighting originates in the terrain-oblivious route of the Roman road cutting across the minor valleys and spurs that lay close to the river Chelmer. The clay soils on the hillsides could be improved by optimising the natural watercourses and supplementing them with additional ditches located to drain wet lying areas into the river. Even without supplementary drainage, water would wash down the clay slopes and onto the valley floor, and this when combined with river flooding would also periodically overwhelm the lighter loamy soils in the valley and ditches would help to drain the floodwaters faster. Overall, the importance of optimising the drainage on the land around Little Waltham outweighed the relatively minor inconvenience of a road cutting through a relatively small number of field boundaries.

How the Land Lies

Relict field systems in East Anglia

The clay-land countryside of north Suffolk and south Norfolk contains several examples of boundaries, lanes and fields which appear to conform to a somewhat regular pattern. The relict field systems in Scole–Dickleburgh and the Elmhams are the two most well-known examples in the region and have been

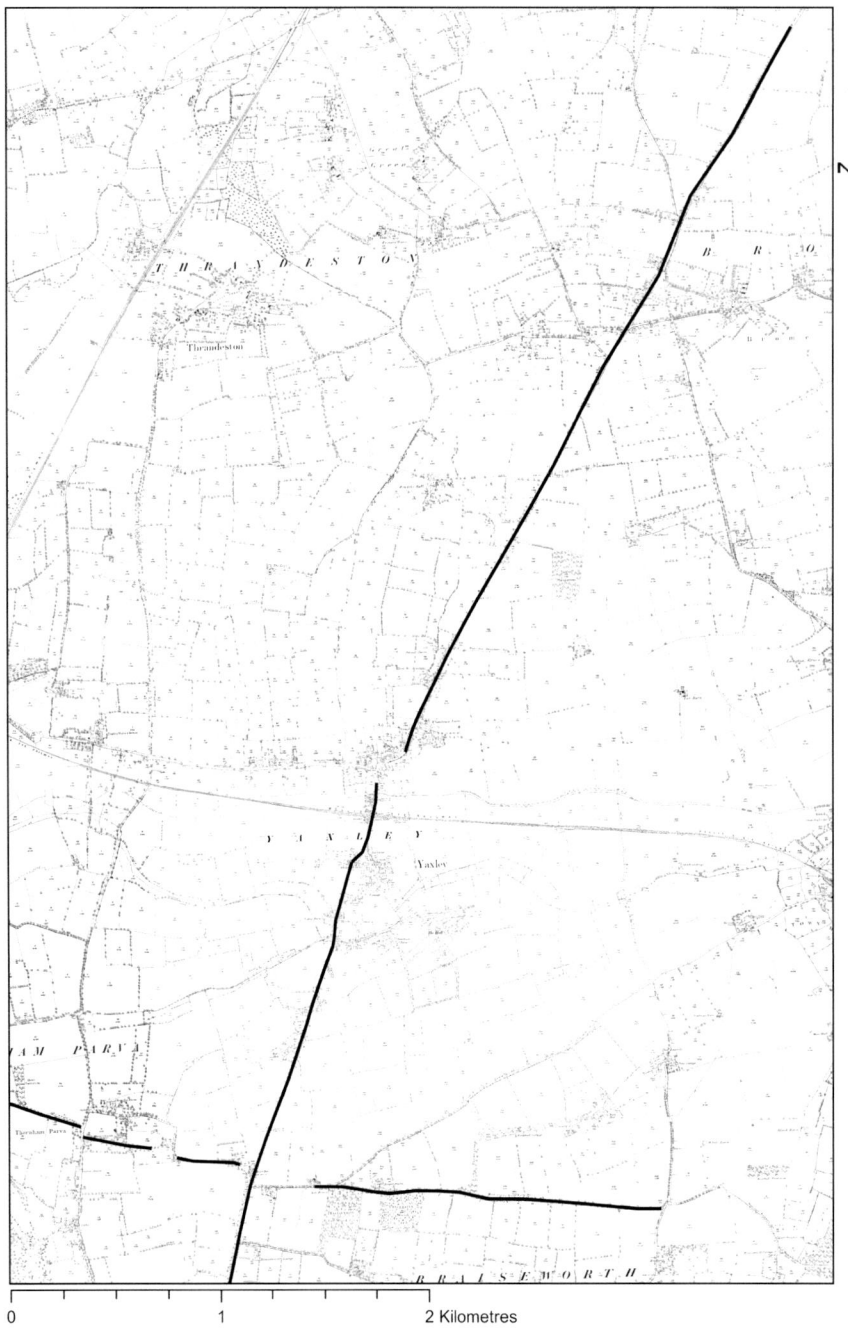

FIGURE 3.4. The landscape around Yaxley, Suffolk shown on the First Edition Ordnance Survey 6-Inch map, Roman Pye Road and the possible location for Grimms Ditch (after Williamson 1987).

mentioned already, but another grid-like landscape albeit smaller in scale was identified by Williamson, in the area around Yaxley (Williamson 1987, 427). Although included within Williamson's analysis of co-axial field systems in East Anglia, the Yaxley landscape has been overlooked in favour of the better known Scole–Dickleburgh system, which remains one of the foundational pillars of research into relict field systems.

Williamson's analysis of the 'regular' field pattern lying south of Eye in Suffolk had a particular focus on the area where the rough grid of lanes and boundaries appeared to have an unconformable relationship with the path of a Roman road. Williamson highlighted two large-scale linear features within the somewhat regular pattern of fields: the Roman Pye Road, which ran on a northeasterly trajectory through the centre of Yaxley; and a lost earthwork called Grimms Ditch, its course previously identified by Norman Scarfe, ranged roughly perpendicular to it (Williamson 1987, 428). Topographically the area around Yaxley, illustrated in Figure 3.4, is one of a clay plateau cut by a few gentle valleys, with land heights varying from approximately 50 m on the plateau to 30 m in the valley.

The environment around Yaxley is typical of the Norfolk and Suffolk clay lands, the principal soil type in the parish is the Beccles Association, an impermeable but fertile clay soil and in the valley, close to the settlement and lying on either side of the minor watercourse that passes west to east through the centre of the parish is a narrow area of Melford Association soils, naturally well drained loams (Hodge 1984, 246). Although the Melford soils would have been relatively easy to work even for the earliest farmers, the Beccles soil on the higher ground would have required some level of surface drainage, in order that the risk of waterlogging and thereby drowning the crop over winter was reduced (Hodge 1984, 118). Although the soil water levels would reach capacity during the winter months

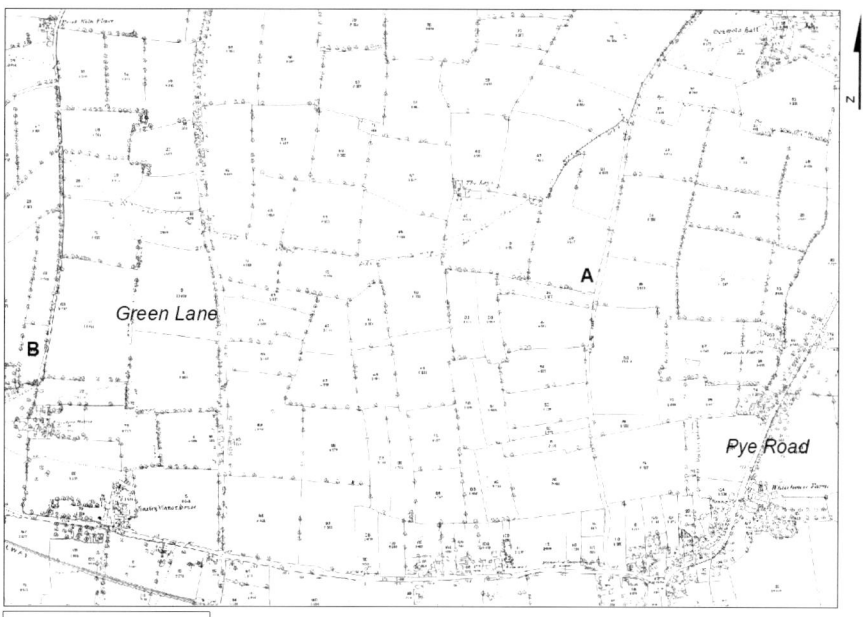

FIGURE 3.5. Detail of the northwestern portion of Yaxley, Suffolk shown on the First Edition Ordnance Survey 6-Inch map.

the low rainfall levels in the region meant that there were few environmental limitations on using the clay soils for growing crops, at least for societies with access to a plough capable of turning a furrow and a need for increased production.

The initial impression on viewing the nineteenth-century field pattern illustrated in Figure 3.4 supports Williamson's contention that both the Roman road and the possible boundary earthwork have been 'superimposed' upon a pre-existing semi-regular pattern of fields. Williamson argued that the semi-regular landscape around Yaxley resulted from prehistoric planning of agricultural land (Williamson 1987, 428). The Yaxley field pattern bears more than a passing resemblance to the Little Waltham landscape discussed previously. However as in the earlier analysis a closer examination highlights potential problems.

Even at the large scale shown in Figure 3.5 the orientation of the grid in Yaxley differs to the north and south of the settlement (in the centre of the plot). Despite their close proximity to one another, in general, the small squarish fields to the north follow a north–south orientation, while those to the south of the village were more closely aligned to a north-northwesterly to south-southeasterly direction.

This difference is further highlighted in the pattern of lanes, the northern portion of Yaxley parish contains three parallel north–south lanes, and two are shown in Figure 3.5, the third lane close to B is in the neighbouring parish of Mellis. The three lanes dominate the field pattern to the northwest of the village, so much so that the regular pattern of field boundaries appear to be slotted in between them. The First Edition Ordnance Survey 6-Inch map names one of the roads as 'Green Lane', on the map this route appears to be slightly wider than the other roads as well as being shown densely lined with trees. Green Lane appears to share morphological similarities with the linear commons, discussed previously. Green Lane appears to lead toward areas of probable former common pasture with Thrandeston's Little and Great Greens likely remnants of a much larger area of 'waste'. While Green Lane, perhaps, retains more of its original form than the other Yaxley roads, it and the other lanes fossilise the repeated journeys made by the villagers to access more distant resources. In this way the lanes in the northern portion of Yaxley parish appear to conform to Williamson's later re-interpretation of the Scole–Dickleburgh field system. Williamson noted the numerous parallel transhumance tracks that led from the valley to the higher ground, the so-called co-axial tracks, due to their morphological similarity to Dartmoor reaves, which Williamson concluded formed the primary spines of the grid-like landscape within which the field pattern was slotted (Williamson 1987, 425; 1998, 27).

It is notable that in Yaxley with the exception of the three lanes found in the north of the parish, there was little evidence for a pattern of continuous features that stretched over many hundred metres, and in particular the long boundaries providing uninterrupted divisions for two or more fields. Instead, a north–south field boundary in Yaxley rarely formed the edge of more than two parcels before terminating on another crosswise feature. Williamson explained similar small imperfections in the Scole–Dickleburgh field system as resulting from later small adjustments (Williamson 1987, 425). This is a possible interpretation, but in Yaxley while the north–south field divisions tend to be frequently interrupted, the same is not true of the east–west aligned boundaries. There are several groups of five or more fields that share the same long east–west boundary feature and upon which the north–south divisions terminate. It would seem unlikely that this apparent distinction could arise solely from piecemeal adjustment. Applying the rules of regression analysis would indicate that the east–west features predate the north–south boundaries, but although long and continuous the east–west alignments are not particularly regular and provide little supporting evidence for a planned field system.

As touched upon previously there is no similar pattern of parallel lanes visible in the landscape that lies south of the village. In this area comparatively few of the field boundaries even extend beyond the edge of a single parcel. This is evident even in Figure 3.6a, which shows the fields Williamson used to illustrate his conclusion that the Roman Pye Road cut through the vestiges of a prehistoric field pattern (Williamson 1987, 429). In common with many who write upon relict landscapes Williamson based his analysis upon the Tithe map, the earliest surviving map of the parish. Tithe maps were drawn to provide a visual index to the accompanying Tithe Apportionment and illustrate the boundaries of areas upon which Tithes were owed. 'First Class' maps, those which were considered to be sufficiently accurate to be useful in boundary disputes, made up only a small proportion of the whole; for example, they account for just over 10 per cent of all Tithe maps in the neighbouring county of Norfolk (Norfolk County Council 2012).

A comparison of Figure 3.6a and b illustrates subtle but significant differences in the field pattern as drawn by the surveyors of the Tithe Commission in 1842, and four decades later by the Ordnance Survey. Several field boundaries appear to have been lost, those shown in grey in Figure 3.6b, but the most significant

FIGURE 3.6. a) Detail of the field pattern south of Yaxley, Suffolk illustrating the unconformable relationship with the Pye Road (after Williamson 1987, 429; taken from the Tithe Map 1842, Norfolk County Council 2012); b) Detail of the field pattern south of Yaxley, Suffolk on the First Edition Ordnance Survey 6-Inch map, highlighted boundaries (after Williamson 1987, 428).

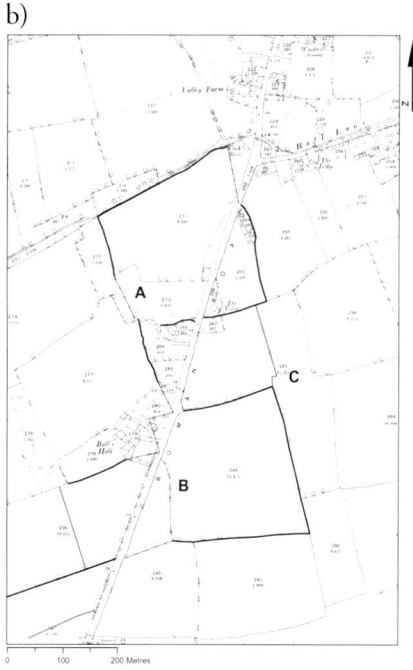

difference between the two maps in Figure 3.6 is found in the relative regularity of the boundaries, and an example of this is visible by comparing the area around point A in Figure 3.6b with the same location in 3.6a. The field boundaries drawn in the Tithe Map are generally straighter and more regular in form than those mapped by the Ordnance Survey 40 years later. Although field boundaries are likely to be altered and adjusted over time with changing agricultural practices, during the nineteenth century it was more typical for sinuous boundaries to be made straight, rather than the reverse. Furthermore, many of the curving 1880 boundaries indicate the presence of trees along them, which suggests that they have been present in the landscape for some time before being surveyed, and this when combined with the absence of in-field trees that would indicate lost hedges suggests that the First Edition of the Ordnance Survey 6-Inch map was the first accurate representation of the Yaxley Field pattern.

In his discussion of the relict landscape in Yaxley, Williamson highlighted the fields shown in Figure 3.6a, which he observed on the Yaxley Tithe Map as illustrative of the action of Roman Pye Road in cutting through the prehistoric field pattern, and the map does initially at least provide an attractive argument, particularly with Williamson's lost elements shown as dotted lines (Williamson 1987, 428). As noted previously there is little evidence for direct continuation of boundaries from one field to the next, and while two millennia of changing agricultural systems, not to mention priorities, will undoubtedly lead to changes, there is little to suggest that there was ever a single coherent field plan, beyond a very approximate tendency towards a north–south grain in the landscape.

One of the key elements of Williamson's argument is that the Roman road was imposed upon the earlier field pattern and created inconveniently shaped

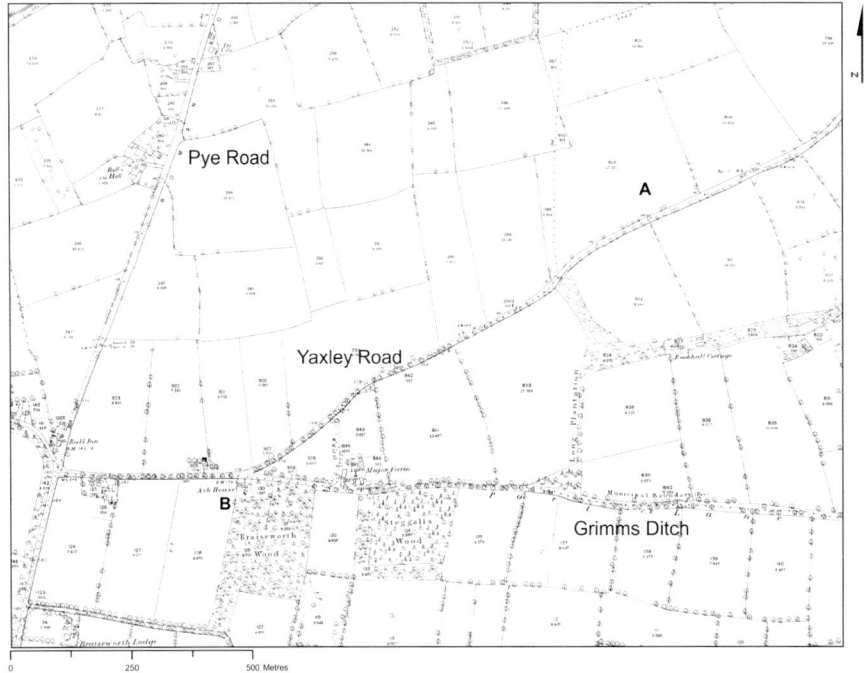

FIGURE 3.7. Detail of the First Edition Ordnance Survey 6-Inch map showing Yaxley Road, Braisworth, Suffolk.

fields, and one of the prime examples used as evidence for this interpretation was the area shown in Figure 3.6a. Considering the same fields shown on the Ordnance Survey First Edition 6-Inch map suggests that far from having a prehistoric origin, several of the field boundaries resemble the reverse 'S' curve so characteristic of medieval open-field strips and were presumably created by late medieval or post-medieval 'piecemeal' enclosure.

These sinuous boundaries are particularly noticeable to the west of B and the east of C in Figure 3.6b, but they are common throughout the Yaxley field pattern. An example of how significant this is to an understanding of the origin of the field pattern can be discerned by comparing the two maps in Figure 3.6. On the Tithe map the area close to B forms a narrow triangle made up of straight sides, but on the First Edition Ordnance Survey 6-Inch map the same boundary is shown as sinuous following the reverse 'S' curve previously noted. This indicates that the field was ploughed up to the Roman road and further that it was likely that the headland ran parallel to the road in this parcel. Although the triangular form is noticeable on the modern maps as noted previously in the discussion of a similar landscape in Caxton, Cambridgeshire, it is useful to remember that in earlier times the land would have been divided into narrow strips and the additional inconvenience of ploughing a 12 yard strip that had an oblique angled end, is very much less than it is perceived to be when viewed at the scale of a whole field, or furlong.

Perhaps the most noticeable interruption in the field pattern, other than the Roman Pye Road, is caused by a lane, now called Yaxley Road, which travels east from the location of the possible earthwork. Yaxley Road is clearly visible on the extract from the First Edition Ordnance Survey 6-Inch map shown in

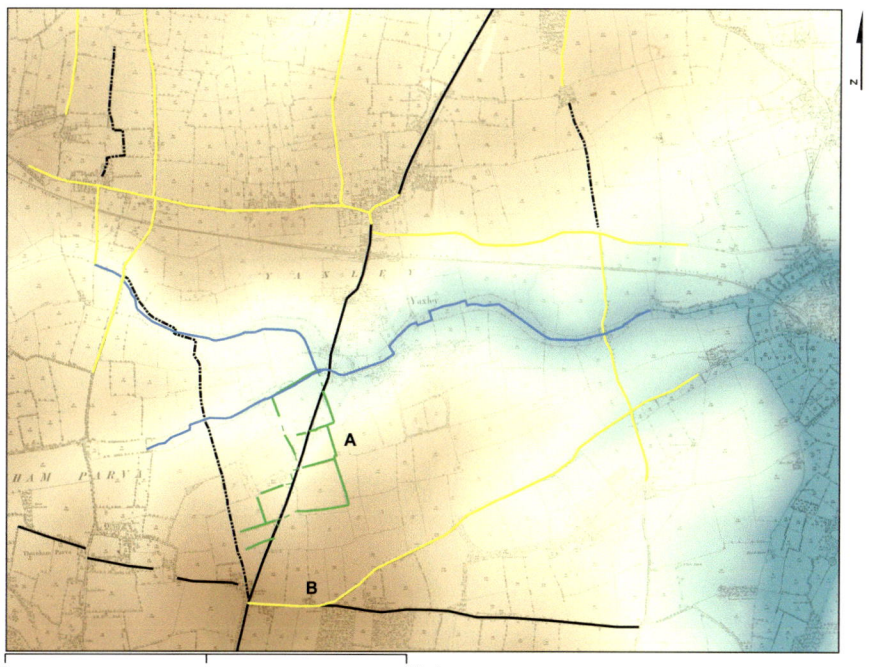

FIGURE 3.8. The topography close to Yaxley, Suffolk and the First Edition Ordnance Survey 6-Inch map. Local lanes shown in yellow, watercourses in blue and parish boundaries by black dotted line. Also included are Roman Pye Road and Grimms Ditch Earthworks in black and 'slighted' fields in green (after Williamson 1987).

Figure 3.7, starting close to B and travelling towards, and beyond A. At point B, where Yaxley Road meets the Grimms Ditch earthwork, there are numerous sub-triangular fields, which would have been just as inconvenient to plough as those parcels supposedly slighted by the Roman Pye Road. In his analysis of his purportedly ancient landscape, Williamson incorporated only a few short sections of Yaxley Road typically including only those parts which were conformable with the relict field system (Williamson 1987, 429). In common with Drury and others, Williamson removed much of the length of the road from the landscape analysis and as a result, he was able to exclude Yaxley Road, and the troublesome triangular fields from his discussion.

Certainly, within the context of a surviving relict landscape it is difficult to imagine a reason why a presumably later route that was conformable with the supposedly prehistoric field pattern close to point A would then take a path towards point B creating triangular fields. Yaxley Road appears to have functioned primarily as a link between Roman Pye Road and the nearby town of Eye, and therefore there would seem to be little need for the route to apparently cut through the fields to reach point B when with only a slight diversion it could have followed a feature to the north of B and better conform to the boundary pattern. Closer examination indicates that Yaxley Road also corresponds with a slight disruption in the field pattern. Figure 3.7 illustrates that the general alignment of boundaries that lie to the north of Yaxley Road differs, albeit subtly, from those to the south. Furthermore, there is no evidence to suggest that these field boundaries initially continued from north to south. This suggests that the road did not cut through a pre-existing field pattern, but that the regular arrangement of hedges and boundaries that terminate at right angles postdate the lane. Notably a similar adjustment in the orientation of the field pattern occurs again, albeit more obviously, south of the Grimms Ditch earthwork. Given the earlier discussion it is not surprising to find that, once again, there is no evidence in the field pattern that indicates that it pre-dated the earthwork. In Yaxley, and in common with many other supposedly ancient relict landscapes, the regularity of form that provides the evidence of prehistoric, or later, planned countryside, tends to dissipate the more closely the pattern of fields, lanes and boundaries are examined.

If the rough grid of fields around Yaxley did not originate as vestigial remains of a prehistoric field pattern as Williamson originally concluded, could it instead have developed within a loose framework of equally ancient tracks, as he later suggested in his reassessment of the Scole–Dickleburgh landscape? Certainly, the parallel lanes found in the north of the parish suggest that this is a possibility, although, in common with those discussed in Cambridgeshire, many of these lanes appear to be aligned upon topographic features, either passing along minor watersheds or dry valleys. This makes it very difficult to suggest an origin date, as these features would have been both visible and useful to local communities as natural divisions until quite recently.

As discussed above the field pattern to the south of Yaxley village is less regular than it is to the north, reflecting the more complex topography. Figure 3.8

illustrates that Yaxley Road follows a dry valley and it is likely that the slight difference in the orientation of the field boundaries to either side of it reflects attempts to optimise drainage of the clay soils using the natural slope. This conclusion is supported by the slight adjustment in the alignment of field boundaries seen north of the lane starting at point B shown on Figures 3.7 and 3.8. The boundaries lying closest to Pye Road on the clay plateau follow a direct north–south alignment matching neither Pye Road nor the surrounding field pattern but appear to follow a rough compromise orientation. As the boundaries move toward the dry valley their orientation gradually shifts until they are aligned perpendicular to the valley and watercourse. This is reminiscent of the migration of alignment of the boundaries of the Roman fields lying close to Ermine Street in the Cambourne Development Area and discussed in Chapter 2.

The importance of this right-angled relationship between boundary and watercourse is visible at point A in Figure 3.8. Williamson highlighted this small section of the Yaxley field pattern in his analysis to illustrate how the Roman road divided parcels unequally, leaving sub-triangular remnants of land. Figure 3.8 indicates that these fields, shown in detail in Figure 3.6, clearly share the same perpendicular relationship to the minor watercourse seen in Caxton, Cambridgeshire. Little evidence has been found for ridge and furrow earthworks in northeast Suffolk, even upon the clay soils but it is likely that plough ridges were lost through post-medieval enclosure and cultivation (Liddiard 1999, 6). However, even the absence of ridging would not in itself preclude the slope being used for surface drainage, in this low rainfall area the simple action of ploughing up and down slope, especially if individual strips were separated by a deep furrow would provide some improvement. Once again, the importance of using the natural slope to facilitate field drainage and improve the land for agriculture far outweighed any inconvenience caused by farming a strip, or even a field that terminated upon an oblique angle.

So far this chapter has reconsidered whether two notable examples of English relict field systems are in fact instances where an ancient landscape has been slighted by the imposition of later features. The evidence instead suggests that the loose semi-regular pattern of lanes and fields derived from the importance of topography in improving early agricultural landscapes. While not all so-called relict field systems contain a feature that slights the landscape, they do all presume a large degree of landscape planning, whether this was local covering a few adjacent parishes or large scale sub-regional arrangement, for example, the Dengie Peninsula, the Elmhams, and Scole–Dickleburgh. Despite the difference in scale, examples of these two different scenarios have tended to be subject to direct comparison. Similarly, explanations of the origins of the individual relict field systems have been extrapolated or applied to historic landscapes of varying size, perhaps unwisely. There must be, after all, significant variations in precisely how a regular landscape was established over a few hundred hectares near a farmstead or settlement, to ones that encompass many square kilometres and communities.

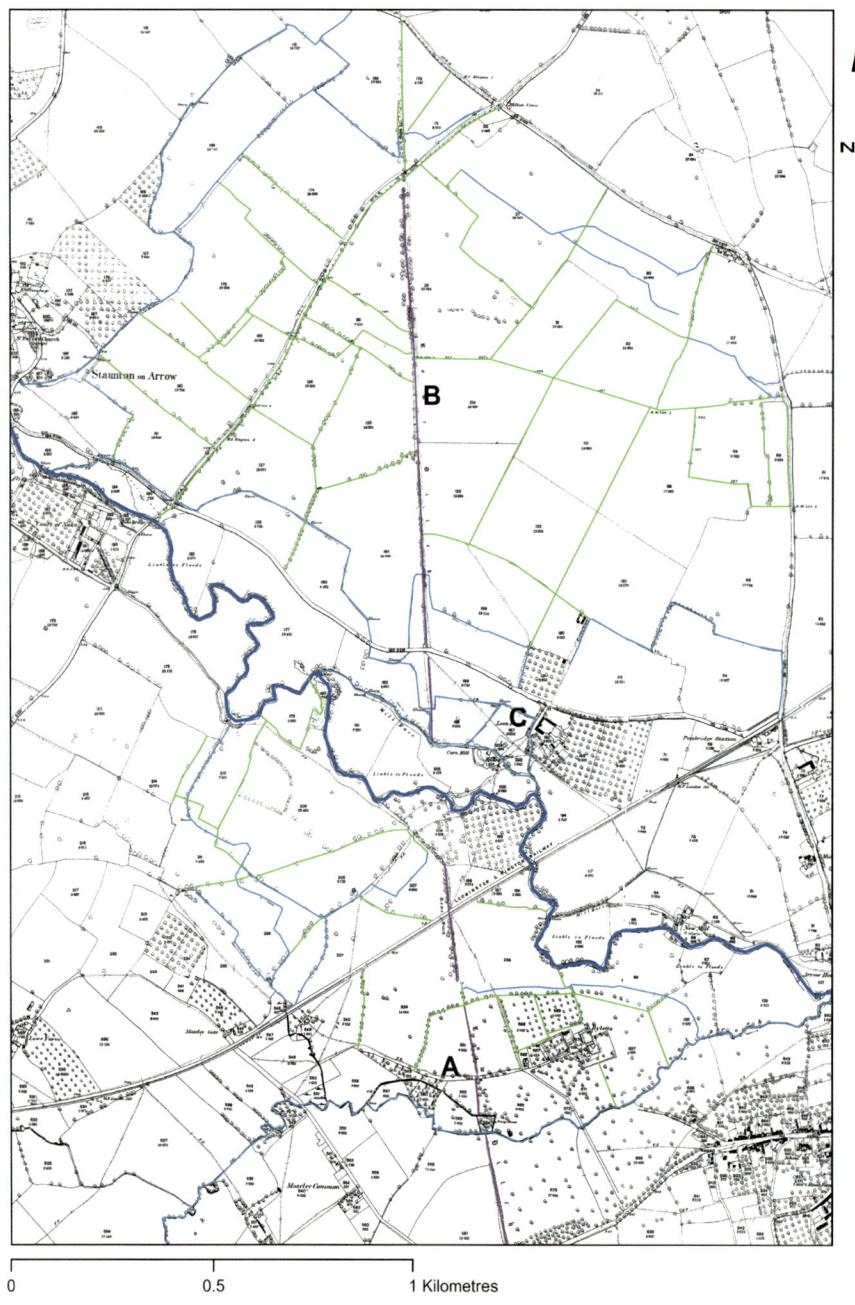

FIGURE 3.9. Rowe Ditch (in violet) on the First Edition Ordnance Survey 6-Inch map. The river Arrow is the thick blue line in the lower half of the map. Modern field ditch boundaries shown in green (dry) and blue (wet).

Late Iron Age or Romano-British field systems in the Arrow Valley?

While a disharmonious relationship between a Roman road and field boundaries is perhaps the most frequent indication of the presence of a so-called relict landscape in the Arrow Valley in Herefordshire, the regular field patterns instead encounter two linear earthworks. These earthworks, one a ditch, the other a bank are both of early medieval origin and have each been used to provide a *terminus ante quem* for the fields that surround them.

Lying close to Pembridge is Rowe Ditch, although the first written record dates from 982 CE but it is thought to be of late Roman or very early medieval origin as it cuts through an early Romano-British farmstead. The relationship between Rowe Ditch and the landscape of the Arrow Valley was discussed in detail by Paul White in *The Arrow Valley, Herefordshire: Landscape, Change and Conservation* (2003a, 45). Approximately 6 km further west, Offa's Dyke – the giant boundary earthwork constructed during the 780s CE – crosses the river Arrow near the modern town of Lyonshall.

Although both earthworks date from the first millennium CE, their relationship with the surrounding field boundaries differs. Rowe Ditch cuts across the field pattern in much the same way as a Roman road, which it resembles in its straight form. Conversely near Lyonshall, Offa's Dyke has a generally conformable relationship within the surrounding landscape and this despite being a large-scale defensive earthwork rather than a relatively small local feature (White 2003a, 42).

Climatically the local environment between Lyonshall and Pembridge is very different to that of the case studies discussed previously, lying in one of the wetter zones of England and the average annual rainfall recorded by the Met Office in Shobdon, just north of Pembridge, is almost 800 mm, by comparison the weather station in Writtle, Essex near Little Waltham, receives less than 600 mm of rain in an average year. Close to Pembridge the Arrow Valley contains numerous northeast–southwest brooks, which run roughly parallel to the river and intersect north–south watercourses, caused by higher ground lying both west and north of the low lying plain. This land formation can be seen in Figure 3.9, which shows the wider topography around Rowe Ditch. The valley topography is extremely muted with a fall of only 5 m in height over a distance of 1,300 m and much of the land lying on either side of the river Arrow is prone to flooding. Further upstream the landscape surrounding Offa's Dyke near Lyonshall differs significantly, with narrow valleys around the main watercourses with landfalls of 60 to 100 m.

Despite the difference in local topography both areas are dominated by the same type of soil, namely free draining, slightly acid loamy Rowton Association soils, which are somewhat infertile but being easy to work would be attractive sites to early farming communities. The light soils would be at risk of erosion by rainfall or flooding, but they drain quickly after inundation (Landis 2020). White noted the easily erodible soil caused sedimentation in the ditches (White 2003a, 58). This would appear to confirm the importance of controlling drainage on the land in the Arrow Valley, as well as highlighting the requirement for regular maintenance to keep ditches functional.

As touched upon above, the valley topography west of Pembridge has a fall of only 5 m in height over a distance of 1,300 m and this must have made surface draining the soils extremely challenging. This section of the valley contains numerous northeast–southwest brooks, which run roughly parallel to the river Arrow. These brooks intersect several north–south oriented watercourses of natural origin that transport the water draining from the higher ground that surrounds the west and north of the plain. This land formation is illustrated in Figure 3.12, which shows the wider topography around Rowe Ditch. As noted above, the Rowton

Association Soils that are found in the valley are predominately light and free draining, which could imply that additional drainage would not necessarily be required (White 2003b, 4). Modern descriptions of Rowton Association Soils are of loose silts overlying gravels, which makes them free draining but as previously discussed, prone to erosion. Despite being light and easily workable the opportunities for spring cropping are limited, particularly as after light rains the silt is prone to 'cap', creating a hard surface that prevents the new shoots emerging.

Even freely draining soils benefit from drainage if there is significant annual rainfall and ditches would help to return the land to a workable condition more rapidly after wet weather, particularly as the area is also prone to flooding by the river Arrow. From archaeological fieldwork on land close to the river Arrow at Leen Farm, indicated by point C in Figure 3.9, White noted significant periods of sedimentation of the ditches. This appeared to be particularly pronounced during the wet periods, which he dated to between 40 BCE and 480 CE and 600 to 1280 CE (White 2003a, 58). In his discussion of the Arrow Valley White noted that Rowe Ditch cut obliquely through the modern field pattern, following a straight course, and even passing through the remains of a Romano-British farmstead, although White believed the ditch was more likely to be of early medieval date (White 2003a, 42). Certainly, the First Edition Ordnance Survey 6-Inch map (in Figure 3.9) makes a compelling case that the earthwork has disrupted what appears to be a somewhat regular pattern of similarly aligned boundaries. However, it is worth noting that although Rowe Ditch appears to slight the overall landscape pattern, there is once again little indication of disruption to individual field boundaries. As noted previously in the case of Little Waltham there are no examples where the divisions appeared to fossilise as a previously continuous boundary that has been cut by the earthwork. There is only one boundary that appears to have any claim to have once been a continuous line, seen on Figure 3.9 north of point B.

In the course of his archaeological fieldwork at Leen Farm (close to point C on Figure 3.9) White noted that most of the boundaries shown on the First Edition Ordnance Survey 6-Inch map appeared to be of medieval or post-medieval origin. Using aerial photography White was able to locate a number of crop marks in the fields surrounding the farmyard, which appeared to have a rough northeast–southwest alignment. White was able to excavate two of these crop marks, indicated by A and C in Figure 3.10. Close to point A on Figure 3.10 White located a deep, 1.8 m ditch, which led him to be confident that the site was occupied during the Late Iron Age (Caulfield *et al.* 1997, 14). His investigation of the crop mark close to C found a ditch just beneath the modern plough soil and this contained artefacts dating to the second and third centuries CE in the ditch fill (White 2003b, 15). Similarly, White noted that a visible scatter of pottery dating from the Romano-British period was found in the field marked D. From the archaeological field work at Leen Farm, White concluded that the field pattern probably originated during the Roman occupation (White 2003b, 17). Crucially, White also noted that the Romano-British field pattern revealed by the crop marks matched the orientation of the wider

FIGURE 3.10. Archaeological features near Leen Farm, Pembridge (after White 2003a and drawn on the First Edition Ordnance Survey 6-Inch map). Cropmarks in light pink, surviving earthworks in mauve.

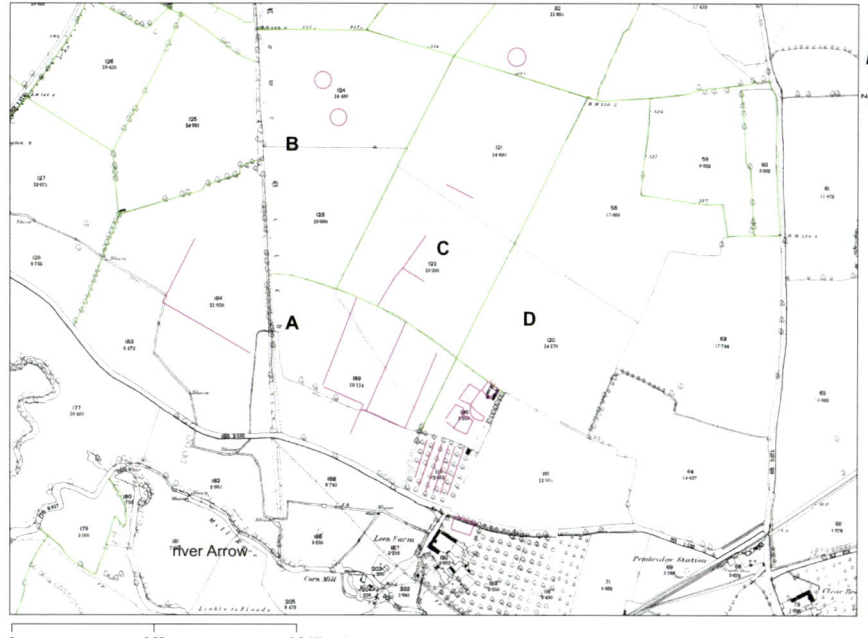

valley landscape. This led White to conclude that the boundary pattern of the Arrow Valley had a 'general trend of northwest-southeast' which would 'appear to continue through successive historical periods' up to the present day (White 2003b, 17). White queried whether this was simply coincidence or if it reflected 'a continuity of landscape organisation' (White 2003b, 18).

White was correct in assuming that the persistence of the dominant orientation in this section of the Arrow Valley was not a coincidence, but not because later generations of farmers respected ancient field boundaries. White's conclusion took results from a small excavation of a ditch section and applied it to the wider landscape on the basis of similar orientation, and without reference to the local topography and drainage patterns. The methodology used by White has become one of the pillars supporting the discovery of relict field systems by matching the alignments of small sections of excavated ditches with modern field boundaries.

The loosely analogous relationship noticed between the Iron Age and Romano-British boundaries White identified to the north of Leen Farm and the modern field boundaries in the nearby area is directly comparable to that found in the Cambourne Development Area discussed in Chapter 2, specifically that while some of the crop marks share similar orientation to the modern boundaries many more do not. Furthermore, the Late Iron Age or Romano-British features around Leen Farm cover a very small area, just a few square metres.

These early boundaries were clearly closely associated with their contemporary settlements (White 2003b, 11). There is no evidence in the form of crop marks or other archaeological data that would indicate that they extended far into the surrounding landscape (White 2003b, 11). White's presumption is based upon the observation that the modern field pattern

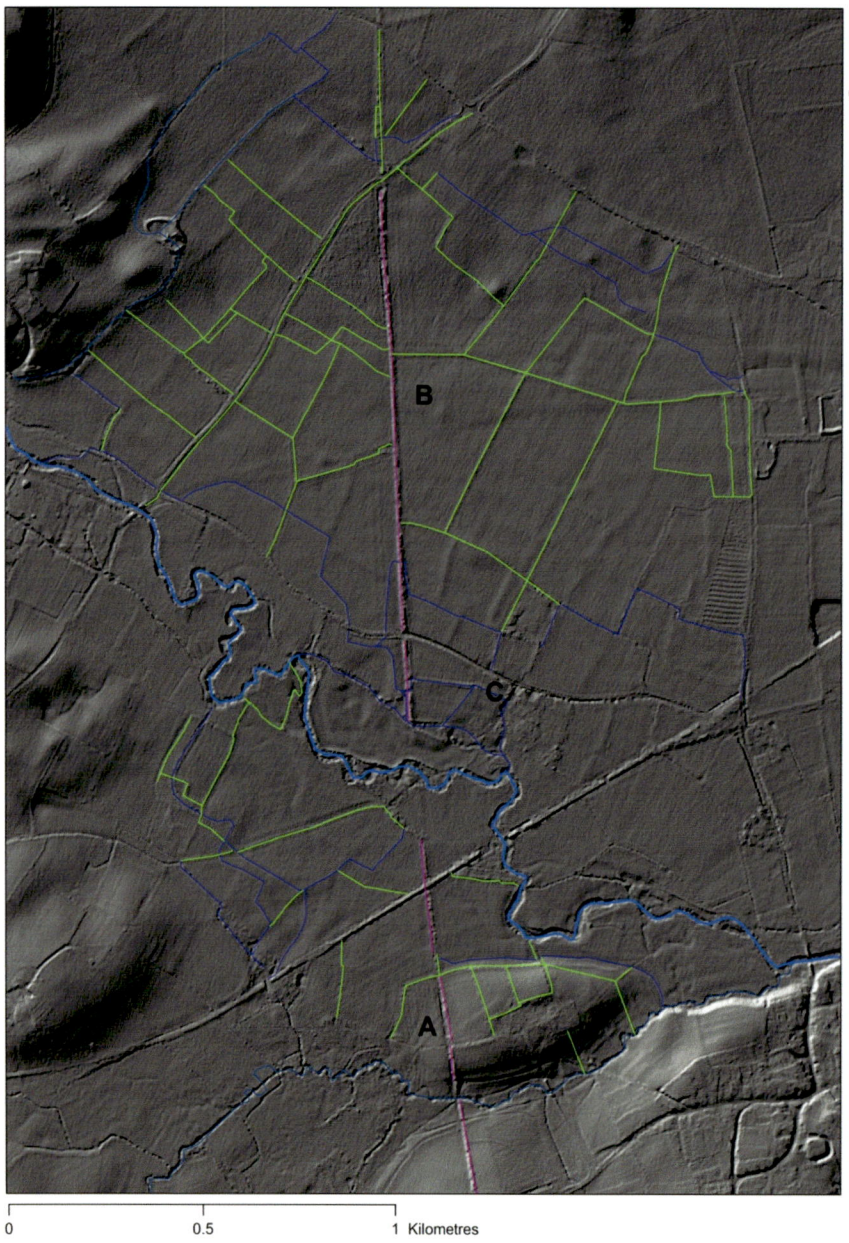

FIGURE 3.11. LiDAR (Composite DTM 2 m) covering the area of Rowe Ditch in the Arrow Valley. The river Arrow (mid-blue), field boundaries (green) and brooks (dark blue) from the First Edition Ordnance Survey 6-Inch map.

also has a preference for a general northeast to southwest alignment. The conclusion that a relict field system dating no later than the Romano-British period covers the Arrow Valley rests principally upon the First Edition Ordnance Survey 6-Inch map, and particularly the slighting of the modern field boundaries by Rowe Ditch.

The disharmonious relationship between Rowe Ditch and the adjacent field pattern is also visible on the LiDAR (DTM 2 m) plot shown in Figure 3.11. By removing the majority of the modern features from the image the significance of the local environment is highlighted; in particular the way in which Rowe Ditch intercepts the river Arrow at an oblique angle. The field boundaries that lie to the north of the watercourse, by contrast, have that by now familiar right-angle relationship with it.

Although Rowe Ditch does cut obliquely across the dominant orientation of field boundaries, there are some fields that do not fit easily into a neatly planned grid. Just north of point B the boundaries of several narrow fields appear to have slightly sinuous edges, which resembles the reverse 'S' created by piecemeal

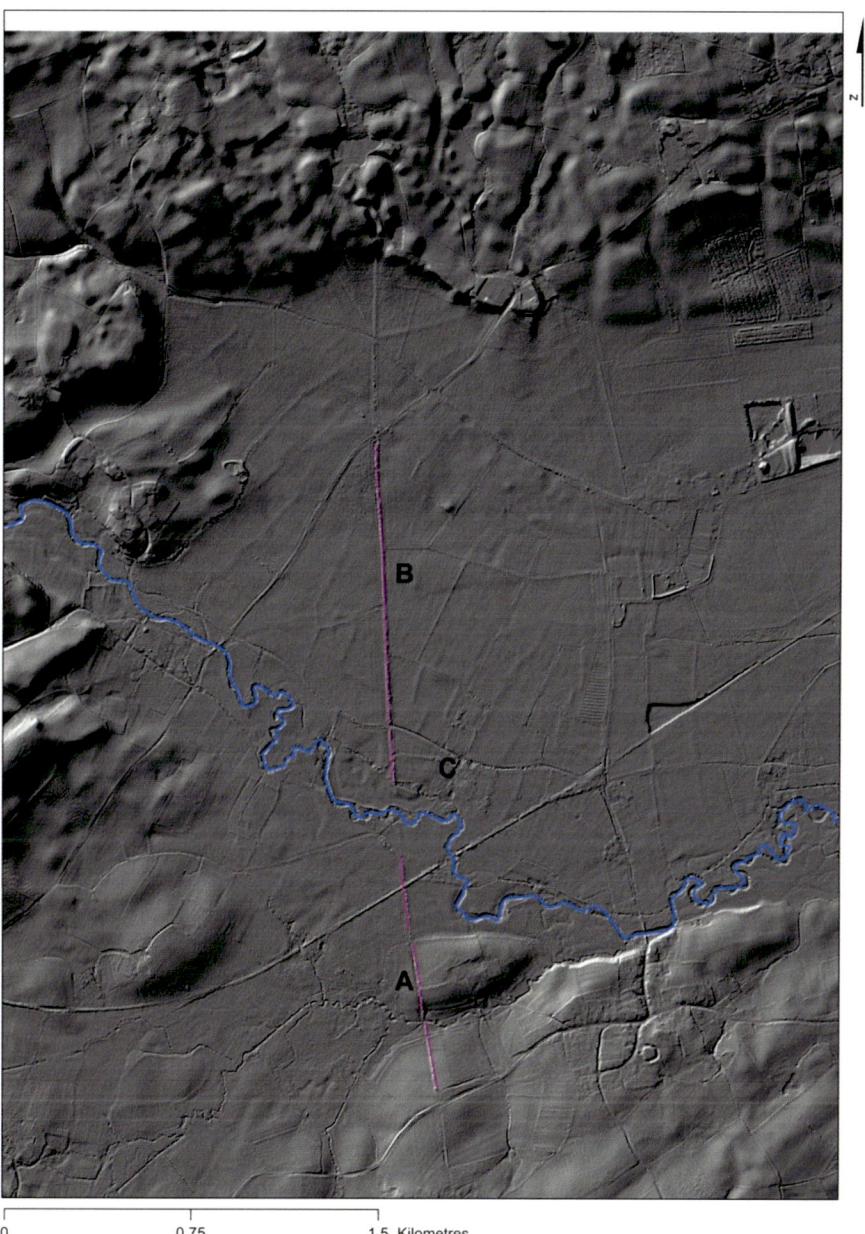

FIGURE 3.12. Wider topography of the environs of Rowe Ditch in the Arrow Valley (LiDAR Composite DTM 2 m).

enclosure of former open field strips. The field ditches appear to adjust their course very close to Rowe Ditch in order to meet it at a right angle, presumably to facilitate the flow of water into it. Immediately south of B in Figure 3.10 and visible in Figure 3.11 is the earthwork of Bagley Lane, a lost medieval route, which also appears to slight the modern field pattern in some places, and yet be incorporated into it elsewhere (White 2003b, 12). Figure 3.11 also indicates the extent to which the area lying closest to the river, and in the vicinity of Leen Farm (C in Figure 3.11), is crossed by watercourses and wet ditches, their predominately angular form indicating either a post-medieval origin, or that they have been 'improved' over the centuries; either way, their density indicates an area that is prone to flooding and waterlogging, despite the freely draining soil types discussed previously.

This locally wet environment is likely to greatly benefit from improvements in surface drainage in all historic periods, and a desire to improve the land could be the reason for the digging of the numerous small enclosure ditches identified by White through crop marks and excavation (White 2003b, 11).

The wider focus of the LiDAR plot in Figure 3.12 illustrates a feature of Rowe Ditch that is considerably less noticeable on the First Edition Ordnance Survey 6-Inch maps, namely that the alignment of the earthwork alters at the river. The southern section of the earthwork is slightly misaligned with the northern portion, and it appears to be deliberately located to cut across the end of a small island in the flood marshes at point A. It is also notable in Figure 3.11 that the relationship between Rowe Ditch and the local field boundaries close to point A appears to be generally conformable. This is almost certainly because Rowe Ditch crosses Curl Brook, the minor watercourse that flows to the south of the island shown in Figure 3.11, at an angle close to 90°. This is in direct contrast to the earthwork's relationship with the river Arrow, which lays just a few hundred metres to the north. In general, the pattern of modern field boundaries that lie to the south of the river Arrow appear much less regular than those found to the north and it is difficult to incorporate these southern boundaries into a convincing relict field system without a great deal of selection. A comparison of Figures 3.9, 3.11 and 3.12 illustrates that the field boundaries south of the river Arrow, like those to the north tend to relate to the local topography, streams and watercourses.

The plot of the wider area shown in Figure 3.12 also illustrates just how small the area covered by the group of fields slighted by Rowe Ditch actually is. Within Figure 3.9 it is possible to see two lanes, one on either side of the group of regular fields that lie to the north of the river Arrow. The road on the west takes a southwest to northeast route through the fields and its route is conformable within the surrounding pattern of field boundaries. In contrast, the lane lying around 750 m to the east of B appears to lie roughly parallel to Rowe Ditch and it shares the earthwork's north–south orientation. Despite this, this road does not slight the surrounding field pattern as might be expected, because the orientation of the proximal field drainage ditches has altered and the boundaries in this area follow a north–south alignment. The north–south aligned boundaries cover another small area before the boundary alignments shift once again just a few hundred metres further east. This pattern of gradual adjustments to accommodate changes in the local topography is in line with the findings from the Bourn Valley discussed previously.

The presence of Rowe Ditch cutting through the seemingly regular pattern of field boundaries makes the landscape preserved upon the First Edition Ordnance Survey 6-Inch map particularly arresting, but the Arrow Valley contains a second early medieval earthwork. Fragmentary remains of the bank known as Offa's Dyke are found in the Arrow Valley and lie approximately 6 km west of Rowe Ditch. In *The Arrow Valley, Herefordshire: Landscape, Change and Conservation* White includes a photograph of Offa's Dyke, which appears to indicate how the earthwork fitted within the surrounding pattern of boundary hedges, very different to the situation around Rowe Ditch (White 2003b, 46).

In a surviving section of the bank lying close to Lyonshall, Offa's Dyke does indeed appear to be incorporated within the farming landscape, and Figure 3.13 illustrates how the surviving sections of the early medieval earthwork are linked by modern field boundaries that appear to fossilise the ancient route of the earthwork. According to the generally accepted rules of landscape stratigraphy this would indicate that Offa's Dyke was either contemporary with or predated the fields. The field boundaries in the small area close to Lyonshall have the typical perpendicular arrangement to the local watercourse, Curl Brook. Notably the route of Offa's Dyke also crossed the brook at 90° and as a result there is no appearance of divergence between the early medieval earthwork and the surrounding field pattern. The field ditches, aligned to facilitate drainage,

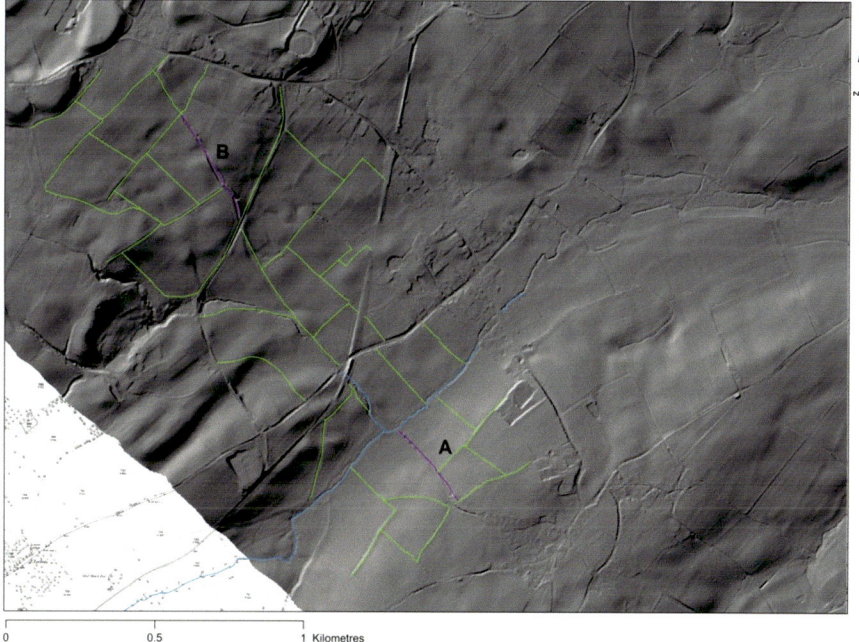

FIGURE 3.13. Offa's Dyke near Lyonshall (LiDAR Composite DTM 2 m), modern field boundaries from the First Edition Ordnance Survey 6-Inch map shown in green, watercourse, Curl Brook shown in blue. Surviving earthworks of Offa's Dyke at points A and B.

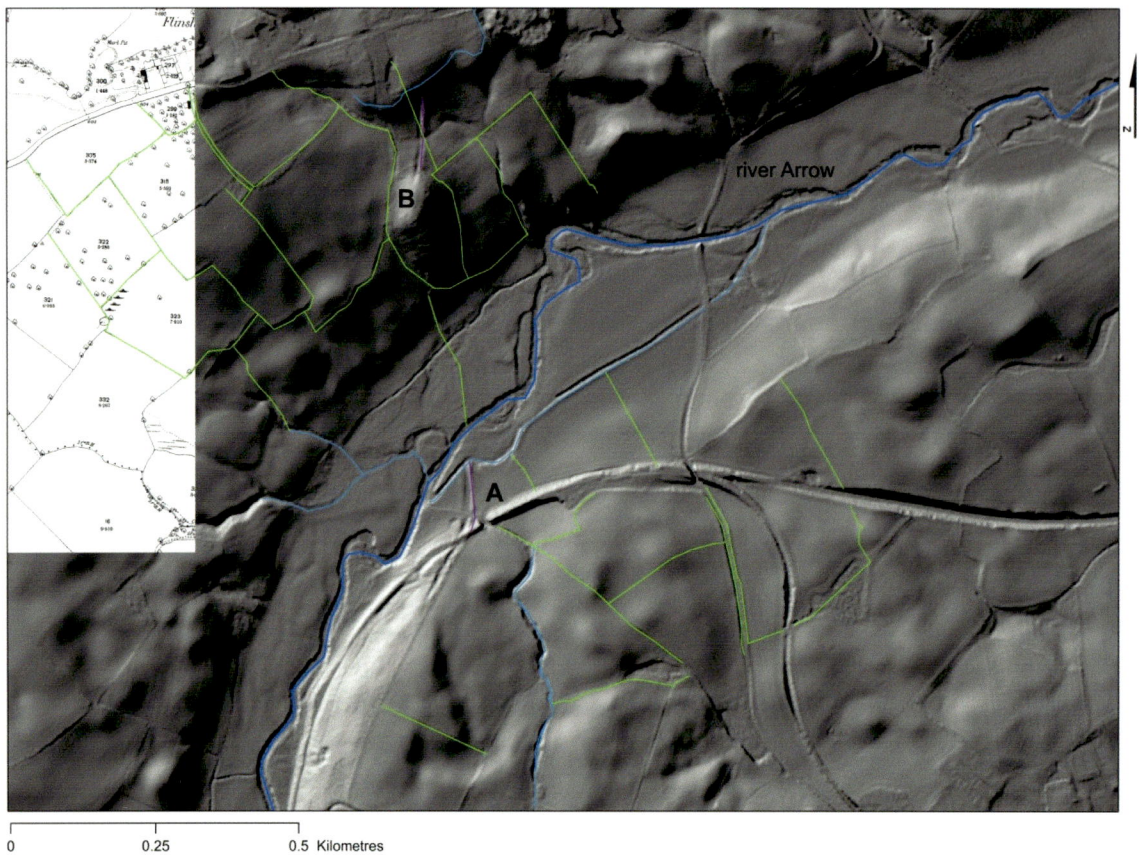

FIGURE 3.14. Offa's Dyke crossing the river Arrow (LiDAR Composite DTM 2 m), modern field boundaries from the First Edition Ordnance Survey 6-Inch map shown in green, river shown in blue. Surviving earthworks of Offa's Dyke at points A and B.

follow the slight slope and meet the minor stream at the characteristic right angle found in all the field systems discussed so far. It is the shared alignment that gives rise to the apparently conformable relationship between the field boundaries and earthwork.

This conclusion is further supported by another surviving section of Offa's Dyke, just a few kilometres to the north, where the earthwork crosses the river Arrow (see Figure 3.14). In this small section Offa's Dyke is not conformable with the modern field boundary pattern. The field ditches have the characteristic perpendicular relationship with the watercourse that has been noted elsewhere in the Arrow Valley, but the earthwork intercepts the river Arrow at an oblique angle. This leads to a disharmonious relationship between the earthwork and the surrounding field pattern. Over the space of just 2 km Offa's Dyke goes from appearing to fit neatly within the modern field boundary pattern to cutting obliquely across them close to the river Arrow. The difference would appear to originate from the angle at which the earthwork encountered or crossed the local watercourse. Where the relationship is perpendicular the earthwork conformed with the general trend for field boundaries to drain towards the river or brook and led to a harmonious relationship. In contrast, where the earthwork 'crossed' the river at an oblique angle then the greater importance of efficient field drainage ditches meant that even a large pre-existing feature would be ignored if it was on the 'wrong' alignment.

'Bronze Age' landscapes on the London Clays

The three previous examples of relict fields systems were identified by the authors due to the disharmonious relationship of the datable Roman road with the surrounding pattern of field boundaries clearly visible on the First Edition Ordnance Survey 6-Inch map. In the following example the major Roman road, Ermine Street, which runs through the grid pattern has been erased from the local landscape, a useful reminder that regionally significant features could be diverted, replaced or even removed entirely.

Wormley lies in the Lea Valley to the north of Cheshunt in Hertfordshire, to the east the parish reaches the banks of the river Lea. The settlement is strung along the road that runs parallel to the river and links Cheshunt to Broxbourne and beyond. Approximately 1 km west of the river the well-drained, fertile and easily workable silts of the Hamble Association soils that cover much of the lower Lee Valley change abruptly to the seasonally waterlogged clays and loams of the Essendon and Windsor Associations, as the land rises to a height of over 100 m OD (Hodge 1984, 207 and 184). Still further to the west, as the ground levels out into a dissected plateau, Beccles Association soils – the fertile clay soil discussed previously in Yaxley – occur. The First Edition Ordnance Survey 6-Inch maps, surveyed in the 1870s, show that much of this higher ground remained as woodland. Within the woodland area the maps show a dominant

FIGURE 3.15. Wormley, Hertfordshire from the First Edition Ordnance Survey 6-Inch map.

'grain' in the landscape, with long boundaries running east–west, and shorter ones aligned north–south. This landscape was identified by Bryant, Perry and Williamson in 2005, who noted its resemblance to the Dartmoor reaves, particularly in the presence of the long co-axial tracks linking the river and watershed, along which a long, continuous line of parish boundaries ran.

The authors suggested that to the east, where the ground fell away towards the river Lea, much of the co-axial field pattern had been erased by the creation of Cheshunt Park in the thirteenth century, something that had also removed the possibility of examining its relationship with Ermine Street (Bryant *et al.* 2005, 12). The authors noted the presence of numerous earthworks within the woodland, banks that were typically 5 to 8 m in width and ditched on either side (Bryant *et al.* 2005, 6).

Bryant, Perry and Williamson suggested that the co-axial landscape had developed within a framework of parallel drove-ways, which had linked the valley floor to the wooded uplands. They argued that the layout was, at least in part, a planned imposition on the landscape, rather than an organic development, on the grounds that in places the east–west tracks were, to use Fleming's phrase, 'terrain oblivious' to the local landforms. To support this argument, they highlighted the relationship between one of the tracks and the stream at point B in Figure 3.16 (Bryant *et al.* 2005, 12). Figure 3.16 illustrates that for much of its length the track runs roughly parallel to the north side of the stream, passing through Wormley West End, before moving closer to the stream and crossing it. This apparently unnecessary crossing of the stream does appear to suggest that the track ignores the local environment, in order to remain roughly parallel to the other east–west features, although one wonders just how easily either the distance between paths could be judged within a well wooded landscape and without surveying equipment.

It is probably useful to note that the drove-way close to B in its continuation eastwards passes Wormleybury and the parish church, and so may fossilise a route between an early medieval settlement site and the watershed resources, as well as linking the hamlet of Wormley West End to the church and main valley settlement. If it did originate in such a way this could suggest it is a later addition to the landscape: it is perhaps significant that this lane terminates in Wormley Wood rather than reaching the watershed. More fundamentally does the fact the lane crosses the stream necessarily make the entire route of the path 'terrain oblivious'? After all, there is a limit to how responsive to local topography a route covering several kilometres can be, without becoming so convoluted as to be unusable.

Figure 3.17 shows the features of the relict landscape overlying a modern terrain model and this highlights how the route of the drove-way near point B relates to the local environment. Reference to the modern flood risk maps indicates that land on either side of the small stream is prone to flooding. Floodwaters can reach the edge of the lane on the north but cover a much larger area to the south, which suggests that the path taken by the lane deliberately avoids the low-lying land. None of this explains the reason for crossing the brook however, and it may simply be that the inconvenience of having to ford

3. Revisiting some famous relict field systems   77

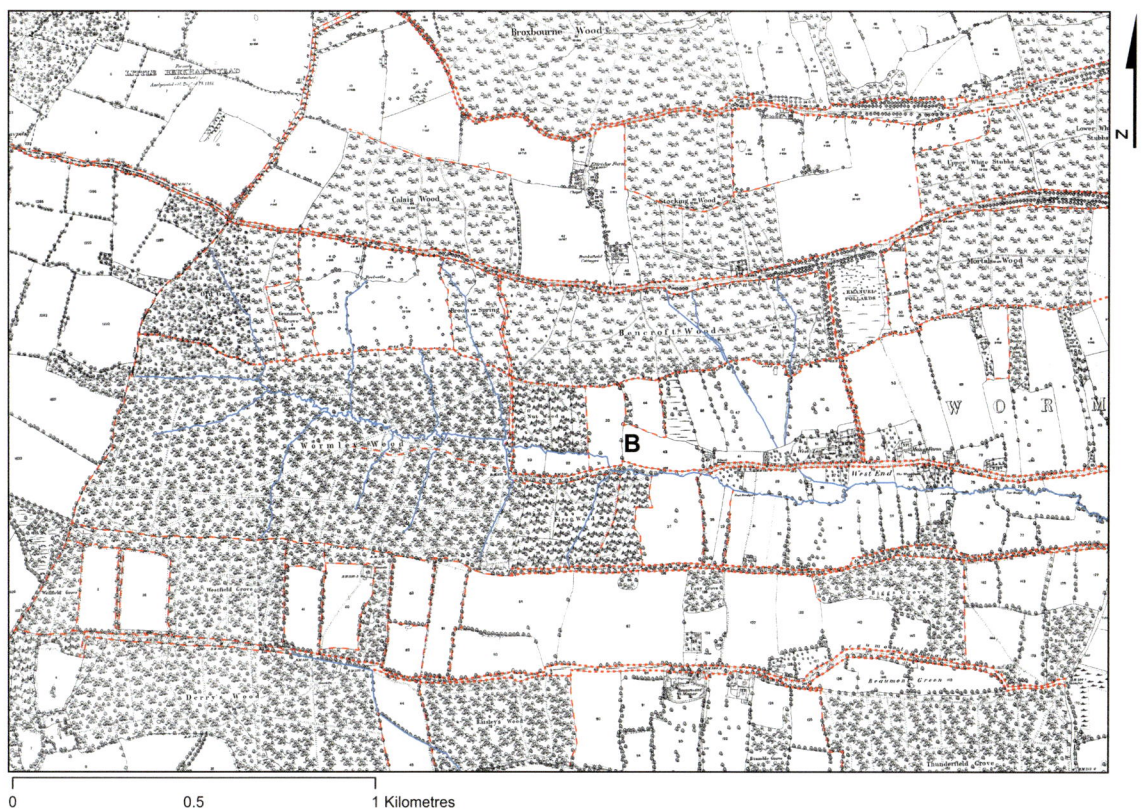

FIGURE 3.16. The earthworks (in red) identified by Bryant *et al.* (2005) on the First Edition Ordnance Survey 6-Inch map. Streams and other minor watercourses shown in blue.

the stream, was outweighed by the 2 km of a relatively direct and level path linking the manor and church to the woodland.

Overall, the terrain model indicates that the east–west features are far from terrain oblivious even at the local level. The spacing that appears so regular in Figure 3.16 seems to be if not determined then heavily influenced by the local landform. Three of the drove-ways run along roughly parallel hill spurs. Notably the long axis C, which is followed by the parish boundary, takes a level path close to the 90-m contour through Wormley Wood and terminates upon the western watershed. Is it the regularity of the local topography that gives rise to the roughly even spacing of the co-axial tracks? The naturally well ordered parallel valleys could even explain the relationship of Beaumont Road and the parish boundary indicated by point A in Figure 3.17. This section was highlighted by Bryant *et al.* as an indication of the 'careful planning' of the landscape and the two axes do appear to be evenly spaced for approximately 750m. This may have originated in deliberate planning or may have resulted from gradual woodland assarts combined with the rationalisation of wide ancient zones of transit into narrow rights of way.

As has been noted previously the relationship between watersheds and tracks is an ancient one but also something that has been both rediscovered and repeated through the ages, as indicated by the results of the large-scale archaeological field work in the Cambourne Development Area. Many of the shorter boundaries in the Wormley area run north–south, and these also appear to relate to the local terrain as they pass downslope to end at or near a watercourse. It is also notable that these short boundaries are generally absent from areas where the landform is bisected by numerous spring fed streams, causing the deep cuts in the hill slopes. Bryant *et al.* suggested that the regular landscape pattern in Wormley resulted from the addition of small field boundaries during the medieval period, which respected the much sparser and earlier framework of tracks and this would explain much of the regularity of the landscape of the lower valley slopes (Bryant *et al.* 2005, 14). As previously discussed, the soils in this area are prone to waterlogging and therefore any surface drainage will improve the value of the land whether for cultivation or pasture. Even where it is not disrupted by minor streams the valley landform is not a simple continuous slope; the fall from White Stubbs Lane and point C in Figure 3.17 is approximately 10 m, while the decline between C and the stream is double that. This may seem a subtle change, but the slightly steeper lower slope will undoubtedly encourage run off and the efficacy of field ditches, all of which would have made assarts in this area more likely to succeed and thus persist as fields in the modern landscape.

As we have seen in the previous chapter resource linkage routes or linear commons have tended to develop organically as the formerly wide zone of transit was gradually restricted by converting the 'waste' to farmland. It has also been noted that subsequent intakes will respect and reflect the form of earlier enclosures or fields by incorporating pre-existing boundaries where they are available. In the Wormley area it is the roughly perpendicular nature of the two valleys belonging to the river Lee and its minor tributary with headwaters in Wormley Wood that created the illusion of regularity which extended even to the short north–south field divisions. Several of the principal co-axial features were located upon the minor watersheds, while others travelled across the hillslopes and appear to roughly maintain a level path, almost as if they followed a specific contour. As features that appear to be influenced by the local topography it is not possible to suggest a date of origin based solely upon morphology. A possible exception to this, however, could be the lane that passes through Wormley West End. It is the only co-axial track that is located in the minor valley and this distinction when combined with the fact that it appears to have linked Wormleybury and the parish church to the West End hamlet and Wormley Wood would suggest its origin was associated with these early settlements.

Although the common drove-ways in Wormley have an unusually regular grid-like arrangement, relict landscapes are not uncommon in South Hertfordshire. Just a few kilometres west of Wormley lie the clay land parishes of Shenley, Ridge and Arkley. They contain numerous place-names that indicate that this area was formerly well wooded like that around Wormley. The First Edition Ordnance Survey 6-Inch map records that in the nineteenth century the parishes still contained the vestigial remains of former linear greens, some

FIGURE 3.17. The earthworks (in red) identified by Bryant *et al.* (2005), overlaid on a terrain map. Streams and other minor watercourses shown in blue.

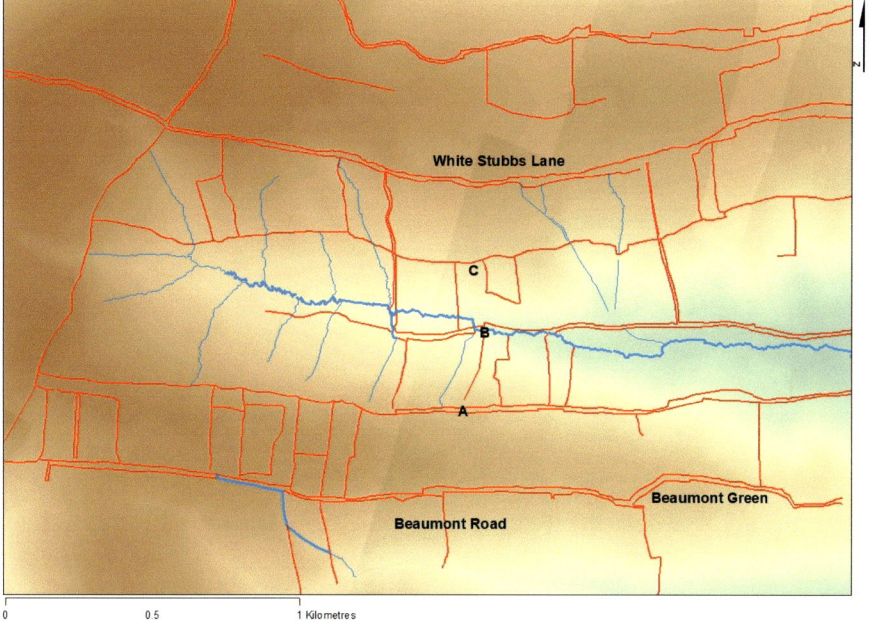

even fossilised in place-names such as Green Street in Arkley. Clues to the pre-enclosure widths of the narrow commons are also provided by the late nineteenth-century First Edition Ordnance Survey 6-Inch maps in the form of the locations of older farmsteads, which generally lie a little way back from the modern lanes.

Jonathan Hunn proposed that the area around Arkley also contains an anciently laid out regular landscape, into which the post-medieval field pattern has been slotted (Hunn and Turner 2004, 110). Although much of Hunn's analysis focused on the small area near Saffron Green, the pattern of sub-parallel, northwest/southeast aligned long roads and boundaries extends beyond the parishes of Arkley, Ridge and Shenley, illustrated in Figure 3.18. They link the valley of the river Colne, which lies north of Shenley, to the clay hills that lie south of Arkley. Hunn suggested a prehistoric origin date for the regular landscape due in part to the apparent scale of the arrangement (Hunn and Turner 2004, 117). He concluded that the sparse grid was established in the Bronze Age to 'apportion land [in a] predominately pastoral society' (Hunn and Turner 2004, 118). The continued importance of pastoral farming in the local area, and the associated need to drove livestock between different environmental zones, had served to preserve the prehistoric boundaries. Over time the spaces between lanes were gradually infilled with fields through piecemeal enclosure (Hunn and Turner 2004, 118).

The soils around Saffron Green are much the same as those found on the wooded slopes in nearby Wormley, namely the Windsor and Essendon Association soils, which are, as previously noted, seasonally waterlogged (Hodge

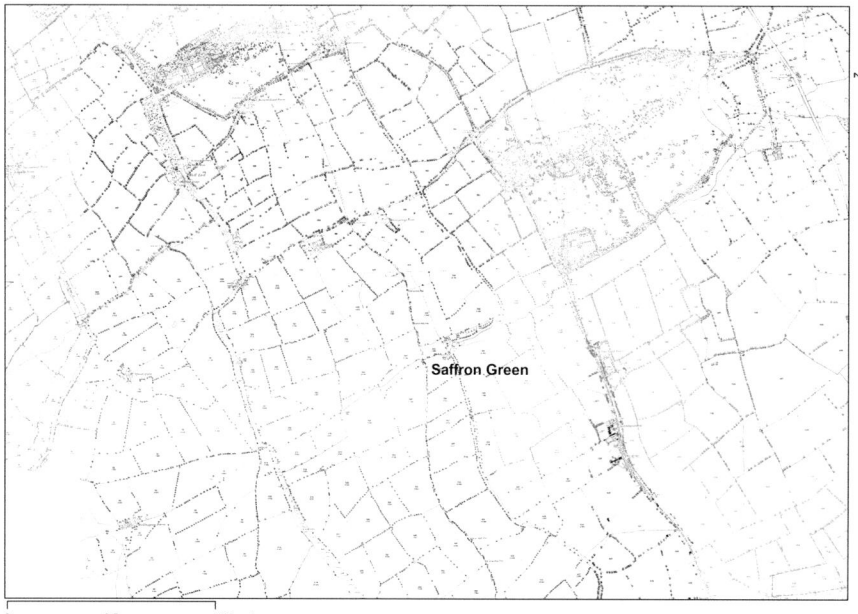

FIGURE 3.18. The semi-regular field pattern around Saffron Green in Arkley, Hertfordshire shown on the First Edition Ordnance Survey 6-Inch map (Hunn and Turner 2004, 115).

1984, 184, 358). In Wormley, where the valley of the river Lea provided lighter and more easily worked soils, this heavy land was considered marginal enough to be retained as woodland into the nineteenth century. By contrast in Arkley and Ridge, where heavy clay soils were found throughout the parishes, comparatively little woodland survived to be mapped in the nineteenth century. As noted above the frequency of woodland place-names in the vicinity, particularly those ending in *-leah* indicate that this area too, had once been a well-wooded landscape (Gelling 1993, 198).

The First Edition Ordnance Survey 6-Inch map for the area around Saffron Green in Arkley shows a field pattern comprising small sub-rectangular hedged closes, interspersed with parallel albeit slightly sinuous lanes, giving the landscape a somewhat regular appearance. The field pattern contains little evidence for the irregular and curving boundaries that are typically considered to be characteristic of woodland assarts.

As is typical of relict field systems, Hunn's diagrams showing the supposedly ancient landscape omitted nonconforming elements that did not fit the model and included sections, drawn with dotted lines in Figure 3.19, which filled in presumed gaps in the grid (Hunn and Turner 2004, 115). This does not necessarily undermine Hunn's central conclusion (Hunn and Turner 2004, 118). But a comparison of Figures 3.19 and 3.20 illustrates the extent to which the landscape grid was formed by the juxtaposition of lanes, several of which ran along watersheds, and streams. This would indicate that both the local and more intermediate landform led to the Arkley grid.

The long northwest aligned boundaries linked the clay watershed in Arkley to the valley of the river Colne 9 km away: one of these features appeared to

3. *Revisiting some famous relict field systems*   81

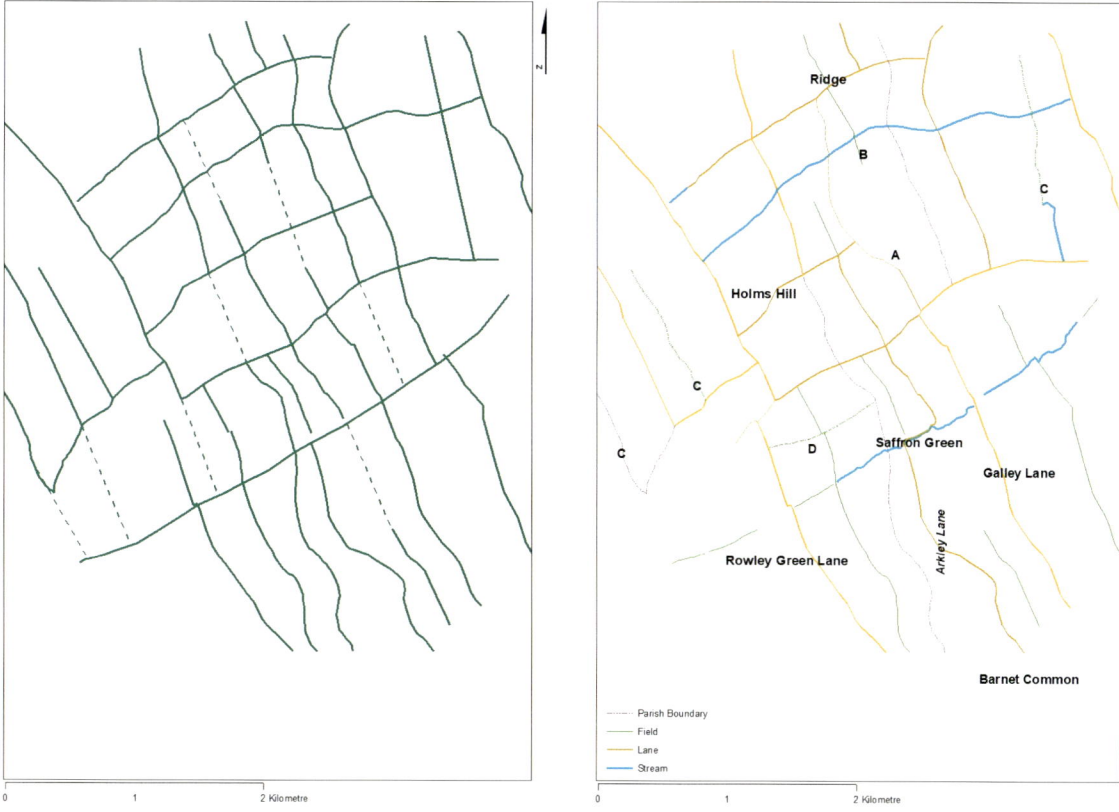

FIGURE 3.19. (*left*) The 'co-axial' pattern in the area of Saffron Green. Those shown as dotted lines are assumed (after Hunn and Turner 2004).

FIGURE 3.20. (*right*) The Arkley co-axials identified by Hunn and Turner (2004) and categorised by type after the First Edition Ordnance Survey 6-Inch map.

follow a minor watershed ridge, most did not. The land height rose between the valley and Arkley, but the incline was not planar; instead it was bisected by a number of parallel valleys aligned approximately east–west, and several of the east–west streams, and minor watersheds, formed the transverse elements of the grid. A curious element of the Arkley landscape is how many of the northwest/southeast aligned boundaries and lanes appear to travel along the east–west features for short distances before departing. This arrangement is characteristic of a later feature meeting an earlier one and would suggest that the east–west boundaries and lanes are the earliest features in the landscape.

An unusual feature of the Arkley landscape is that relatively few of the 'pre-historic' axes are preserved in the form of field boundaries, particularly when compared to the landscapes discussed previously in this chapter. Although at a large scale the field boundaries appear continuous, closer examination indicates that very few extend beyond a single field, unless they follow a natural feature such as a watershed or stream. During his fieldwork Hunn observed that the Arkley fields were hedged and ditched and that the latter contained water at the time of his survey (Hunn and Turner 2004, 10). This suggests that the field pattern in Arkley is closely linked to local drainage patterns, and this can be confirmed by laying the First Edition Ordnance Survey map over a modern LiDAR DTM 2 m. The relationship between the immediate slope and the field

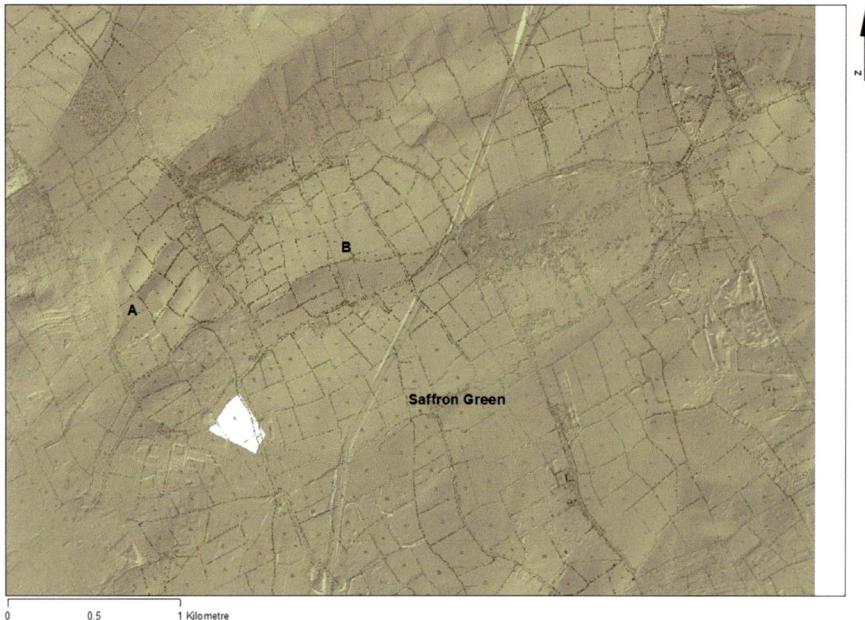

FIGURE 3.21. The First Edition Ordnance Survey 6-Inch map over a modern LiDAR Composite DTM 2 m.

boundaries is clear and is particularly noticeable on Figure 3.21 close to points A and B. The overriding concern with maximising drainage should be of little surprise given the poorly draining character of the local soils.

Within this sparse network of long tracks, the field pattern developed gradually and as the field boundaries responded to their immediate topographic conditions it gave rise to the Arkley landscape's unusual appearance. The pattern of field boundaries and lanes developed from the two common factors found across all the examples discussed so far, namely routes providing access to more distant resources and the local requirement to drain the soils.

CHAPTER FOUR

Summary and conclusion to Part 1

The previous chapters have reconsidered a number of so-called relict field systems located in lowland England and proposed an alternative explanation to the traditional view that they are anciently planned landscapes. The reassessment of Susan Oosthuizen's detailed description of the relict field system in the Bourn Valley, Cambridgeshire was possible in part because of the extensive archaeological fieldwork caried out in advance of Cambourne new town. The published reports provided an unusual opportunity to analyse a well-known and influential relict field system and incorporate the new archaeological evidence with landscape analysis. Oosthuizen had carried out such a thorough and well-argued investigation into the relict landscape of the Bourn Valley using documentary and map sources, that reviewing her argument was a useful way to test many of the founding tenets of relict field systems.

Despite the Cambourne Development Area covering a significant portion of the relict field system, the archaeological fieldwork found no evidence for the planned landscape Oosthuizen had identified. Instead, evidence of the importance of topography could be observed through comparison of Oosthuizen's 'linears' over a local terrain map. This exercise indicated that both the routes and spacing of the long alignments was directly related to topographic elements such as minor ridges and watersheds and dry valleys. Such features provided convenient routes for trackways linking resources in the valley and the watershed or at least ideal corridors to which such tracks became increasingly confined as movement gradually became more restricted as land was taken into arable production or enclosed.

Similar processes, creating networks of parallel roads running from 'river to wold' underlies most of the other relict landscapes briefly explored in Chapter 3. In places such multiple tracks, variously running along valley and ridges, may have provided alternate routes for different seasons and ground conditions, as perhaps at Wormley in Hertfordshire. In such systems of 'resource-linkage routes' some and perhaps many, of the individual examples might have ancient, even prehistoric origins. Some may have originated in the early Middle Ages although, as Mark Gardiner has argued, they must have been in place before 1200 CE (Gardiner 2018, 113).

Where the topography is planar the groups of parallel lanes and boundaries can lead to the development of a rough grid-like pattern of fields, as land was gradually enclosed, something that is visually striking on an Ordnance Survey map, if not always that visible in the landscape. In a number of cases such grids appear to be assigned a *terminus ante quem* by the fact that they are slighted by

Roman roads or an analogous dated linear feature, an approach pioneered in Drury's discussion of the Little Waltham field pattern. The analysis presented in the previous chapter highlighted a number of problems with this approach, including enhancement of the 'grid' by discounting boundaries that do not conform to it, and a failure to perceive the functional necessity of field boundaries in terms of land drainage.

This is apparent in the relationship between the furlongs and the Roman road in Caxton at the head of the Bourn Valley. Incorporating the land height information into the landscape analysis showed that the Caxton furlongs, and later field ditches were principally concerned with encouraging water to flow downhill and into the stream. The importance of drainage far outweighed the minor inconvenience of an oblique ended furlong. This relationship was repeated in many of the relict field systems discussed in the previous two chapters where a Roman road or another feature was thought to slight a regular field pattern. In the Arrow Valley the same feature, Offa's Dyke, slighted one field pattern but was conformable with another a few kilometres south. The difference between the two locations was the angle at which the earthwork crossed the stream; when it met the water course at a perpendicular angle there was no slighting.

The previous chapters have, perhaps above all, illustrated how incorporating GIS mapping technology and especially LiDAR data allows for a detailed analysis of the boundary and lane pattern with reference to the underlying topography. This technology was not available to Drury and Williamson when they carried out their research into the regular landscapes they identified. Although both commented on the local topography, their source information was restricted to the contour lines on Ordnance Survey Maps and physical site survey.

So-called relict field systems remain a popular area of research for historians as the publication of *The Fields of Britannia* has illustrated. They provide evidence for social organisation on a large scale and are particularly popular with those historians and archaeologists who argue for continuity during the centuries that followed the departure of the Roman army from Britain. The most fundamental element of the study of relict landscapes is the presumption that regularity can only come from planning and not from organic development nor gradual accretion. The case studies discussed in the previous chapters have illustrated how in these examples the eventual regularity of the field pattern was a response to the local environment, with planar topography leading to regular landscapes and more bisected landforms having a more irregular appearance. It remains useful to keep in mind that the neatness of form visible on an First Edition Ordnance Survey Map is far more noticeable than it is at ground level, which after all reflects the experience of earlier communities.

Part 2
Planned open fields

CHAPTER FIVE

The origins of open fields

The superficially homogeneous appearance of the modern English lowland landscape masks a great division in the countryside that survived until the middle of the eighteenth century. Two hundred and fifty years ago a traveller through the Midland counties would have seen a countryside that has since disappeared. Village settlements were surrounded by two or three large 'open fields' that stretched to the parish boundary (Rackham 1986, 5). The origins of this champion landscape – at least in the sense of the boundaries of fields and furlongs – have until recently been sought in the Middle and Late Saxon periods, rather than earlier ages. Nevertheless, the deliberations on the origin of open fields share a number of common themes with the debates around relict field systems. This chapter will attempt to summarise these specific elements of the open field debate by focusing upon the discussions around planned fields and settlements.

Farming in the champion regions was carried out in large open fields that were subdivided into numerous strips or selions. During the Middle Ages these open fields were communally ploughed, a process known to modern historians as 'co-aration', with the individual farmers contributing resources to the village plough teams. In many areas and particularly on the Midland clays, the land was ploughed to form narrow raised earthwork strips, usually referred to as 'ridges', which were separated from adjacent strips by a shallow ditch or 'furrow'. The furrow acted as a boundary marker as well as providing a degree of drainage for the soil forming the ridge. Repeated ploughing of the strips to the same boundaries eventually created a low bank at the narrow ends of the strips, which was called a 'headland'. One of the open fields would be left fallow each year and functioned as a temporary common pasture, while the remaining field or fields would be cropped. This had a dual benefit; it provided grazing for the livestock of the vill and allowed the land to rest and gain nutrients through manuring on the hoof (Fox 1981, 66).

In a typical Midlands vill, each individual farm or holding comprised a collection of strips that were scattered evenly across the open fields. The strips, 'selions' or 'lands' were grouped together in furlongs or shots, which were subdivisions within the open field (Hall 2014, 3). Each landholder would have a strip in every furlong in all of the open fields. The arrangement of the strips could be highly organised with evidence from manorial records indicating that in some manors the husbandmen had the same neighbours in every furlong, and occasionally this extended to the village street (Homans 1941, 42; Harvey 1978, 14). This apparent regularity may reflect a preference for order by medieval administrators rather than the reality of a typical vill, as such a tidy arrangement would frequently be disrupted by changes to holdings through inheritance and land sales (Lewis *et al.* 2001, 149). Surviving medieval manorial and parish documents record the ordinary details of individual holdings, rights and obligations, sometimes over centuries. This wealth of information, much of it dating from the thirteenth century onwards, has been mined to illuminate the organisational detail of the open fields (Ault 1972, 18). For antiquarians writing in the late nineteenth century there was another source, the testimonies of the landholders who farmed the late surviving open fields (Seebohm 1883; Orwin and Orwin 1938; Fox 1981, 66).

As noted previously, well into the twentieth century it was understood that the withdrawal of the Roman garrisons led to much of the English countryside reverting to woodland. The arrival of settlers from north Germany and Scandinavia – conventionally, the Saxons, Angles and Jutes – was accompanied by the destruction, enslavement or western exile of the indigenous population (Hoskins 1988, 38). The early debate in the origins of open fields was between those who believed gradual evolution of native farming systems and the introduction of a new continental system by the Germanic settlers (Seebohm 1883, 410; Maitland 1907, 349). In the late nineteenth century Seebohm combined documentary research with the testimony of farmers to conclude that open-field farming was domestic in origin (Seebohm 1883, 410). By contrast Maitland concluded that open fields developed from kin group farming systems in villages settled by Angles, Saxon and Jutes (Maitland 1907, 349). In 1915 Gray carried out a detailed geographical analysis of the English open fields, which showed that the classic open field arrangement was found only in the Midlands. Gray concluded that this was because the European settlers were able to impose the open-field farming system on a comparatively empty region through sheer force of numbers and overcome any resistance to change (Gray 1915, 418). Later the focus shifted away from such cultural or ethnic interpretations towards a consideration of the utility of the open fields. The Orwins stated 'there is very little in the characteristic features of the Open Fields which cannot be explained […] by the common sense of farming practice' (Orwin and Orwin 1938, 14).

Writing several decades later Joan Thirsk also considered the practicalities of medieval farming. Thirsk suggested that dispersed holdings had resulted from the assarting of land from the 'waste' as pressure on resources increased through population growth. The expansion of the ploughlands into the former 'waste' reduced the area of the common pasture that was available for grazing by the livestock of the vill (Thirsk 1973, 252). The resulting holdings were made up of piecemeal intakes of the 'waste' and this was further complicated by a custom for partible inheritance leading to the fields being subdivided amongst the heirs. All this led to farmers holding numerous small fields that were scattered across the parish lands, although Titlow pointed out there was little documentary evidence for partible inheritance in England (Thirsk 1964, 12; Titlow 1965, 86). The holding pattern became more and more complex, and the land available for pasture was reduced. The scattered holdings had another problem, namely the task of manuring the ploughlands that lay furthest from the vill (Thirsk 1964, 15). Thirsk believed that the 'Midland' form of open-field farming had been devised in order to provide grazing for the livestock of the vill and increase agricultural production through rotational manuring on the hoof (Thirsk 1973, 235). The adoption of a two- or three-field system would have necessitated a wholesale re-allocation of holdings for which Harold Fox found documentary evidence from settlements in Bedfordshire and Cambridgeshire that appeared to support Thirsk's conclusions. The records detailed the deliberate reorganisation of scattered fields and indicate that the motivation for the change was to improve yields through the use of rotational fallow and grazing (Fox 1981, 314). Thirsk also concluded that open-field farming reached a zenith in terms of organisation during the thirteenth century. She noted that the regularity and complexity of the arrangements recorded in the medieval documents was unlikely to reflect the origin of open-field farming. Thirsk suggested instead that the original patterns of land allotments in disparate villages became more similar over time due to greater frequency of communication between manorial administrators (Thirsk 1973, 274). Thirsk's conclusions were persuasive and influenced many of the authors of chapters in Baker and Butlin's volume on early field systems (1973).

Thirsk's chronology for the emergence of the 'Midland System' was, however, challenged by the results of archaeological fieldwork carried out by Glenn Foard in the late 1970s. Foard found pottery scatters that indicated settlements of Early Saxon date within the areas of former open fields in a number of Northamptonshire parishes, but none of later Saxon date (Foard 1977, 76). This led Foard to conclude that the Early Saxon farmsteads migrated to form nucleated villages by the Late Saxon period. This indicated the point in time when, following Thirsk's model, holdings were re-allotted and extensive open fields laid out. He concluded that the open fields must therefore have been created in conjunction with this settlement re-organisation. Brown and Foard called this event the 'great re-planning' and concluded that it took place during the ninth and tenth century CE (1998, 76).

Planned open fields

In the late 1970s Mary Harvey carried out detailed documentary research into the open field system of the parish of Preston in East Yorkshire. Here she found evidence for an extremely regular open field system, the surviving documents describing how the squarish parish was divided into two main fields that were separated horizontally by an east–west lane, along which many of the village farmsteads and closes were located. The sources recorded that the two open fields were sub-divided into 'seven bydales' (Harvey 1978). Unfortunately, no pre-enclosure maps survive for Preston, but the descriptions contained within several terriers indicated that each bydale contained a strip belonging to each holding, and that the order of the holdings in each bydale was consistent, following the same sequence throughout the fields. The documentary sources also detailed the layout of the individual strips, apparently describing how all followed the same north–south alignment. This led Harvey to conclude that the selions were very long, extending unbroken all the way from the village closest to the parish boundaries, a distance of over 2 km (Harvey 1978, 4).

The regularity of strips, bydales, fields and settlement in Preston suggested to Harvey that this arrangement could only have arisen through large-scale landscape planning. And as Preston retained evidence for this activity then neighbouring parishes should contain similar evidence. During the 1970s and 80s Harvey expanded her research to take in more of the settlements of Holderness, and she identified numerous other parishes that shared similarities with Preston, and in particular the very long strips (Harvey 1983). Elsewhere in the Vale of York Harvey identified more examples of similar strip arrangements, which she named 'long furlongs' as they could be up to 550 m in length (Hall 1995, 131).

In Preston the earliest sources that provided evidence for the field system linking the long furlongs with regular land tenure dated from the mid-thirteenth century. Harvey surmised that the origin of the furlongs and tenurial system were likely to be contemporary and settled upon a ninth-century origin for the layout, following Danish settlement (Harvey 1983, 91–103). She further concluded that the landscape must have been 'fully exploited' in order to establish the long furlongs stretching from settlement to boundary and furthermore that the population of the vill needed to be sufficiently large to justify cultivating all the available arable land (Harvey 1983, 94). Harvey noted that there were difficulties for the early origin date; indeed she later suggested that population pressure had only maximised cultivation in the early eleventh century (Harvey 1983, 98). Harvey concluded that fluctuations in population led to individual holdings being combined and divided without physical alteration of the long furlongs (Harvey 1983, 102).

Harvey's conclusions were influential and David Hall, working in Northamptonshire, enthusiastically took up the concept of 'long furlongs'. These features appeared to correspond with a number of his own discoveries in the Northamptonshire parish of Wollaston. The destruction of a former open field headland in the parish through modern ploughing had revealed that the selions or lands had originally continued uninterrupted. This indicated that the furlong division that had been preserved in the headland was a later insertion truncating the originally longer strips. It presumably resulted from an adjustment or rearranging of the Wollaston fields at an unknown date (Hall 1981, 31). In Wollaston the insertion of transverse headlands across the long furlong must, Hall concluded, have resulted from an adjustment needed to take account of the very localised field drainage requirements, which had been overlooked when the open fields, furlongs and strips had originally been laid out.

Hall's identification of the long furlongs in Wollaston led him to look for similar arrangements elsewhere in Northamptonshire and identified evidence for the former presence of long furlongs in nine further parishes and townships (Hall 1995, 133). In Raunds he identified a former long furlong that was over 1 km long (Hall 1995, 133). Looking outside the Midlands, Hall suggested that further examples of long furlongs could be seen in the Fens, where strip fields over 1 km long had originally been a common feature of the landscape (Hall 1995, 132). Although he considered the possibility that the long furlongs resulted from piecemeal development, in the end Hall concluded that the evidence for later adjustments, particularly to improve drainage, argued against it (Hall 1995, 133; Partida *et al.* 2013, 36). He concluded that long furlongs had originally been widespread and constituted the original layout of the fields. Over time the strips had been modified to create the more typical 'checkerboard' appearance, with 'cross' furlongs with ridges running at a right angle to one another (Hall 1995, 133). Hall, like Foard perceived that the planned open fields had been laid out as part of the 'great re-planning' during the Middle or Late Saxon period, accepting in broad terms Thirsk's model for the emergence of champion landscapes in the reorganisation of an earlier holding pattern, but not its chronology or details.

Like Harvey, Hall concluded that parish open field arrangements are inherently stable, and he concluded that in Northamptonshire field and furlong names had great longevity. Hall noted that the place names listed in the post-medieval field books and terriers could also be found in some of the earliest parish records dating from the twelfth and thirteenth centuries. This apparent stability was maintained through all the changes in population and fortune over the intervening four or more centuries, Hall perceived that the furlongs first glimpsed in the twelfth-century records must have resulted from a deliberate and planned earlier organisation of the landscape (Hall 1981, 12; 1982, 26). Hall, like Harvey argued that the open fields must have been laid out centuries before Thirsk suggested they reached their pinnacle in the thirteenth century (Thirsk 1966, 145).

In the long furlongs in England, both Harvey and Hall saw similarities with roughly contemporary field systems in Germany and particularly those around Hassegau in eastern Saxony. Following the defeat of the Saxons by the Frankish army at Hochseeburg Castle in 743 CE, the Franks imposed a new territorial arrangement on their newly acquired dominion. They set up a very regular pattern of rectangular townships each with long boundaries that ran upslope from valley to upland, and the settlements were established along the river side. The farmland was sub divided into narrow strips or furlongs that ran the full length of the township boundaries (Nitz 1988, 154). Matzat extended his analysis and carried out a comparison of long furlongs in Germany and Yorkshire. This further influenced Hall who concluded that landscape re-planning was possible and had occurred in England and in Mainland Europe (Matzat 1988; Hall 1995, 132).

The suggestion that the open fields resulted from a 'great re-planning' in the mid-eighth century was taken up enthusiastically by historians interested in the development of rural settlements. Roberts created a morphological classification scheme for English rural settlements ranging from 'agglomerations', which were unlikely to have been planned, to 'rows' that had been. The model of planned settlements and open fields was combined to form the concept of the 'village moment'. This event was thought to have taken place during the eighth and ninth centuries and led to the population leaving their dispersed farms and relocating to a core settlement. Debate continues as to what the catalyst for this change was, and local, seigniorial and other pressures that led communities to seemingly leave their farms, migrate to nucleated settlements and reorganise their fields have all been considered (Lewis *et al.* 2001, 13).

John Blair, Stephen Rippon and Christopher Smart presented evidence for planning in settlements and adjacent fields in *Planning in the Early Medieval Landscape* (2022). The 'short perch' is a unit of measure identified by Blair when examining the plans of churches constructed in the early seventh century CE (Blair *et al.* 2022, 102). By laying a grid based upon the 'short perch' over the plan of the surrounding settlement he concluded that several ecclesiastical and royal sites dating from the late seventh and eighth centuries contained evidence for planning based upon the 'short perch' (Blair *et al.* 2022, 149). This methodology was extended to settlements that had been identified as having a regular morphology using the First Edition Ordnance Survey Map (Blair *et al.* 2022, 46). A short perch grid was placed over the nineteenth-century Ordnance Survey map for the selected settlement, frequently orientated upon the church and immediate surroundings. Comparison of the nineteenth-century boundaries to the grid led the authors to perceive the initial settlement plan (Blair *et al.* 2022, 175). The authors noted that the grid and map could be unconformable and suggested that the original plan was a 'guiding principle' with discrepancies between the streets, boundaries and the grid resulting from the builders and ditch diggers (Blair *et al.* 2022, 175) possibly indicating the planned layout had not been respected by all those constructing the vill.

Alternative explanations for 'planned settlements'

As with the planning in the open fields, the concepts of planned and nucleated settlements have been subject to debate. There are many champion villages that display few signs of planning and in a number of cases settlement regularity has been interpreted in different ways. In West Cambridgeshire, Oosthuizen noted that the regular layout of several villages had been caused by the loose grid of co-axial tracks and linear greens in the Bourn Valley. Tofts and crofts were strung along the lanes and clustered around junctions giving settlements the appearance of a grid layout, but she concluded this pattern had developed organically as the settlement grew (Oosthuizen 2006, 60). The influence of the surrounding fields on the village layout was explored by Williamson, Liddiard and Partida when they analysed the morphology of apparently planned villages in Northamptonshire and in particular the relationship with the surrounding furlongs and strips. They found a clear correlation between strips abutting the village streets and the arrangement of tofts, which led them to conclude that the regularity resulted from the settlement expanding over pre-existing open field strips as population waxed and waned (Williamson *et al.* 2013).

Williamson *et al.* questioned several of Hall and Harvey's conclusions and in particular that the open fields were stable in form and function from at least the twelfth century until enclosure. Documentary evidence suggested that open-field farming systems were frequently remodelled to take account of changing priorities (Williamson *et al.* 2013, 124). Change was further confirmed by details recorded in Domesday Book, that less than half the land in most Northamptonshire vills was under the plough in 1066, but by the early thirteenth century ploughland had increased to cover all or almost all of the land area (Williamson *et al.* 2013, 124). The increase in ploughland area must have come from gradual extension of cultivation into the 'waste', until it reached its limit. This increase in area under the plough must have necessitated changes to the existing open-field system, and Williamson *et al.* suggested that the regular pattern of open field holdings that is preserved in documents is likely to result from the re-allotment of strips in the centuries after the Norman Conquest. Perhaps surprisingly the results of their research also suggested that a lack of available pasture was not the catalyst for the development of regular open fields as suggested by Joan Thirsk, as many Northamptonshire villages had access to abundant reserves of grazing land (Williamson *et al.* 2013).

Conclusion

This chapter has briefly introduced the ideas of a number of historians and archaeologists who have argued that 'Midland' open fields were established through a 'great replanning' of settlements, land and farming. There is no doubt that a number of manorial sources preserve evidence that some fields contained repetitive rotations of holdings in each furlong, and this indicates a level of organisation that cannot have developed organically. Thirsk as well as Fox and the Northamptonshire Project all found plentiful documentary evidence for adjustments and sometimes reorganisations of existing open field allotments and activities. This, however, is very different from the notion that many or most open fields originated as planned systems of land allotment featuring very long furlongs. This argument, like those for relict field systems, is essentially based on topographic analysis and on the interpretation of shapes and forms still present in the landscape, recorded on maps or described in early documents and a perception that regularity in the landscape must indicate planning. But as discussed in previous chapters much of this stems from a failure to consider a regular landscape within its environmental context. This has led to patterns being interpreted as resulting from planning rather than an organic response to topography and the environment. The following chapter will reconsider several of the most well-known examples of planned open fields using the same techniques that were applied to the so-called relict fields systems.

CHAPTER SIX

Open fields and 'planned' agricultural landscapes

The previous chapter introduced some of the debates around the origins of open fields, and specifically how historians such as Hall and Harvey who argued that the system resulted from landscape planning employ arguments that are familiar to those with an interest in relict field systems. In particular the suggestion that landscapes with a regular pattern of boundaries, lanes and other man-made features could only have originated as part of a planned system of land allotment. Unlike the so-called relict field systems most examples of planned open fields are small in scale and cover land belonging to single parish or township. With the exception of Mary Harvey, few English historians have argued for a wider landscape plan for the English open fields, although as discussed previously this argument has been made for areas in Mainland Europe (Matzat 1998).

A difficulty with the study of planned open fields in England is that the landscape evidence for open field farming in many parishes is limited and while documentary sources can survive, there often remains little physical evidence for the lost strip pattern, particularly in areas of Parliamentary Enclosure. In some places clues to layout of the open field strip can be found in earthwork evidence that preserved the furlong pattern at the time of enclosure. To summarise, the strategy of searching the First Edition Ordnance Survey maps looking for unusually regular boundary patterns which underpins the study of relict landscapes is less likely to be successful in former champion countryside. Nevertheless, in some areas nineteenth-century field boundaries appear to fossilise some of the former open field furlongs, as seen previously in West Cambridgeshire and further examples will be discussed in this and the following chapters.

Long furlongs in the East Riding of Yorkshire

As briefly explained in the previous chapter, during the 1970s and 80s Mary Harvey studied the landscape history of various parishes in Holderness. Her interests were expansive, incorporating Viking land settlement, the local economic effects of the Harrying of the North ordered by William of Normandy and the division of the region into administrative units based upon wapentakes. Harvey's examination of the tenurial structure of parishes in Holderness has proven to be especially influential in the study of open field farming through her introduction of the concept of 'long furlongs'. Subsequently Harvey has found evidence for planned open fields in parishes in Holderness and the Vale of York, but the work she carried out in Preston in Holderness formed the foundation for much of her later work, and it is to that we turn now (Harvey 1978; 1983; 1985).

Harvey carried out a detailed examination of the open-field farming system in the parish of Preston in Holderness. Within the surviving parish documents, she discovered an extremely regular open-field farming system. Most of the parish ploughland was located in two large fields. Within the fields there was no mention of furlongs as would be typically expected in an open field, instead each field was divided into seven 'bydales'. Documentary sources further recorded that almost all the strips in Preston's open fields were aligned north–south. To further add to the sense of regularity, the 'lands' or strips belonging to the 'oxgangs' (the measure of farm holding in Preston) were located in the same order in every bydale. Some of these lands were very long, stretching from the settlement to the parish boundary over 1500 m. Detailed though Harvey's analysis of Preston was, it resembled many of the examples of relict field systems discussed previously in that she does not include the environmental conditions within the parish in her considerations. As illustrated in previous chapters concerning relict landscapes, climate, soil type and drainage were (and are) of great importance to husbandmen and farmers and therefore this section will begin with a brief environmental analysis of Preston in Holderness.

The region of Holderness lies in the East Riding of Yorkshire, between Kingston upon Hull and the North Sea coast. The land is low lying, much of it is barely above sea level and even the briefest comparison of historic and modern maps indicates the number of coastal parishes that have lost land and even entire settlements to the sea. To the north of the region the land height rises and forms islands of slightly higher ground which reach around 25 m OD, and these have tended to be the preferred settlement sites. In between the islands of higher ground are valleys with land heights close to sea level. The proportion of this low-lying land increases in the parishes into the south and west of Holderness and much of the southern shore of the promontory is now protected from inundation by sea walls.

The large sub-rectangular parish of Preston lies to the west of the Holderness promontory and is closer to Kingston upon Hull than it is to the North Sea coast. In the southwest the parish land lay alongside the saltmarshes of the Humber Estuary. In the eighteenth century the village settlement resembled a stunted 'T' in shape, as is visible in Figure 6.1. Farmsteads were strung along lanes that linked the main settlement with the hamlets of West and East End. Approximately halfway along this route was a lane that led south, past the church, to the neighbouring settlement of Hedon. Preston was one of the grid-planned settlements discussed by Blair *et al.*, although as one that was initially thought to be more 'ambiguous' (Blair *et al.* 2022, 185). By orienting a grid based upon four short perches upon the parish church and its immediate environs, Blair *et al.* perceive a grid stretching into the surrounding fields (Blair *et al.* 2022, 185).

FIGURE 6.1. *A Copy of the Enclosure Plan of Preston in Holderness by John or William Iverson* (DDCK 35/1/f) and strip orientations (after Harvey 1978).

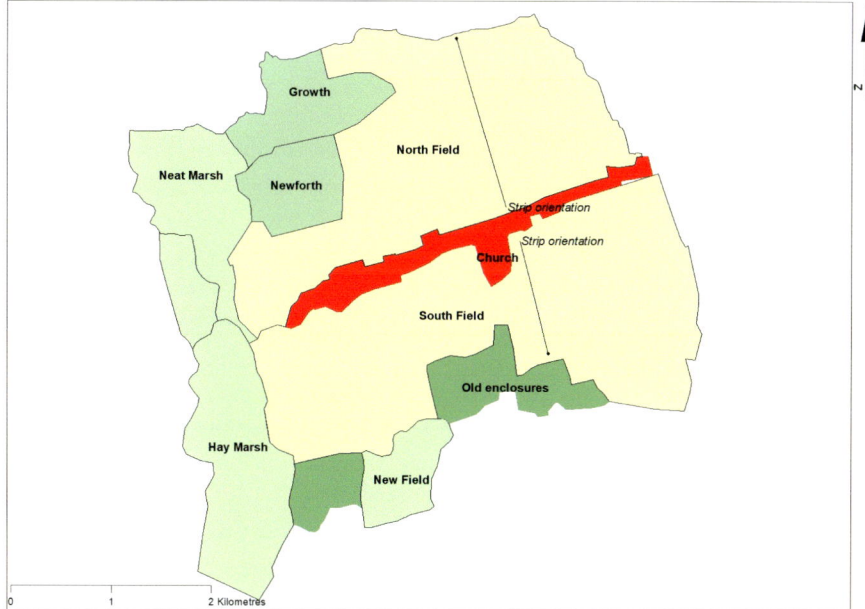

The elevation in the parish is extremely muted; near the church the land height is approximately 11 m above sea level, while in the southwest corner of the parish close to the salt marshes it is less than 2 m OD. The slight undulations in the modern fields are all but invisible when passing through the landscape.

Modern land drainage techniques have allowed the ploughlands and the previously waterlogged low lying fen meadows, marshes and damp pastures to be converted into highly productive arable land, and the fertile clay loams suit the production of root vegetables. Modern water management will have altered the natural drainage patterns. These changes are of quite recent origin, the nineteenth century tithe maps depicting a very different landscape to the one visible today, they still show a landscape that contained large areas of fen and marsh.

The principal slope in the parish runs from north to south. The earliest surviving map of Preston dates from the late eighteenth century and is the Parliamentary Enclosure Map. It records a parish that contained a large proportion of 'waste' in the form of common grazing, meadow and fen (IA/126). Comparing the eighteenth-century map to the modern topography indicates that the common meadows, marshes and fen lay on the lowest lying land and covered somewhere between a quarter and a third of the parish (IA/126).

Comparison of the early survey with modern soil maps indicates that the area that remained as 'waste' in the eighteenth century typically overlaid Wallsea Association soils. The Wallsea soils are a clay type and, lying at or near sea level, before modern underdrainage would have remained waterlogged for much of the year (Hodge 1984, 336). Elsewhere in the parish the soils are a mix of clay loams of the Burlingham 2 and Holderness Associations. Both soil types are slowly permeable but fertile clay loams. They also suffer from seasonal waterlogging and before modern drainage cultivating the land in springtime after the winter rains would have been very difficult (Hodge 1984, 132 and 214). The parish lies on the east coast of the British mainland and as such annual precipitation is lower than the national average, providing a window for cultivation in the autumn.

As noted above the soil classifications are modern and farming the fields in Preston was likely to have been more difficult in the past. This would have been especially so in the area where the open fields abutted waterlogged marshland as this would likely have further hindered soil drainage by slowing the outfall. As touched upon previously the modern, drained, agricultural landscape in Preston is one of arable and horticultural cultivation and the majority of the modern field boundaries have a north–south alignment and still use the slight natural fall to aide drainage. Could the simple and very muted topography in Preston have been the cause of the unusually regular arrangement of lands that was noted by Harvey?

Harvey's initial research into the Preston open fields used several post-medieval sources and in particular two mid-eighteenth-century land terriers which detailed two separate holdings. The terriers preserved details of Preston's open-field farming system just a few decades before the parish was subject to Parliamentary Enclosure in 1773. The records showed that Preston's landholders were still farming their land in two open fields in the mid-eighteenth century. The two-field system has been considered as the most restrictive of all the regular open field arrangements (Postgate 1964, 23). Preston's fields were called the North and South Field, and they lay on either side of the settlement. The terriers recorded village farms that were held in the form of named oxgangs and in the eighteenth century around half of the 130 oxgangs were still copyhold. By the eighteenth century there were fewer landholders in Preston than there were oxgangs. As a result, larger farms were made up of several oxgangs, giving Preston a total of 47 named holdings.

As noted previously a curious element of the Preston open fields is that there were no documentary records of furlongs in the Preston terriers. The named lands belonging to the oxgang were repeated in the same order seven times, east to west, across the open field. Each full repetition of the lands formed a bydale (Harvey 1978, 7). In the south field there were two additional bydales encompassing around 30 acres of east–west aligned lands.

The eighteenth-century terriers make clear that the lands were not combined but treated individually in the records even when they were held by the same farmer. Harvey found that although the widths of the lands recorded in the separate bydales differed, they typically appeared to measure around 30 ft (9 m) (Harvey 1978, 16). This is roughly consistent with the width of the ridge and furrow on the LiDAR layer. Another unusual element of the Preston system is that despite the detailed records of the number of oxgangs that belonged to each named holding, Harvey found that all the Preston lands were a standard width (Harvey 1978, 17).

6. Open fields and 'planned' agricultural landscapes   99

As touched upon previously the terriers described the layout of the strips. From this Harvey was able to deduce that most of the lands in Preston followed a consistent north-south orientation. Furthermore, from the descriptions in the terriers many of the lands appeared to cover the full extent of the field from settlement to the parish boundary (Harvey 1978,4). Although only one was actually described as stretching from town to boundary and containing over 2 acres, the others were all detailed in relation to their adjacent parcels (Harvey 1978, 9).

Harvey noted that 'despite being frequently broken by marshy areas, dykes or roads the common north–south orientation' of the lands was unaltered (Harvey 1978, 4). The descriptions in the terriers convinced Harvey that many of the individual lands must have been very long, stretching more than 1500 m.

Although there is no evidence for the locations of the bydales, in order to illustrate the way that they functioned in Preston's fields, Harvey depicted them as long rectangular field divisions that stretched from the settlement to the boundaries (Figure 6.2). To Harvey the 'simplicity and uniformity' of lands indicated that the Preston open fields must have been laid out in a single planned event (Harvey 1981, 188). A field pattern that developed through gradual expansion of the cultivated area, Harvey contended, would create a complex pattern of furlongs between which she expected the direction of the strips would change (Harvey 1980, 4).

Harvey returned to the documentary sources in order to determine when the seemingly planned field system first originated (Harvey 1978, 7). Another curious element of the Preston open fields was that the names of the individual holdings as listed in the eighteenth century did not relate to the contemporary

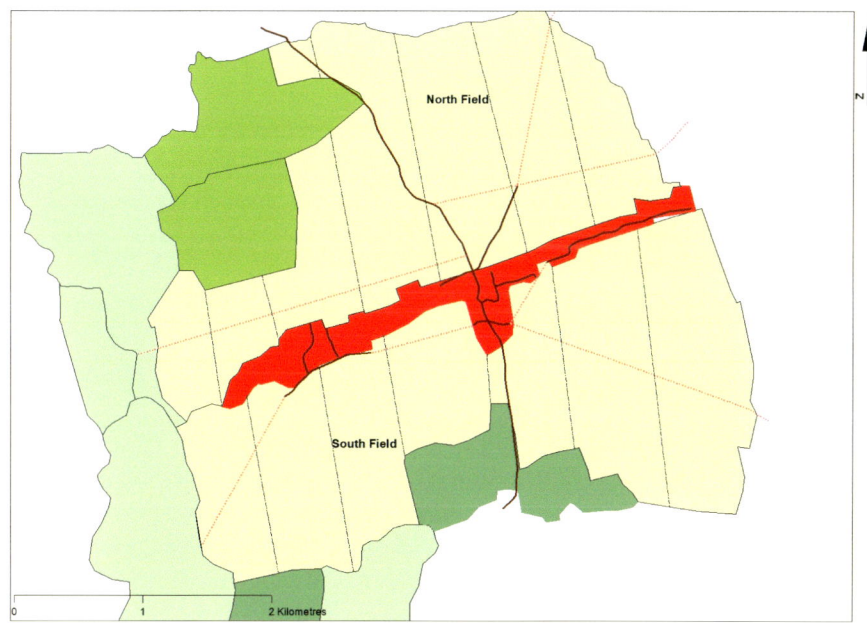

FIGURE 6.2. *A Copy of the Enclosure Plan of Preston in Holderness by John or William Iverson* (DDCK 35/1/f) and the approximate location of the main 'bydale' boundaries (dotted lines) (after Harvey 1978).

land holders, as indicated by entries such as: 'a land called Robert Clarks of William Bursall's owner and occupier' (Harvey 1978, 7).

Harvey compared the early modern terriers with surviving fourteenth-century manorial documents and found she was able to link around 14 of the 47 holding names in the 1750 terrier to recorded surnames of Preston's medieval inhabitants. This led her to conclude that the oxgang names must date from roughly the same period (Harvey 1978, 7). From this Harvey concluded that the fields and strips must have been created before the mid to late thirteenth-century when these names were first recorded (Harvey 1978, 10). Although Harvey was able to link a third of the strip names to the surnames of medieval inhabitants, there was no mention of bydales in the same early sources. Indeed, Harvey noted that the widths of the eighteenth-century lands appeared to be based upon contemporary measuring technology rather than those typical of the medieval period (Harvey 1978, 18).

Although Harvey found the first documentary evidence for the oxgangs or holding names in the thirteenth-century surnames she suggested the open fields were likely to have been laid out during the eleventh century. Harvey concluded that the open field was originally laid out with long strips leading from settlement to boundary (Harvey 1978, 23). Unfortunately, Harvey was unable to find information on how this system of land allocation was implemented (Harvey 1978, 13). She considered that it was likely that there was a period of reorganisation of the open fields around the time of the earliest surviving records (Harvey 1978, 24). Harvey proposed that the bydale system would allow for population growth by reapportioning the holdings within the fields (Harvey 1978, 19). This corresponded to the evidence found by Thirsk and Fox, which indicated that open-field farming systems were frequently subject to alteration (Thirsk 1964, 9; 1973, 233). The reorganisation of a parish's open field farming did not necessitate a physical rearrangement of the fields, furlongs or even individual strips, it simply altered the way the strips were farmed (Fox 1981, 89).

As briefly noted above the earliest surviving map of Preston is the late eighteenth-century Parliamentary Enclosure map (IA/126). Although it included the 'waste' it did not depict the layout of the former open fields, bydales and lands. The map depicts a few 'old enclosures', mainly lying close to the village but also in the south of the parish. Several of the village crofts appeared to have been enclosed from former open field strips, as they have the characteristic long narrow form of an open field strip, but they were short in length, and while some were aligned north–south, others followed an east–west orientation. The eighteenth-century map evidence indicates that the newly enclosed parish land was being rationalised. Comparison of the building line of the village houses to the new enclosure lanes indicated that a more complex and winding pattern of settlement lanes had been altered, although a few survived as public rights of way. Moving away from the settlement any traces of the pre-enclosure routes had been lost, replaced by new straight roads and drains that ran through the fields (IA/126). There was nothing in the post enclosure field pattern that could provide any further insight into the location and layout of the bydales. Many of the boundaries of the newly enclosed fields followed the same approximate north–south alignment detailed in the eighteenth-century terriers, but despite this similarity they were not noticeably long, and none stretched the entire distance from the settlement to the parish boundary.

Harvey perceived regularity as a characteristic of deliberate planning, just as Rodwell and Drury, Rackham and Oosthuizen did when considering relict field systems. However, unlike relict landscapes the evidence for the regular field pattern in Preston is based primarily upon documentary sources and not on surviving maps. Therefore, it would be useful to see if there is any evidence for the former strip arrangements visible using modern LiDAR.

Unfortunately, in Preston most of the evidence for ridge and furrow has been lost through continuous ploughing and the cultivation of root crops but there remain a few clues to the earlier strip layout. Evidence to support the north–south alignment of strips can be found in the far south of the parish, where ridge and furrow has survived in several of the fields described as 'old enclosures' on the eighteenth-century map. All the strip orientations visible in Figure 6.3 share the same approximate north–south alignment.

More curious is that none of the strips in these examples extend any great distance. This may be because they are all within the old enclosures; the strips near points B and C appear to end upon headlands, which suggests either that they were not part of a continuous long strip before they were enclosed, or that they continued to be ploughed after enclosure. Given the description of the north–south aligned lands in the documents it is perhaps curious that many

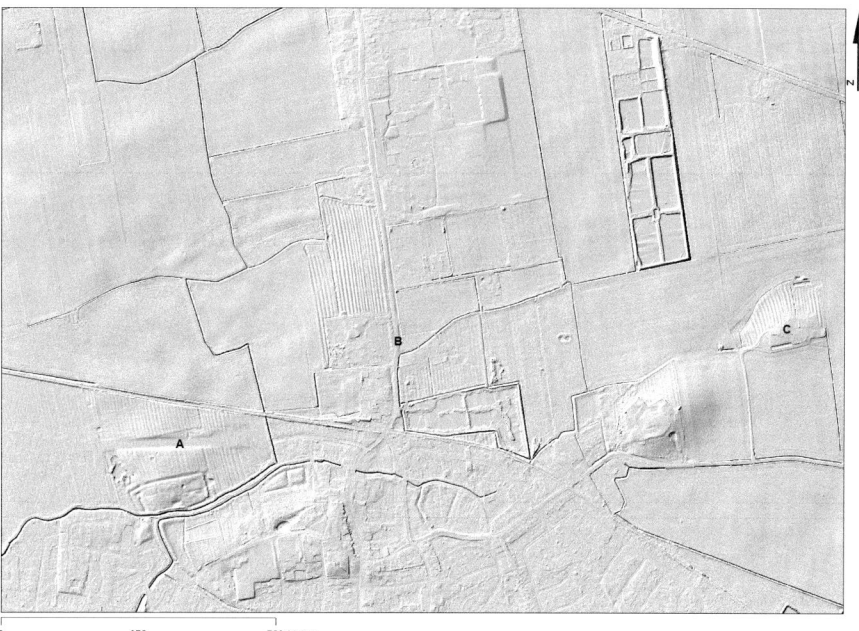

FIGURE 6.3. LiDAR Composite DTM 50 cm for Preston in Holderness.

of the old enclosures had noticeably irregular boundaries, suggesting that they may fossilise old breaks in the strip pattern. As noted previously the documents indicate that many of the lands in Preston were interrupted by natural features or roads that must have caused a break in the ridge and furrow. In other places the resulting group of shorter strips might have been called a 'furlong' but in Preston the land holding appears to have continued across the marsh, ditch or lane into the next strip that lay to the north or south. In other words, while the land was continuous and long stretching from the settlement to the parish boundary or the 'waste', the length of the ridge and furrow strips that made up the land were likely to be shorter and interrupted by both natural and man-made features.

The First Edition Ordnance Survey 6-Inch map preserves evidence of several of these possible interruptions to the plough strips that survived in the form of suspiciously sinuous transverse field boundaries. They cut across the otherwise regular enclosed fields and examples are highlighted by 'A' in Figure 6.4. These modern ditches may relate to some of the natural streams referred to in the terriers. They were not drawn in the eighteenth-century enclosure map, which only appears to depict a ditch when it forms the boundary of a holding. Nevertheless, they would have formed a break in the strip pattern. For all the detail recorded in the terriers, the precise way Preston's lands were arranged is somewhat obscure. As Harvey noted most lands were located according to the neighbouring strips, but how did that work when a stream, marsh or lane interrupted the field? Were the strips on each side of the feature precisely aligned or was it simply that the order of strips remained the same in the subdivisions. Unfortunately, the sources provide no further evidence.

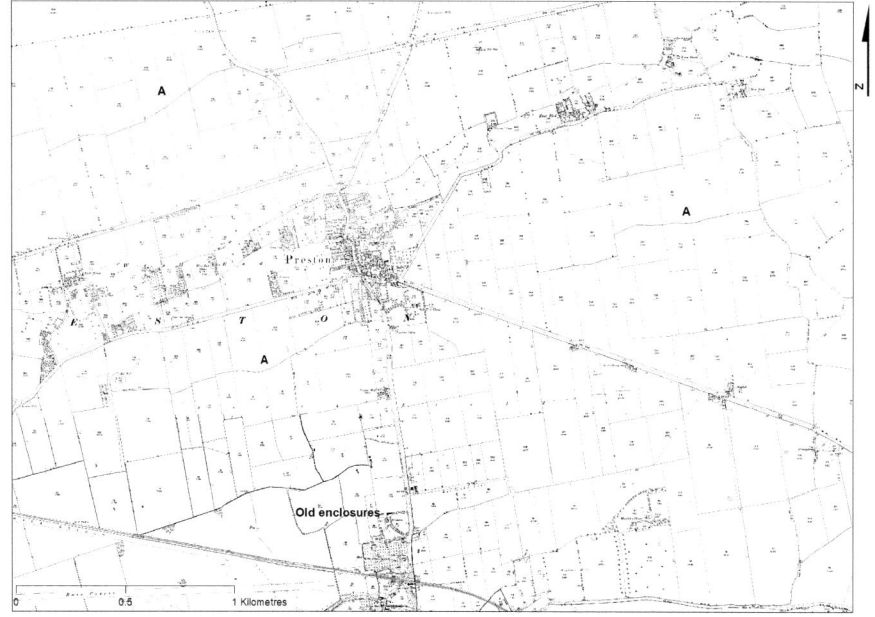

FIGURE 6.4. Detail of the First Edition Ordnance Survey 6-Inch map for Preston in Holderness.

Harvey's analysis of the open fields in Preston indicates that by the eighteenth century the layout of oxgangs and lands was very regular and organised, particularly in relation to the repetition of the order of the lands within the bydales. The bydales provided a method by which individual holdings could be evenly distributed across the open fields in the absence of furlongs, which performed a similar function in a typical Midland open field. As noted previously the medieval documents contain no references to bydales; they first appear in the records in the seventeenth-century terrier. Harvey noted that in the eighteenth century the bydales contained 130 oxgangs, while Domesday Book records 93 oxgangs in Preston. The details of oxgangs in the medieval records are inconsistent, for example only eight freehold oxgangs are listed, but if one accepts Harvey's assumption that the roughly 60 copyhold oxgangs recorded in medieval documents relate directly to the 65 copyhold oxgangs in the eighteenth century this would indicate that the Preston oxgangs must have been reorganised sometime after the eleventh century. Another indication of reorganisation is perhaps visible in the standard strip widths of lands in the eighteenth century. Not only do the widths appear to ignore the oxgang unit, but they were also likely to have been based upon a post-medieval measure.

Reorganisation of Preston's holdings may not have required a physical replanning of the open fields. The bydale and long lands system in Preston would have been an elegant way to simplify scattered holdings, particularly as cultivation extended to boundaries of the parish and 'waste'. In the muted planar landscape of Preston, the vast majority of ridge and furrow would have been aligned north–south to aid drainage. Therefore, even if the fields had originally been organised into furlongs separated by the few streams, marshes and lanes it would be a simple administrative action to convert that to the system of bydales described in the seventeenth- and eighteenth-century terriers. However, although there is plenty of evidence for shared north–south alignments in the Preston open fields there is far less evidence for long strips themselves. Only one land is described as such in the eighteenth-century terriers, and both the documentary sources, and the evidence of transverse ditches indicate that the lands were made up of shorter sections of ploughed ridges following the same alignment. Harvey's conclusion was that Preston's long lands had been laid out following a single plan either in the eleventh or fourteenth centuries. It seems more likely that Preston's ploughlands expanded gradually to meet the needs of a growing population, and the simple topography meant the vast majority of strips were aligned north to south. The absence of detailed medieval records does not indicate whether the fields were farmed in furlongs or not, but certainly by the seventeenth century the strips belonging to the holdings were regularly ordered and repeated seven times across the fields in the bydales.

One of the challenges for Harvey's analysis of the open fields in Preston was the absence of a map showing the early strip pattern. In nearby Skeffling a surviving early eighteenth-century estate map depicted land held as long strips stretching from the village to the edge of the parish. This appeared to correspond well with the documentary evidence in Preston. In Skeffling the cultivated land was divided into two open fields, the East and West Fields located on either side of the settlement (DDCC/155/2). Just as in Preston, the strip orientation was not altered even when the fields were bisected by streams or lanes (DDCC/155/2). To Harvey this was further evidence for deliberate planning of open fields (Harvey 1981, 185).

A closer examination, however, shows that while the selions maintain east–west alignments there is abundant evidence that the individual strips are not themselves continuous. An example of this is visible in the East Field shown in Figure 6.5, where the selions shown in the In Field do not line up with those located in the Out Field. This is contrary to what would be expected if the lands had been laid out as a deliberate plan. Evidence for similar strips that share alignments but are not continuous can be seen in the West Field. Although the majority of the strips in the Skeffling open fields share the same east to west orientation due to the topography, the evidence from the Skeffling map indicates that the majority of the strips did not stretch the full distance from settlement to parish boundary (DDCC/155/2). This has potential implications for the understanding of the long lands in Preston.

Harvey's work in Preston led her to identify 'long-furlong' open fields where the strips extended from the villages to the watershed or streams without deviating from their course for several kilometres. Fundamental to this was Harvey's interpretation of the documentary sources in Preston: however, as noted above, this analysis overlooked the environmental influences in the parish. The efficacy of surface drainage would have undoubtedly been of significant concern to the medieval inhabitants. In both Preston and Skeffling the shared alignment of strips over long distances results from the muted, planar topography and the

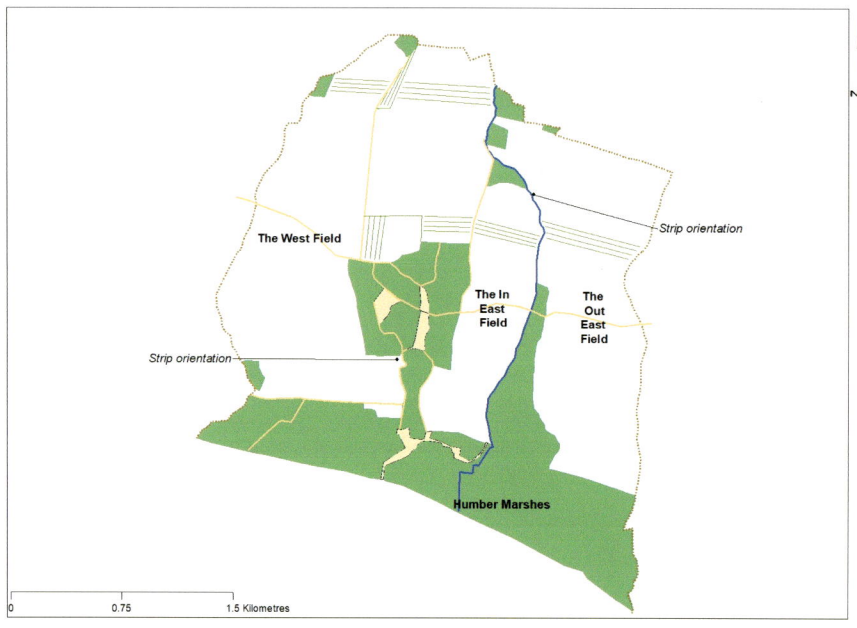

FIGURE 6.5. *A Copy of the Enclosure Plan of Skeffling in Holderness by John or William Iverson* (DDCK 35/1/b and strip orientations (after Harvey 1978).

need to use the slight slope available to drain the land. This created an appearance of regularity which Harvey interpreted as characteristic of deliberate planning, rather than the response to the local environment.

Long furlongs in the Midlands

Harvey's research in Holderness has proven influential, and inspired archaeologists such as David Hall to seek similar landscape evidence for planned field systems in Northamptonshire. In Holderness little landscape evidence for the former strip pattern had survived in the continuously ploughed landscape, but in Northamptonshire much of the former open field land had been converted to pasture following enclosure. This preserved the layout of strips and furlongs as ridge and furrow into the mid-twentieth century, when much of the grassland was returned to arable cultivation. The late survival of the earthworks allowed much of the strip pattern to be recorded through aerial photography before it was destroyed by modern ploughing, and this has allowed the field and furlong patterns to be examined in detail.

David Hall identified several examples of long lands in Northamptonshire, two of which were located in the parishes of Raunds and Wollaston (Hall 1995, 133). Hall noticed that in these parishes there were areas where the orientation of ridge and furrow appeared to be continued across several succeeding furlongs. Hall believed that the matching strip alignments must have been created when larger furlongs were subdivided by the insertion of headlands (Hall 1982, 48). The original long strips would have stretched over thousands of metres and reached the township boundaries. Hall concluded that his Northamptonshire long furlongs were very similar to the examples Harvey had previously identified in Holderness, and as such they were likely to have the same origin, namely that they reflected the original layout of the open fields (Hall 1995, 135).

Hall surmised that the insertion of the headlands into the former long furlongs was likely to be in response to localised drainage requirements. This, Hall believed, explained the checkerboard pattern of furlongs commonly seen in Northamptonshire, where strip alignments change from furlong to furlong (Hall 1995, 133). This appears to be logical but what explained the motivation for inserting headlands into a long furlong while keeping the same strip alignment?

Although Hall commented upon drainage of the open fields there is little to indicate that he considered the field pattern in relation to the local environmental conditions. As the previous examination of the strip patterns in Preston and Skeffling have illustrated topography was a major influence in the arrangement of strips and furlongs. Six furlongs in the parish of Raunds were identified by Hall as originating as a single long furlong. Figure 6.6 depicts Hall's six furlongs and the underlying topography.

Hall's numbered furlongs, 1–6, are marked on the map, as is his point 'A', marking the ends of the headlands which he believes were inserted to break up the original long furlong (Hall 1982, 50). Immediately it is noticeable that the alignment appears to continue further, beyond the parish boundary and into

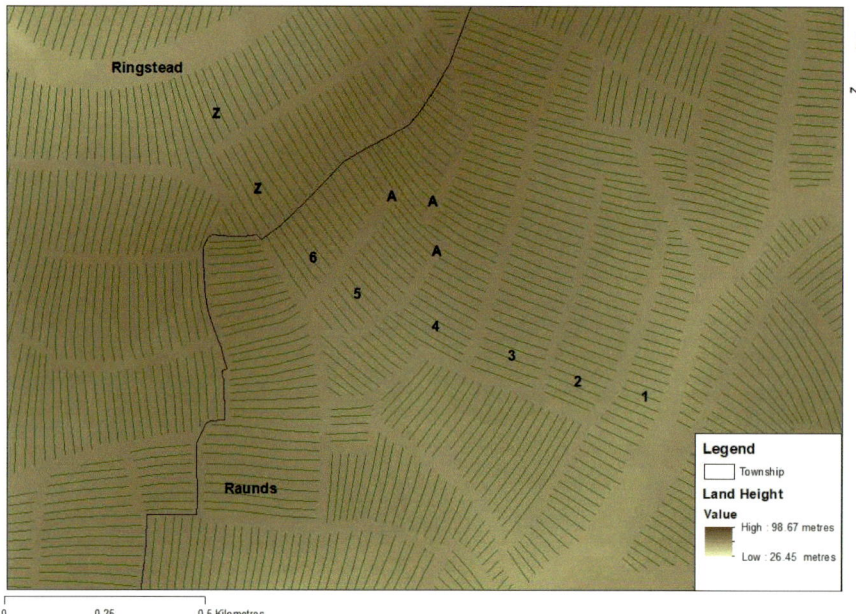

FIGURE 6.6. Long furlongs in Raunds (after Hall 1982, 48–9).

the neighbouring township of Ringstead, as indicated by the two furlongs 'Z', although Hall does not include this in his analysis.

The soil type changes across the furlongs; furlongs 1 and 2 overlie calcareous clay and loam soils of the Moreton Association. They benefit from drainage, as the sub soils are somewhat impermeable, leaving them prone to seasonal waterlogging (Hodge 1984, 257). The remaining furlongs overlie the same fertile glacial clay soil belonging to the Hanslope Association as found in the Bourn Valley and discussed in Chapter 2. The soil is unlikely to be available for spring cropping in this region, but benefits from surface drainage (Hodge 1984, 209).

The boundary between Raunds and Ringstead runs along a minor watershed, to which the strips are clearly arranged at right angles, following the slope. At the other, eastern end of the arrangement, furlong 1 is similarly aligned perpendicular to a natural feature, this time to the stream. Closer examination of the field pattern in Figure 6.6 shows that furlongs 1–4 are all primarily aligned on the watercourse while the strips in furlongs 5 and 6 have a slightly different alignment, which is focused on the watershed. The headland between furlongs 4 and 5 is the place where the orientation is gradually adjusted to ensure the strips have a right angle relationship to both the stream and the watershed. This slightly curving path between terminal points is a common feature in prehistoric co-axial systems and there are many examples of this in the Dartmoor reaves, but in this instance, it is likely to reflect the importance of maintaining an optimum angle to facilitate drainage. As noted previously Hall concluded that the insertion of headlands was to improve drainage, but it is clear from the topography in Raunds that if the original layout had taken the form of a group of very long, curving strips then the subsequent insertion of several transverse headlands would be more likely to hinder than improve the drainage.

In the parish of Wollaston, Hall identified another potential long land by noting how ridge and furrow in two small furlongs ('A' and 'B' on Figure 6.7) appeared to share the same alignment and that crop marks showed them continuing beneath the intervening headland between the two points marked 'q'. This led Hall to suppose that furlongs A and B were originally a single larger unit, subdivided by the insertion of the headland, which, by the eighteenth century at least, formed the course of a local lane called Thatchway (Hall 1982, 48).

It is perhaps useful to take a slightly wider view, and to note that the open field strips in the surrounding furlongs were ranged perpendicular to the slades and valleys, something that is particularly noticeable at the points marked 'd' in Figure 6.7. While the small hillock at point 'Z' creates a complicated strip arrangement, with changes in orientation in order that the furrows follow the slope, this is of relatively limited significance in the field as a whole. More generally the selions in the Wollaston field shared the same approximate direction, despite being divided into numerous furlongs and almost all the strips tended to run down the main slope, which falls from south to north.

A surprising feature of Hall's long furlongs in Wollaston is their small scale: the combined length of the strips in furlongs A and B is only around 250 m, a length similar to the classic 220-yard length of a 'normal' medieval furlong. It is quite possible that a small furlong incorporating the parts of furlongs A and B that lay between the two points 'q' in Figure 6.7 has indeed been subdivided at some unknown point in the past. However, it is also possible that an originally

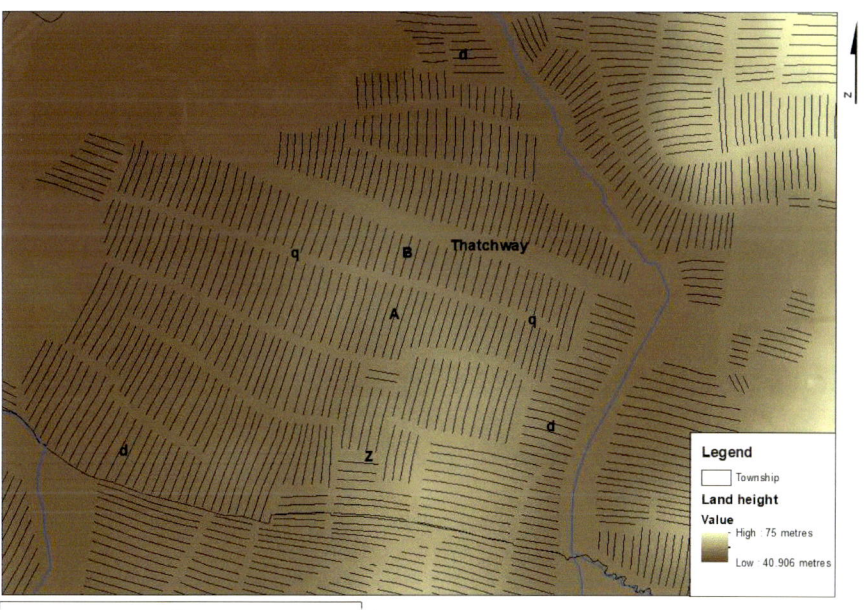

FIGURE 6.7. Long furlongs in Wollaston (after Hall 1982).

narrower headland between furlongs A and B was widened to make room for the Thatchway, thus accounting for the crop marks.

One of the difficulties in interpreting the layout of the supposed long furlongs is the extent to which the strip alignments that appear to be continued in successive furlongs when reproduced in a map or photograph reflects the genuine arrangement. As discussed in previous chapters, in many cases where supposedly ancient field boundaries appeared on an Ordnance Survey or Tithe map to be 'slighted' by Roman roads, closer examination indicated that the boundaries did not line up on either side of the road as would be expected if the road had been imposed on a pre-existing field pattern. Surviving maps showing open field strips appear to indicate that a similar pattern can be seen in the long furlongs, namely that the supposedly continuous strips were actually slightly offset on opposing sides of the headland. To take a practical approach to open field strips this would appear to be an inefficient layout. The frequent appearance of land disputes in manorial records indicates that the strip pattern was subject to both accidental and deliberate damage, even without accounting for large scale changes. Disputes required investigation, and regular confirmation of the strip widths and divisions was required. Measuring land allocations was an arduous and time-consuming process, and any method of reducing the burden, for example allowing two strip widths lying on either side of a headland to be measured at once should surely have been welcomed?

One of the most curious elements of the long furlongs in Northamptonshire are the transverse headlands. They rarely appear to benefit the local drainage, as Hall originally suggested, and generally interrupt it. A more plausible explanation for these patterns – such as successive furlongs, each containing strips oriented in the same direction but separated by headlands – might be that they simply represent repeated expansions of cultivated ground at the expense of common pasture, in contexts where there was no need to change direction to account for drainage. An alternative response would have been for each landholder to extend their strips up to a newly agreed upon point, eliminating the need for additional transverse headlands. This could have gradually created long furlongs, but this is different from their establishment as a deliberate act of large-scale landscape planning. That this was not done in the Northamptonshire fields and instead that the furlongs appeared to have been taken out of the 'waste' as separate intakes divided by headlands is perhaps worthy of further investigation. Hall, like Harvey, interpreted regularity as evidence for planning in the landscape, but this overlooked the importance of optimising the local environment when farming the open fields.

Regular landscapes in the open fields of North Yorkshire

Hall identified long furlongs elsewhere in England, perhaps most notably in Middleton in Ryedale on the edge of the North York Moors. The modern field boundary pattern appears to fossilise the long reverse 's' curve characteristic of medieval ploughing as illustrated in Figure 6.8. To Hall this suggested it

6. *Open fields and 'planned' agricultural landscapes* 109

FIGURE 6.8. First Edition Ordnance Survey 6-Inch map for part of the parish of Middleton in Ryedale, Yorkshire.

originated as an open field landscape deliberately subdivided into long furlongs (Hall 1982, 51).

In *Medieval Fields*, David Hall highlighted the modern field boundary pattern Middleton as preserving the 'ploughing curves' so characteristic of surviving ridge and furrow. He further stated that 'the whole parish seems to have been laid out in two massive blocks with strips … up to 2,000 metres long' (Hall 1982, 48). More recently Stuart Wrathmell, writing about Scandinavian settlement in North Yorkshire, highlighted this same field pattern, noting how the 'reversed 's' shapes of the boundaries gives the appearance of swathes of open fields either created at one time or in successive phases of an overall scheme' (Wrathmell 2021, 4). Wrathmell further noted that the layout of Middleton itself suggests that it is a planned village, echoing comments made by Allerston in the 1970s, and suggested that the entire plan, the fields, territories and settlement dates from the ninth century (Allerston 1970, 97; Wrathmell 2021, 97).

The field pattern recorded on the First Edition Ordnance Survey 6-Inch map, and illustrated in Figure 6.8, does indeed illustrate that many of the fields surrounding the township are in the form of long curving enclosures. They resemble, albeit on a larger scale, Hall's long lands in Northamptonshire discussed previously. This curving field pattern is not unique to Middleton, similar arrangements of long narrow fields are visible in several villages lying to the east of Pickering, as well as in neighbouring Aislaby and Wrelton.

The medieval parish of Middleton contained numerous townships that have since separated into their own parishes, including Aislaby and Wrelton, which are located east of the settlement. The ancient territory of Middleton was much larger than the current parish and stretched from the Costa Beck in the south to Middleton Moor, which lay more than 12 km north (Page 1923). The topography of the early parish varies significantly: the land falls from Middleton Moor at almost 270 m OD, to Costa Beck, which lies just over 25 m above sea level. In the modern parish, the highest land is just over 125 m OD. Middleton village was located in the far south of the ancient parish along the road linking Pickering and Helmsley. The crofts and tofts of the settlement formed a lozenge shape, with the minor lanes, High and Low Back Side lanes separating the village gardens from the surrounding fields.

The curved strip fields highlighted by Hall cover only a small portion of the former parish territory, and all lie close to the settlement. The fields to the north stretch for around 2 km from High Back Side Lane to end up on Broates Lane, with the land falling in height by approximately 80 m across that length (Hall 1982, 49). To the south of the settlement is a similar grouping of curved strip fields lying between Low Back Side Lane and Street Road. These fields are much narrower and shorter than the northern strips, they range in length between 500 m in the east and 1200 m in the west. The change in height here is very slight, approximately 5 m.

Middleton village is located at the junction of two rather different soil types and geologies. A permeable sandstone laid down during the Carboniferous and Jurassic periods lies to the north of the village while the settlement itself and the fields to the south overlie Glaciolacustrine Clay (Soil Survey 1983, Sheet 1). The soils are similarly varied, ranging from the free draining soils that lie on the northern hillsides to impermeable clay soils that lead down to the Costa Beck. The tofts and crofts of Middleton are located upon the northern extent of the clay soil, and High Back Side Lane even appears to follow the approximate boundary of the clay soil for much of its length.

The light lands to the north of the village change in character moving northwards, up the slope. Near to the village lie the free draining acid loams of the Rivington 1 Association (Soil Survey 1983, Sheet 1). These are easy to work and dry out quickly, allowing many field working days, but lack fertility and are prone to leaching, as well as being droughty for cereals and even more so for grass (Landis 2020). Further north the soil type changes to the Elmton 2 Association, and the differing substrate is visible when the soils are freshly cultivated, as the tilth of this lime rich soil contains many white lime pebbles, derived from an underlying outcrop of Jurassic Limestone (Soil Survey 1983, Sheet 1). Elmton soils are easy to work and dry quickly, allowing plenty of days for field working, but again are prone to drought (Hodge 1984, 181). This lime rich loam would have been similarly workable, but also slightly more fertile than the Rivington 1 Association soils that lay closest to the village.

To the south of the settlement the impermeable clay gives rise to the fine loam and clay soil of the Foggathorpe 2 Association (Soil Survey 1983, Sheet 1). Although the soil is more naturally fertile than those lying to the north of the village, the impeded drainage, combined with low gradient and high rainfall, makes this land very difficult to farm without modern under drains. The likelihood of seasonal flooding and waterlogging would even limit the grazing of livestock outside the drier summer months; however, these same environmental conditions would have produced relatively abundant grass growth in the late spring and summer, at least when compared to the droughty soils that lay north of the settlement (Everitt 1977).

The curving narrow fields that were interpreted by Hall to be fossilised long furlongs lie mostly to the north of the village. Although both described the fields as preserving the reverse 's' curves of extended open field strips, it is clear from Figure 6.8 that the field boundaries are perhaps better described as *sinuous* curves. The strip fields lying north of Middleton do not, upon closer examination, really conform to the typical pattern of a medieval plough strip. The latter followed a straight course for most of its length before curving subtly as it neared the end. This does not describe the fields to the north of Middleton, which would appear to curve in the middle of the strip but have a relatively perpendicular relationship to the two transverse lanes. In contrast, it is relatively easy to identify on Figure 6.8 those fields that *do* appear to have originated through the early piecemeal enclosure of open-field strips, most obviously the narrow closes lying south of the settlement, several of which clearly display the characteristic reverse 's' curve as they meet Street Lane: note, in particular, the subtlety of the terminal curve of the south field lands in comparison to the northern field strips. This same pattern is visible on the earliest surviving map of Middleton's fields, which dates to 1730 and includes the tithable land of the parish reproduced in Figure 6.9.

The 1730 map excludes the area to the north of Broates Lane, which at the time was common moorland, as well as much of the common marsh or 'carr' that lay below Street Lane (MIC 2046/118-24 & 1982/276-79). Otherwise, it

112 How the Land Lies

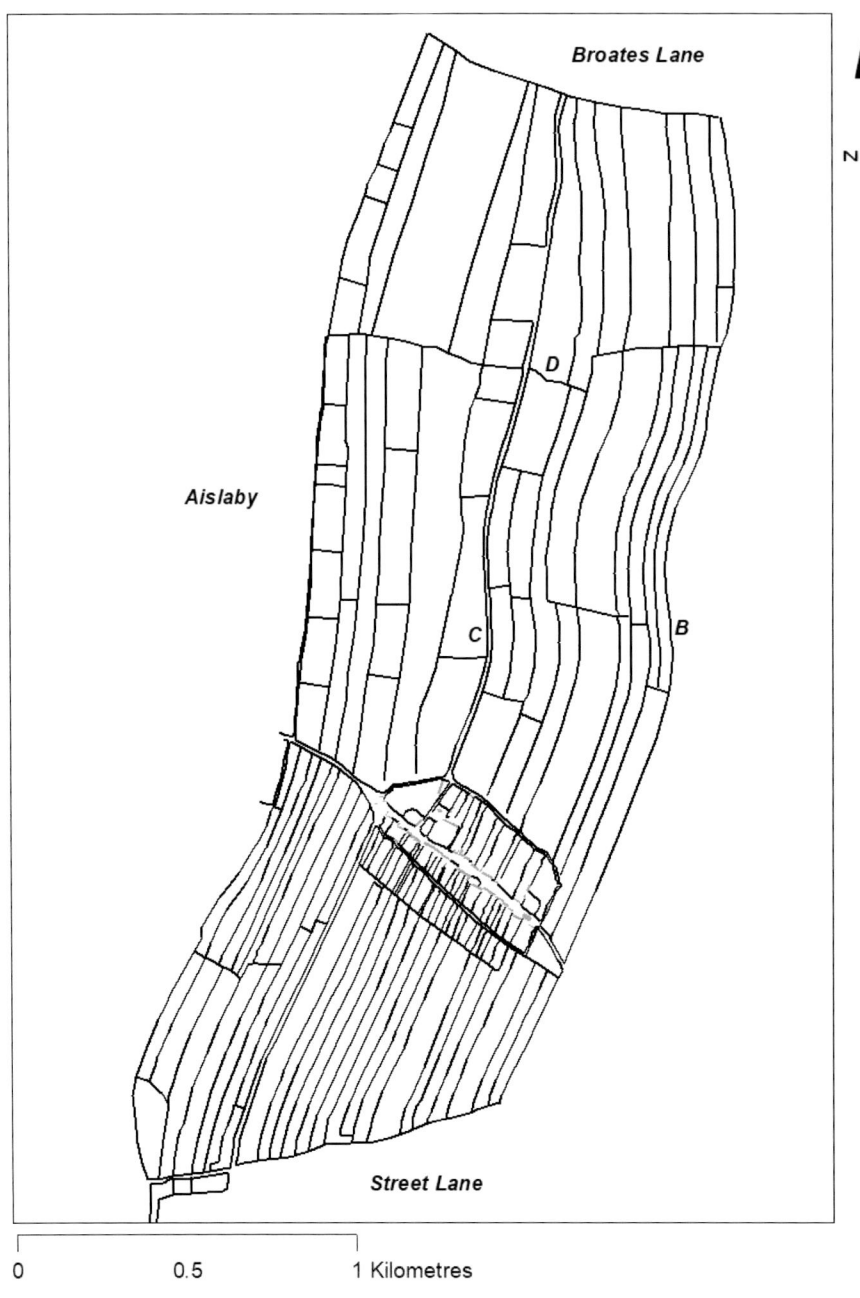

FIGURE 6.9. *A Plan of the Tyth Land at Middleton in the County of York* (MIC 2046/118-24 & 1982/276-79).

indicates that the general framework of Middleton's fields was retained between the early eighteenth century and the time that the First Edition Ordnance Survey 6-Inch map was surveyed in the 1850s, although there was some amalgamation of narrow lands into wider fields. Both maps show a clear difference between the typical widths of the strip fields found to the north and south of the settlement.

6. Open fields and 'planned' agricultural landscapes   113

FIGURE 6.10. Detail of *A Plan of the Tyth Land at Middleton in the County of York* (MIC 2046/118-24 & 1982/276-79).

On the lighter soils to the north groups of former open field strips had been combined into larger, wider parcels than on the heavy clay soils to the south. The 1730 map indicates this process of enclosure and amalgamation was already underway (MIC 2046/118-24 & 1982/276-79). While this distinction is visible on the nineteenth-century Ordnance Survey map it is more marked in the earlier survey. It could be that the wetter land south of the settlement

114   *How the Land Lies*

limited the number of selions that could be successfully grouped together before a field ditch was required. This was not a simple case of creating larger fields on the lighter soils, however, because while the strips themselves were wider, the many were subdivided by transverse boundaries, thereby creating smaller rectangular fields.

An important feature of the Middleton landscape, which is clearly visible on the maps of 1730, is the relationship between the boundaries of the village

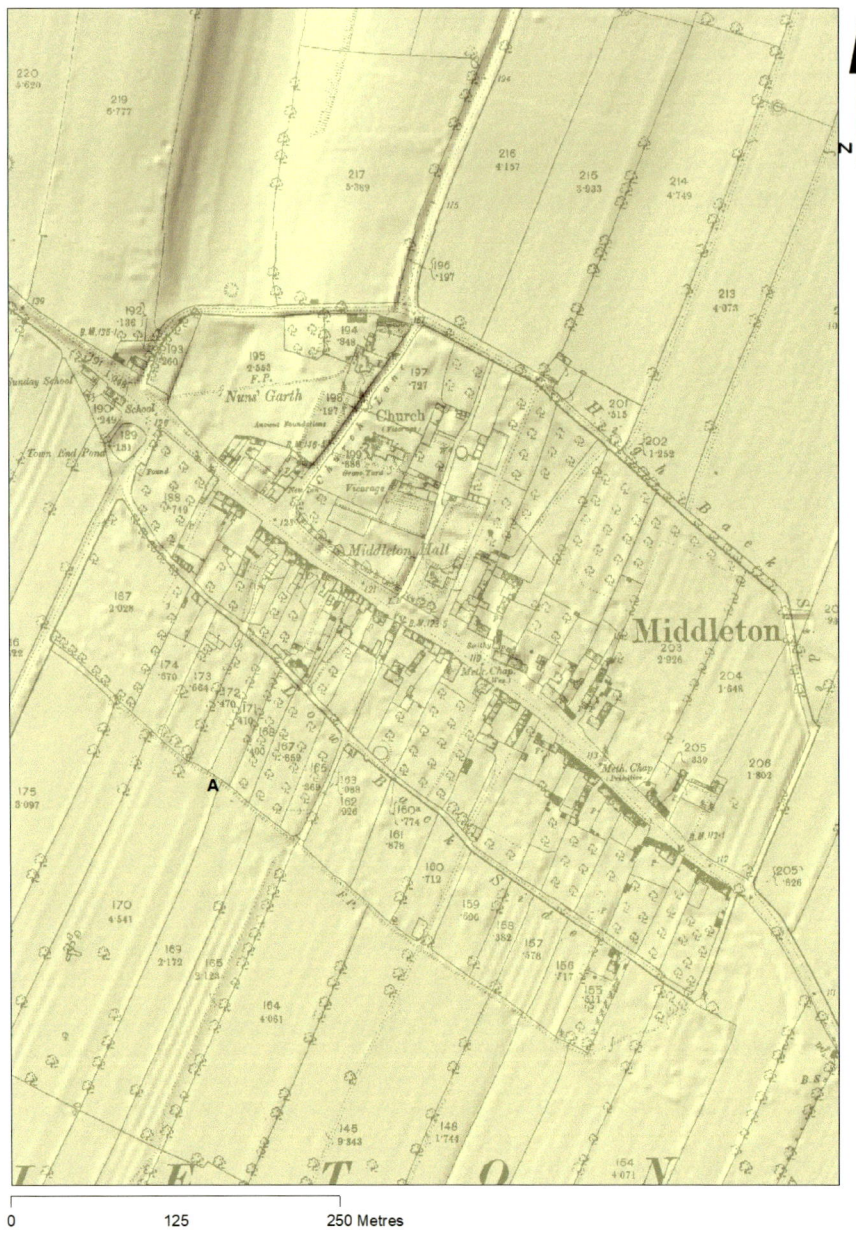

FIGURE 6.11. The village of Middleton in Ryedale, detail from the First Edition Ordnance Survey Map, overlain on a LiDAR Composite DTM 2 m.

crofts and those of the adjacent fields. This is particularly noticeable in the south part of the settlement, several of the boundaries are precisely in line, with more sharing an identical orientation. This relationship was subsequently obscured by amalgamation and adjustment as a comparison of Figures 6.10 and 6.11 illustrates.

Many of the village crofts contain traces of ridge and furrow, both on the north and the south side of the village street. All this clearly indicates that many of the tofts and crofts originally part of open field strips have been enclosed in a piecemeal fashion at a very early date. The extension of settlement along existing lanes and over strips has previously been identified in Northamptonshire by Williamson *et al.* and can give rise to very orderly arrangements of lanes and farms that appear to be the result of 'village planning', despite the settlement having developed organically (Oosthuizen 2006; Williamson *et al.* 2013).

In summary the layout of the Middleton village appears to respond to a combination of local environmental factors and the way in which people have utilised the surrounding landscape. But what of the 'ploughing curves' to the north of the village that attracted the attention of Hall and that he interpreted as evidence for long furlongs (Hall 1982, 48)? Figure 6.12 depicts the relationship of the boundaries to the natural topography and this highlights the critical influence of a north–south valley, visible close to point 'B', which is followed by the parish boundary separating Middleton and Pickering. This minor valley, which follows a sinuous path against the dominant direction of slope, has clearly also had a determining influence on the form of the field boundaries and eventually even Middleton Lane, marked by point 'C' in Figure 6.12, despite the two features being over 500 m apart. These field boundaries that were shown as hedges in 1730, appear to have been set parallel to the curving valley, the consistent width of each field suggests that this was a simple method of apportioning land by measuring an agreed distance from the valley.

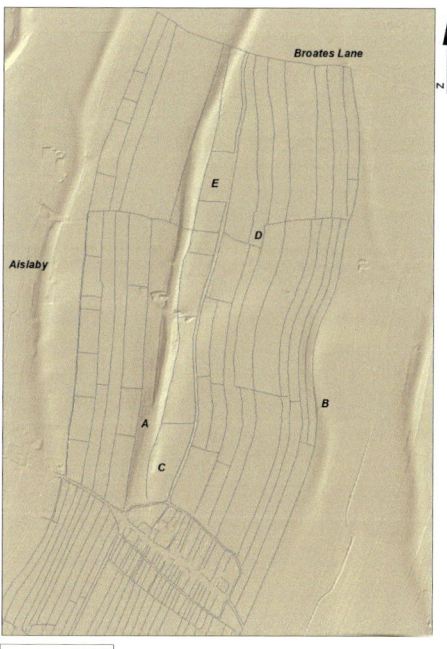

FIGURE 6.12. Detail of *A Plan of the Tyth Land at Middleton in the County of York* (MIC 2046/118-24 & 1982/276-79), overlain on a LiDAR Composite DTM 2 m.

The field pattern that lay to the west of Middleton Dale (point 'A' on Figure 6.12) was morphologically dissimilar to the enclosures to the east in that it was formed of straight rather than sinuous boundaries. This distinction is easily explained if the same measuring methodology was used as the straighter valley form would lead to straight boundaries. The field boundaries in the narrow area between Middleton Lane and Dale do not appear to match either the curving closes, or the straight enclosures. The lane led from Middleton village to distant resources on the high moorland to the north and probably fossilised a former common drove or linear common.

Further evidence of this is visible on the 1730 map, which appears to show a roadside green, albeit very regular in shape, indicated by 'E' in Figure 6.12. North of Broates Lane the field pattern recorded on the Ordnance Survey map is more characteristic of Parliamentary Enclosure. The 1766 Enclosure Act for Cropton in Middleton includes the 'waste' called East Moor that lay to the north of the parish beyond Borates Lane, as well as the marsh or 'carr' in the extreme south, but the fields near the village had already been piecemeal enclosed (I MIC 280).

The 1730 survey shows several transverse boundaries in the area to the north of the village that extend across multiple narrow fields and have the appearance of fossilised headlands or 'head dykes', to use a local term. The long headland near 'D' in Figure 6.12, which stretches into Aislaby's open fields, may also indicate an earlier limit of cultivation, for the field pattern in the area to its north, in both parishes, becomes noticeably more regular, probably indicating more recent enclosure from 'waste'. The other transverse head dykes probably indicate earlier stages in the expansion of the arable, and certainly suggest that the open fields did not, in fact, consist of long, attenuated strips in a single huge furlong, but as in the Northamptonshire examples discussed previously, a group of furlongs, separated by headlands, containing strips orientated the same way following the direction of the slope, and drainage. The curving profile of the strip fields is also clearly a product of the topography, engendered by the sinuous valley 'B': indeed, the pattern of north–south minor valleys, running at right angles to the dominant direction of slope, has more generally influenced the layout of furlongs both in Middleton and in the neighbouring parishes. Hall also included the curving strip fields lying to the south of Middleton in his discussion and as noted above these do resemble the characteristic reverse 's' of medieval arable strips, as can be seen in Figures 6.13 and 6.14. As previously discussed, the area to the south of the village is characterised by impermeable clay loams on very gently sloping ground.

Perhaps unsurprisingly given these environmental challenges, the field pattern here is also strongly aligned upon the local topography, utilising the slight natural slope to aide drainage (see Figure 6.14, which exaggerates a narrow band of land heights ranging from 35 m (pale yellow) to 20 m (blue). The narrow strip fields shown on the 1730 map closely follow the direction of the slope and curve as they meet Street Lane and the ditch at a right angle.

The township of Middleton in Ryedale has been used as evidence for both settlement and landscape planning in the medieval period. Through comparison of the regular features with the local environment it is clear that most of the apparently planned elements arose from the way people responded to the natural environment.

The regular appearance of much of the village derives, not from 'planning', but from the way settlement has expanded organically over former open-field

6. Open fields and 'planned' agricultural landscapes

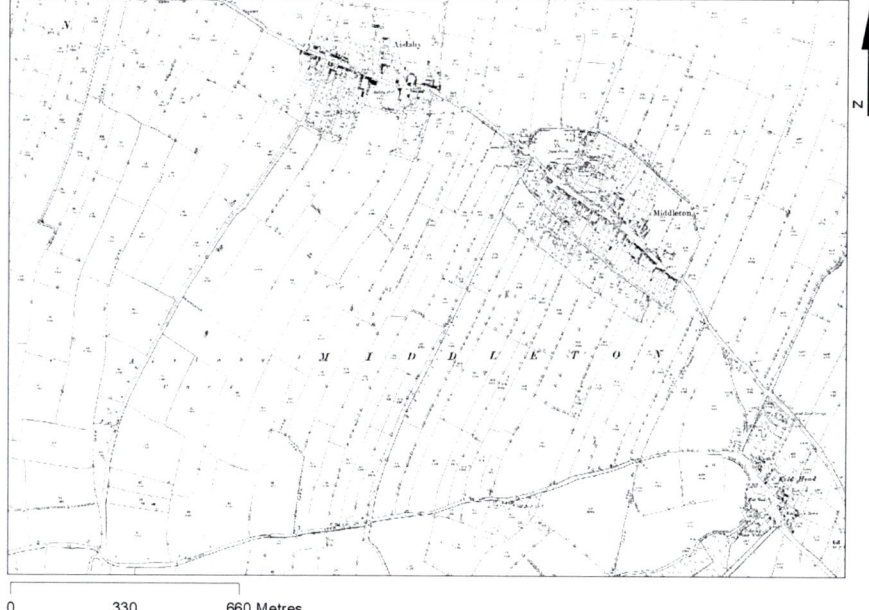

FIGURE 6.13. Fields to the south of Middleton and Aislaby in Ryedale, on the First Edition Ordnance Survey 6-Inch map.

FIGURE 6.14. Detail of *A Plan of the Tyth Land at Middleton in the County of York* (MIC 2046/118-24 & 1982/276-79) and a DTM layer ranging from 35 m (pale yellow) to 20 m (blue).

strips in a manner seen elsewhere, in particular in Northamptonshire (Williamson *et al.* 2013). The long strip fields to the north of the village represent, not long furlongs planned on a large scale, but the fossilised remains of a series of furlongs, separated by headlands, probably representing successive northwards intakes from the waste.

Conclusion

The evidence reviewed above appears to indicate that the long furlongs found in Middleton and the neighbouring settlements resulted from the gradual expansion of ploughland. The local environment and in particular the topographic form and the soil types strongly influenced the form of the new intakes, which was fossilised in the form of transverse head-dykes. A similar pattern of gradual extension is visible in the Raunds and Wollaston strip pattern, where the shared orientation of the ridge and furrow across the furlongs appears to result from a deliberate intent to utilise the natural slope for drainage. The evidence that ploughed furrows had once continued beneath a later headland confirms that the furlong was subject to adjustment, although the motivation and extent of the change remains unclear. The Wollaston evidence acts as a reminder that the existing open field strips and furlongs could be altered and adjusted as the needs of the communities waxed and waned.

Harvey's examples from Holderness illustrate how the allocation and ordering of lands in the open fields could develop into a very regular pattern. The simple layout of strips in Preston almost all followed the same north–south orientation, however, the records also show that the strips were frequently cut through by streams, lanes and marshes into shorter lengths. In other parishes these smaller groups of lands might have been called furlongs, but in Preston the shared strip orientation led to emergence of the bydale system in the late medieval or early modern periods.

The examples from Holderness, Middleton and Northamptonshire have illustrated how apparently regular landscapes are interpreted as resulting from planning and schemes of deliberate land allocation. As discussed in previous chapters this is common in discussions of so-called relict field systems. However, in both cases the regular elements can be explained by the aspects of the local landscape and in particular local landforms. Medieval husbandmen had an empirical understanding of how to farm their fields, and the importance of surface drainage in improving the soils. In areas with planar topography this led to a simple strip pattern where the majority of the furrows followed the slope and thus shared the same orientation. When considered without reference to the local landform the pattern had the appearance of a regular planned landscape, but this is illusory, as becomes clear once topography is included in the analysis.

Harvey and Hall both perceived similarities between the long furlongs of Holderness and Northamptonshire and the planned settlements in Saxony described by Matzat, but these conclusions were challenged by Nitz. Nitz suggested that the long furlongs found in Mecklenburg were not the result of deliberate single event planning but had developed through the gradual accretion of land by the assarting of waste near the township boundaries (Matzat 1988, 143). Nitz further noted that the German farming system was based on three open fields but without a fallow rotation, which was fundamentally different to the situation in England (Matzat 1988, 141; Nitz 1988, 151). These inconsistencies together with the fact that to date no evidence has been found that can support an origin for German open fields that predates their appearance in England, led Nitz to suggest that the German and English open fields are an example of equifinality (Nitz 1988, 158). Nitz concluded that despite their similar morphology the features have independent roots; the long furlongs in England developed from the simplest method of land division, while in Germany from the adoption of the mouldboard plough (Matzat 1988, 145). While the interpretation presented here would partly support these conclusions, in the sense that it would see common alignment of strips over large areas as the consequence of repeated intakes of land from pasture, it would suggest that in most cases these took the form of separate but aligned furlongs, of normal medieval length, rather than long furlongs.

CHAPTER SEVEN

Northamptonshire and its open fields

The previous chapter considered the landscape evidence for planned open fields using several well-known examples. Comparison of the pattern of strips and furlongs with the underlying topography highlighted the close relationship between the strip alignments and local drainage patterns. Perhaps just as informative was the consistent nature of the approach, namely that ridged plough strips were aligned down the slope. In the examples presented in the previous chapter the landform was simple, which led to a regular pattern of strips. As with relict field systems it seems likely that furlong patterns in the open fields were shaped by wider, less immediate topographic and environmental influences, and in particular the presence of 'resource linkage' routes both contemporary and inherited that connected the differing ecological resources. This chapter explores these varied influences on the development of medieval furlong patterns in Northamptonshire and will provide examples on which the broad 'rules' for the development of field patterns presented in the previous chapters can be tested.

Northamptonshire lies at the approximate halfway point of the former champion belt, which originally stretched from Yorkshire to the south coast of England. The county saw the greatest proportion of villages that managed their ploughland according to the regular open-field farming system well into the Early Modern period, with many open fields surviving until Parliamentary Enclosure in the eighteenth or nineteenth century. Possibly more than any other English county, the development of Northamptonshire's agricultural landscape has been studied by historians and archaeologists interested in the origins of open-field farming in England.

The longevity of the county's open fields, combined with the formal manner in which they were removed from many parishes has ensured that Northamptonshire has a rich store of documentary evidence. These predominately local sources recorded elements of the organisation and management of the open fields at a parish or township level. Although in many places the earliest records are dated to the thirteenth century (Ault 1972, 18). Until the middle of the twentieth century the landscape of the county itself provided the greatest resource for those interested in the arrangement of the former furlongs and fields. Upon enclosure in the eighteenth century many of the formerly arable lands were laid to pasture and few were ploughed flat before being converted to grassland. This had the effect of fossilising the raised plough ridges that had previously denoted the individual lands held by the farmers, and thus the layout of furlongs, under the sward. Much of the Northamptonshire farmland remained as pasture for the following two centuries until the pressure for increased food production following the Second World War led to it being returned to arable production. Fortunately, for those with interest in open field farming, by this time a comprehensive series of aerial photographs had documented the pattern of ridge and furrow in many of the county's parishes.

Northamptonshire, therefore, has an abundance of sources available for those interested in open-field farming in the Midlands and, perhaps unsurprisingly, has become the county landscape most studied to answer questions on the development and organisation of communities and their open fields. Many of the sources discussed previously resulted from research carried out in Northamptonshire, particularly the work from the later twentieth century by Hall, Brown and Foard; indeed, Brown and Foard's concept of 'a great re-planning' developed from research in the southeast of the county particularly around the parish of Raunds (Foard 1977; Hall 1981; Brown and Foard 1998). These conclusions were challenged by the Northamptonshire project, based at the University of East Anglia in the early 2010s. The research used GIS technology to map all the archaeological evidence from the county, including David Hall's detailed plans of the layout of strips, furlongs and fields (Northamptonshire County Council 2008). Analysis of this data found little or no evidence for wholesale re-planning, instead suggesting the gradual development of a farming landscape when faced with population change. In *Champion*, which presented the findings of the project, Tom Williamson, Robert Liddiard and Tracey Partida incorporated environmental factors into their discussion and analysis of the Northamptonshire landscape particularly considering the differences in soil types and climate (Williamson *et al.* 2013).

Although *Champion* included a consideration of the combined human and environmental factors in the development of the open fields there was little discussion of topography except in relation to major territorial boundaries. The influence of small-scale changes in drainage patterns and land height was not part of the analysis into the landscape. Previous consideration of the development of Northamptonshire's open fields has generally overlooked the possible influence of elevation and slope and yet when farming clay soils the importance of drainage can hardly be overstated. Writing in the 1930s Orwin and Orwin noted that the layout and height of surviving plough ridges in open fields appeared to reflect the local drainage requirements (Orwin and Orwin 1938, 14). Gervase Markham writing in the early seventeenth century reminded his readers of the vital importance of drainage:

> Now since I have here occasion to speak something of the draining of lands, and the keeping of them from the annoyance of superfluous wet, whether it be by inundation or otherwise, you shall understand that it is the especial office and duty of every Husbandman, not only in this soil, but in all other whatsoever, to have a principal respect to the keeping of his land dry, and to that end he shall diligently (as soon as he has winter-rigged his land) take a careful view of how his lands lie, which way the descent does from when annoyance or water may possibly come, and so consequently, draw certain deep furrows from descent unto descent, by which

means all the water may be conveyed from his land, either into some common Sewer, Lake, Brook or other main River (Markham 1613, 62).

The following chapter will thus consider Northamptonshire's open fields and the extent to which the strips and furlongs were influenced by the local environment and in particular the topography. The influence of routes that linked the settlement to distant resources will also be discussed, and finally it will consider whether there is any evidence to suggest that elements of the open field pattern were inherited from prehistoric or Romano-British farms. In order to do this the chapter will focus upon two case study areas in Northamptonshire:
- the hundred of Orlingbury, which lies in the approximate centre of the county, and which contained several parishes with regular furlong patterns;
- and the Central Nene Valley, made up of a group of parishes that share the regular linear sub-rectangular morphology characteristic of so-called relict landscapes.

The huge amount of data collected, organised and processed by the Northamptonshire project team, including their GIS datasets will be the principal source used in this chapter, combined with primary documentary sources and the many secondary sources that discuss the Northamptonshire open fields (Northamptonshire County Council 2008).

Northamptonshire lies midway between Wales and East Anglia near the widest point of the island of Great Britain. Similarly, the county lies midway between the arable farming in the east of England and predominately livestock farming in the west (Hodge 1984, 35). Although the division between the agricultural zones is a modern one, it is not without an environmental basis, simply put the rainfall in the west of the island far exceeds that in the east (Hodge 1984, 29). Furthermore, the average winter temperatures in the west tend to be warmer, and the summers cooler than those in the east (Hodge 1984, 29). The wetter western climate encourages annual grass growth but makes growing cereals more difficult by encouraging fungal diseases, such as ergot, as well as increasing the potential for losses due to wet harvests and costs for drying the grain when compared to farms in the east. Northamptonshire's central position means that it does not experience either of these extremes of climate and today the county still maintains a reputation for mixed farming.

The discussion of each case study area will begin with an examination of the local environment and the specific challenges and opportunities this may have presented to farmers in the past. This will be followed by a brief review of any archaeological fieldwork, and in particular features that influenced the open field landscape. The case studies will conclude with an analysis of the strip and furlong pattern and how it relates, or otherwise, to the local environment and topography.

Case study: The Orlingbury hundred

The area now included in the modern district of Orlingbury was until the fourteenth century divided into two neighbouring hundreds called Orlingbury and Maleslea.

The medieval hundreds were roughly similar in size and were divided by a long curving watershed. A modern route – Mawsley Road – runs along part of the length, and the modern parish boundaries terminate upon the line of the interfluve. The land height near the road is around 130 m OD and falls to less than 70 m at the river Ise. The medieval hundred of Orlingbury lay to the east of the curving boundary and contained a characteristic pattern of narrow sub-rectangular parishes, with long boundaries following a roughly co-axial alignment, which stretched from the banks of the river Ise to the watershed. The settlements within Maleslea hundred lay within the inner curve of the watershed. The township boundaries were similarly co-axial but the topography in the valley of the minor watercourse gave rise to a fan-like arrangement of territories, as can be seen in Figure 7.1. The parishes of Old and Walgrave, in particular, were roughly triangular in shape with only short distances of access to the stream at the bottom of the slope. In the mid-twentieth century the lower lying land around the brook was flooded to create Pitsford reservoir, changing the valley landscape forever.

Glacial clay soils cover the majority of Orlingbury hundred but lying beneath the impervious surface is porous bedrock. The majority of the substrata is formed by the Great Oolite Group but Inferior Oolite and Lias groups are also present. Soils of the Hanslope Association make up the predominate soil type in the area and are found on the upper slopes and watershed of the landform. The qualities of Hanslope soils have been discussed in some detail in Chapter 2 in relation to the Bourn Valley, Cambridgeshire and in particular the fact that they are fertile and well suited to autumn planting before the soil moisture levels reach capacity in winter. The sloping topography in Orlingbury contributes to the ability of the Hanslope soil to drain excess surface moisture, much as it does in the Bourn Valley, but the climate of Central Northamptonshire means

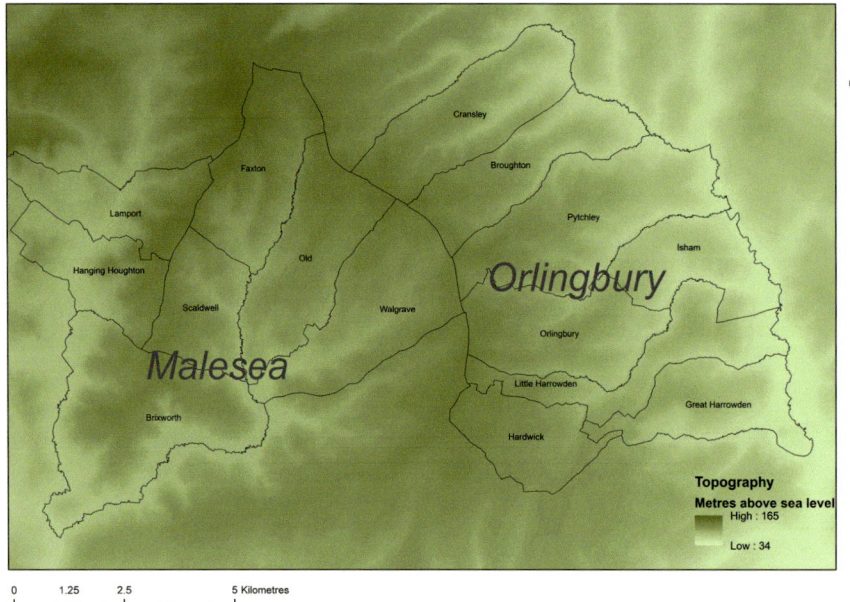

FIGURE 7.1. The topography of the modern hundred of Orlingbury.

that rainfall is both more frequent and of greater volume. This makes Hanslope a more marginal soil type in Orlingbury than it is on the clay plateau lying to the west of Cambridge (Hodge 1984, 209).

Further down slope soils of the Banbury and Denchworth Associations are found. The proportions of the soil types differ on either side of the watershed, as can be seen in Figure 7.2. In the parishes lying east of the watershed, Banbury Association soils cover the largest area after Hanslope. They are typically free draining and, despite being slightly acidic, they are considered today to be suitable for both cereals and spring sown root vegetables (Hodge 1984, 109).

Banbury Association soils retain little moisture, but quickly warm up for spring cultivations, although due to the natural acidity crop yields are likely to suffer unless lime is added. The porous nature of the soil means that stock can be grazed on grass even in wetter periods with limited risk of damage from poaching, although the same characteristic means that grass suffers from drought early in the season, which typically puts on little growth during the dry summer months. In some locations Morton Association soils separate the Hanslope and Banbury soil types. These are another group of free draining soils that are suitable for cultivations in both autumn and spring, although as with Banbury the porous nature means they are not naturally fertile and without regular rainfall crops quickly suffer from drought (Hodge 1984, 421). The Denchworth Association soils are

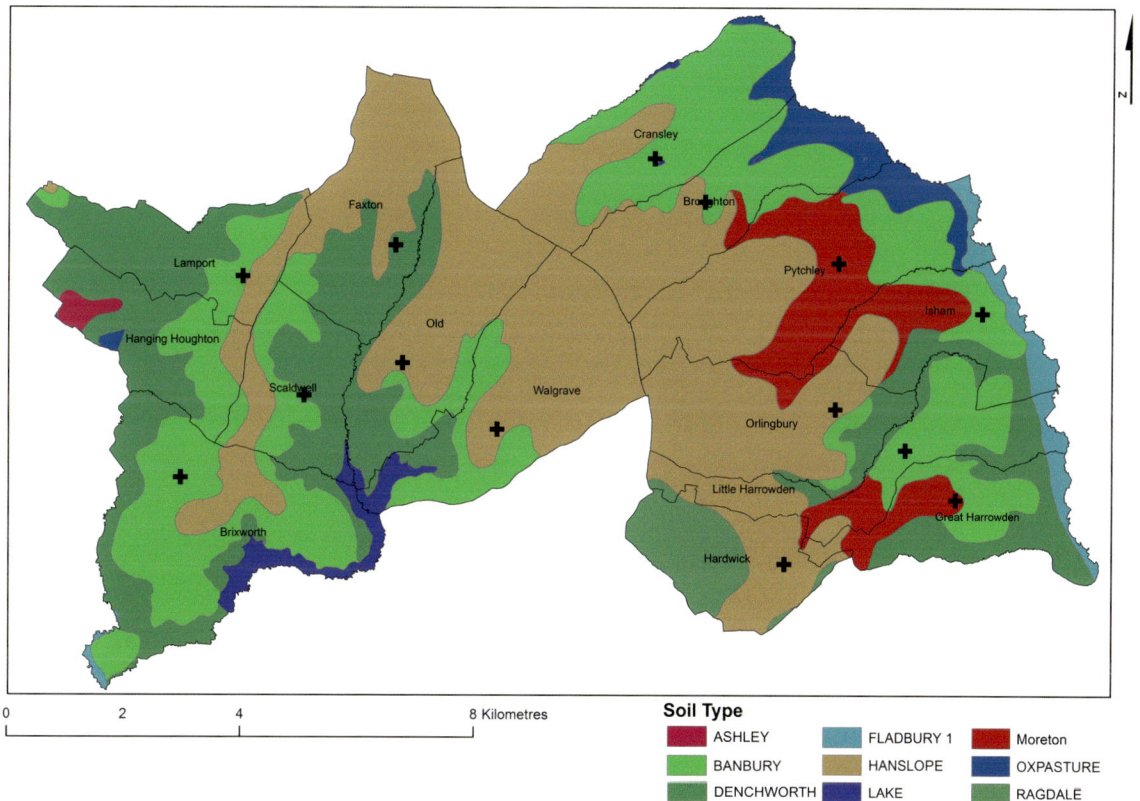

FIGURE 7.2. Soils of Orlingbury Hundred.

poorly draining and prone to severe waterlogging, as well as being only moderately fertile. Even now, with modern forms of under-drainage, there is a very short cultivation window in the autumn. Following the winter rains, Denchworth soils lie wet and are slow to warm up (Hodge 1984, 155). Conversely, the same soil water reserves mean the grass growing season lasts longer than on the neighbouring Banbury and Hanslope soils, although the sward is prone to damage through compaction and poaching in wet weather. Denchworth Association soils are also present in several parishes that lie to the west of the watershed, specifically Great and Little Harrowden, Isham and Orlingbury but here they cover only a small proportion of the land. They tend to lie close to the minor streams or slades and are interspersed with lighter land. Oxpasture Association soils are likewise clayey and seasonally waterlogged and share a similar distribution in the northern half of the hundred where they are located lying close to the minor streams or slades, to use the Northamptonshire term (Hodge 1984, 285).

Comparison of the locations of medieval churches and the modern soil map indicates that the early settlement sites appeared to actively avoid the poorly draining Denchworth soil types. Most of the villages were located on higher ground and lay approximately halfway between the river and the watershed. In the former hundred of Maleslea the majority of settlements are found on, or near, the junction between the Inferior Oolite and older Lias bedrocks; in Orlingbury hundred the settlements are similarly found at the junction of Great and Inferior Oolite groups. Such locations provided a regular supply of water, from springs, although in addition many of the settlements on both sides of the watershed are located next to a slade.

Despite their close proximity, the local environment of the parishes on either side of the watershed differ considerably. In particular, the townships in the former Maleslea hundred had to contend with a larger proportion of the difficult Denchworth soils. In addition, the configuration of the watershed, particularly in the townships of Old and Walgrave, means that much of the land is north facing, reducing soil temperature and both germination and growth rates. Given such a challenging local environment it is perhaps unsurprising that relatively little evidence for Neolithic or even Bronze Age activity has been found in the locality. There are crop marks of barrows and ring ditches on the minor watershed that divides Walgrave from Holcot to the south. A large Bronze Age barrow has been found within 500 m of the major curving watershed in Broughton.

Discoveries of flint axes and pottery through fieldwalking suggest that settlements that may have been associated with the Bronze Age Barrows were located in the valleys. Evidence for Romano-British activity is more widespread and the scatter of Late Iron Age or Romano-British enclosure crop marks indicate that large portions of the lighter soils in Orlingbury hundred were being farmed in this period, with a particularly extensive collection of features recorded in Great Harrowden (Northamptonshire County Council 2008). Unfortunately, the area has not been subject to archaeological excavation which would allow a fuller understanding of the development of the separate phases of the site, but what is of interest is the complete absence of relationship between the medieval

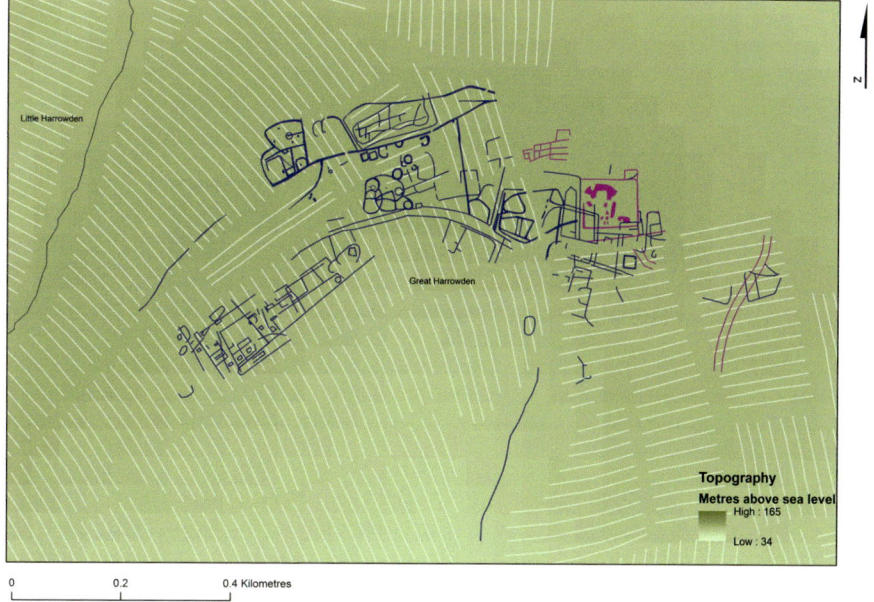

FIGURE 7.3. Phases of landscape in Great Harrowden, showing the late prehistoric settlement in blue, medieval settlement in purple and open field strips in light green (Northamptonshire County Council 2008).

moat, ditches and trackway, shown in Figure 7.3 in pink, and the prehistoric and Romano-British features, shown in blue. Although the square enclosure around the moat may share a similar alignment on the west side to one prehistoric ditch, it would appear that this relationship is either convenient or accidental, as no other medieval features, including extensive areas of now-levelled ridge and furrow, perpetuate or share the earlier alignments.

In the absence of any early medieval charters place-name evidence provides the best source for assessing the extent and distribution of woodland in the early medieval period. The names of Old and Walgrave both derive from –*wold* which, like 'weald', meant woodland (Gelling 1993, 223). *Wold* is usually taken to denote an area that was formerly woodland but that had been mostly cleared to become wood pasture before the settlement was established (Hooke 2013, 33). The name of the Maleslea hundred itself refers to woodland, containing as it does the element –*leah*, 'wood' or 'clearing', which also occurs in the names of Pytchley and Cransley, lying to the east of the watershed. Woodland elements also appear in some minor place-names, such as Badsaddle in Orlingbury, which first appears in a twelfth-century survey as *Bateshasel*, 'Baetti's hazel clump' (Gover *et al.* 1933, 90). Other place-names within the case study area hint at marginal agricultural conditions: for example, several field names in Orlingbury incorporate the element -*moor*, and *Blewberowhyll* in Lamport signifies a cold north facing slope (Gover *et al.* 1933, 91).

The first documentary evidence for the vegetation in the area can be found in Domesday Book. The manor of Brixworth contained a woodland valued at 100 shillings and to the east of the watershed three manors, namely Orlingbury, Pytchley and Wythemail, held woodland that was recorded in furlongs.

The manor of the now lost settlement of Wythemail is thought to have been located near the watershed in modern Orlingbury (Gover *et al.* 1933, 90). The First Edition Ordnance Survey 6-Inch map depicted woodland in the parishes of Orlingbury and Pytchley, most of which lay close to the watershed.

As touched upon previously, the curving ridge that divided the medieval hundreds of Orlingbury and Maleslea is followed by a road (now for much of its length a track or 'green lane'), which, as it is itself followed by the hundred boundary must be of considerable antiquity. Notably none of the parish or township divisions cross the watershed. The use of natural features as territorial boundaries is repeated with many of the minor divisions that separate the parishes that made up the hundreds, following minor watercourses and hill spurs.

When viewed at a large scale the medieval furlong patterns on either side of the curving watershed, as reconstructed from archaeological and cartographic evidence by the Northamptonshire project, appears highly regular. Many of the townships contained very long headlands separating the furlongs, some extending for more than 3 km, and which ran down the dominant direction of slope at right angles to the watershed. The same relationship with the broad topography was shared by the ribbons of pasture, linear greens or commons, that ran through the open fields, frequently following the lines of slades. Many of the settlements in the study area lay alongside a slade and therefore also a linear green, and it is likely that the narrow common provided an access route into the open field furlongs, as well as grazing for the livestock and perhaps even hay. Judging from their configuration several linear greens may once have provided access to larger areas of grazing, and woodland, on the watershed. The slade greens that lay closest to the settlements almost always stretched all the way

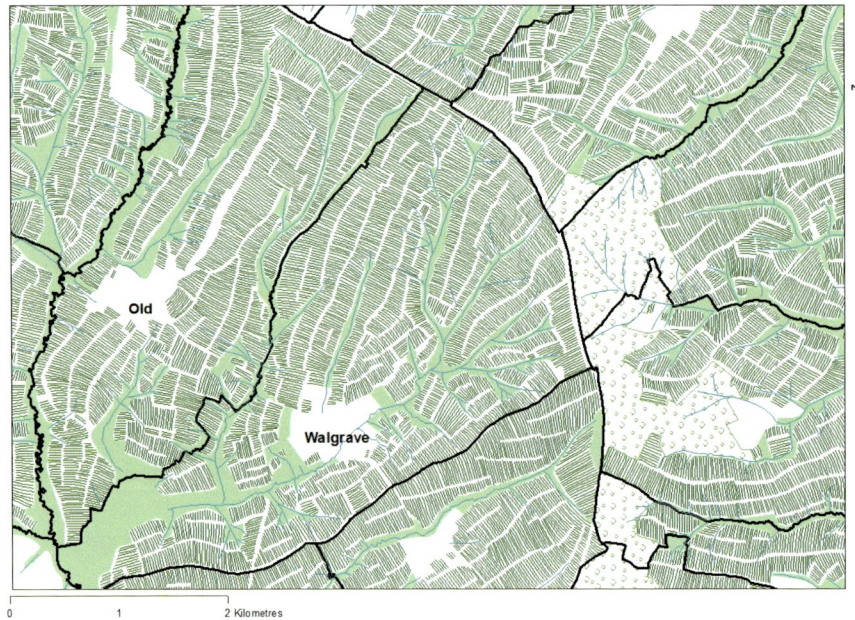

FIGURE 7.4. The landscape of Old and Walgrave at the time of Parliamentary Enclosure (Northamptonshire County Council 2008)

to the watershed, as can be seen in Figure 7.4. The 1758 map of Walgrave shows vestigial traces of such an arrangement; it depicts the linear common lying next to a slade that led from the village to Broughton Common on the higher ground, probably a remnant of a much larger area of watershed intercommon.

The linear greens and slades in Orlingbury hundred combined with the major and minor details of the topography to create a loose landscape framework within which the strip and furlong pattern fitted.

The headlands frequently ran parallel to the slades and, together with the adjacent greens, formed a roughly co-axial pattern running from the river valley to the watershed: that is, a pattern in part structured by the configuration of ridges and tributary valleys and partly by a network of resource-linkage routes, itself structured by broad environmental and topographic patterns. However, when the headlands are overlain on detailed elevation maps it is clear that the alignment of the long headlands was primarily a response to the smaller-scale local landforms and in particular the drainage pattern. The majority of the open field headlands ran along the minor watersheds that divided catchment areas of the township slades or lay parallel to them.

The open field strips were arranged at right angles to the headlands, or more correctly, given that headlands were created through repeated ploughing, the open field strips were set at a perpendicular angle to the streams and slope. This facilitated drainage down the slope, and into the slade so excess water could be carried away (Markham 1613, 62). In most examples the ridge and furrow led directly from the headland to the edge of the watercourse, or more frequently the adjacent narrow green. Occasionally another parallel headland cut across the slope apparently breaking the natural drainage pattern. This would seem to be a particularly curious arrangement in view of the otherwise significant importance of local topography in determining the direction of the strips. These headlands may fossilise earlier stages of piecemeal expansion. If the furlong pattern reflects the gradual extension of arable land into the 'waste' the interrupting headland could be interpreted as preserving an older division between the ploughlands and the commons.

The pattern of furlongs that lay close to the settlement of Old appears to support this interpretation of gradual expansion. The strips that lay to the east of a ridgeway path (A) on Figure 7.5 follow the slope from the minor watershed towards the slade. The individual lands traversed a fall of about 20 m in land height. The slope was interrupted approximately halfway between the watershed and stream by the western headland of furlong C. The strips that lay closest to the vill were even shorter and divided by four separate headlands. Furlong B has the appearance of originating as an intake that has been cut out of a formerly larger area of common pasture. The headland that separates furlongs B and C begins at the southern boundary of the slade-side common and furlong C. It then followed a curving path that ran roughly parallel to furlong C's western headland and by so doing maintained a relatively regular strip length in furlong C. In direct contrast to the regularity of strip length in furlong C,

FIGURE 7.5. Detail of the furlong pattern in Old (Northamptonshire County Council 2008).

the selions in furlong B varied considerably. Rather than creating equal shares they appeared to be primarily concerned with expanding cultivation as far into the waste as possible as the narrow intakes on either side of the small stream near point 'B' attest.

Furlong B perhaps provides the clearest landscape evidence for piecemeal expansion of cultivation into areas of common, but further evidence for similar intakes is visible elsewhere in Figure 7.5. The headlands of furlong C have a sinuous shape and roughly reflect the course of the slade, suggesting that they, too, originated as an intake from the waste. Evidence for the gradual expansion of cultivated land can also be found in records of minor place-names. Several in Walgrave include elements such as *–moor*, *-wold* and *-common*, which all suggest they originated as intakes from the 'waste' (Map/705).

The layout of the open fields within the area just discussed is interesting because it shows, once again, how the interaction of land use patterns and topography can generate an appearance of large scale, co-axial landscape organisation. The strips and furlongs illustrate the complexity of the interactions between society and environment, on a range of spatial scales and developing over a long period of time, which shaped medieval landscapes.

Case study: The Central Nene Valley

The second case study area, the Central Nene Valley, lies to the east of Orlingbury in an area that was similarly converted to pasture following enclosure. The Central Nene Valley area encompasses the townships that lie between the river Nene on the west and the county border approximately 8 km to the east.

7. Northamptonshire and its open fields

From the banks of the river Nene the land rises to a wide watershed at around 70 m OD, the ridge runs from Clopton in the southwest to Warmington in the northeast (Figure 7.6). Beyond Warmington village the higher land begins to fall away towards the low-lying eastern fenlands, and the city of Peterborough 10 km to the northeast.

Many of the townships within the Central Nene Valley exhibit a roughly rectangular morphology. Their narrowest sides lie along the watershed and

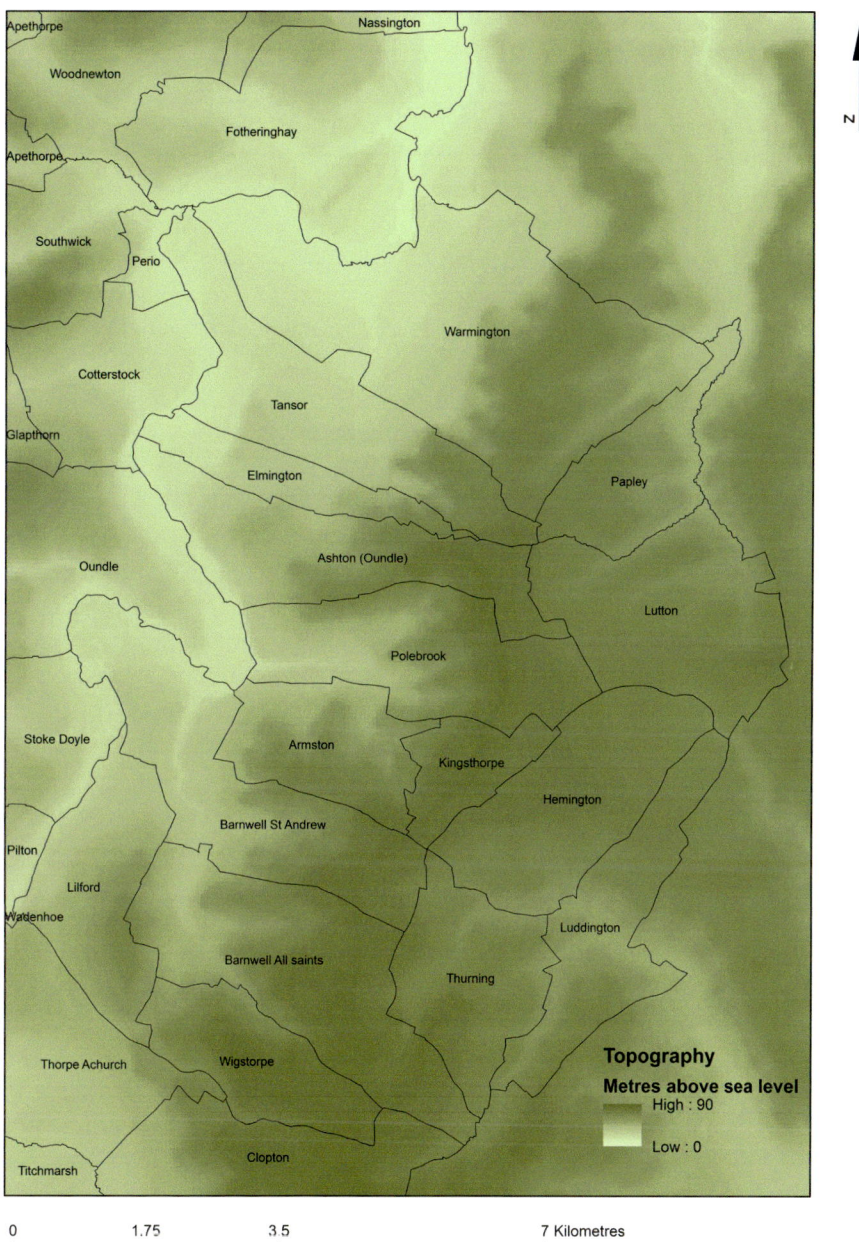

FIGURE 7.6. The topography of the Central Nene Valley.

riverbank, with their longest boundaries passing up the slope. This arrangement of parallel linear territories has been noted previously, particularly in the Essex landscapes discussed by Rodwell and Drury (Drury and Rodwell 1980). It is characteristic of parish boundaries found within so-called relict field systems and these are commonly, but not exclusively, identified in woodland countryside (Harrison 2002). Similar boundary patterns were identified in Cambridgeshire by Rackham, Oosthuizen and Harrison (Rackham 1986; Harrison 2002; Oosthuizen 2006).

There are significant differences in the soil characteristics between the watershed and riverbank in the Central Nene Valley, and this is reflected in both the bedrock and surface geology. The main bedrock is made up of a combination of Kellaways Formation and Oxford Clay Formation. These impermeable bedrocks were laid down in the Jurassic period over the top of the porous limestone Great Oolite formation. Together these bedrocks underlie the entire case study area excepting a narrow outcrop of the Great Oolite formation, which lies close to the modern course of the river Nene.

Overlying the Kellaways and Oxford Clay formations are glacial clay soils visible in Figure 7.7. The majority of the land on the hillside is covered by the same slowly permeable Hanslope Soil Association that has been discussed in previous case study areas. These fertile soils retain nutrients well but can lie wet particularly in the early spring following the winter rains. The soils depend on streams and slopes to drain away excess water, and in the Central Nene Valley the Hanslope soils lie on the hillsides and so the natural landform facilitates the surface drainage (Hodge 1984, 210). Successful cultivation of clay land is not dependent upon the soil type alone, it is also determined by a combination of the climate, and in particular the volume and timing of precipitation, with the topography, and whether this encourages runoff of excess water. The importance of local climate when considering soils may be more apparent in a comparison of the number of days available for fieldwork on the heavy clay soils of East Anglia and the Midlands but the differences can also be significant on a small scale. The climate in the east of Northamptonshire is drier than that in the west and the lower annual precipitation ensures that the clay soils of the Nene Valley are in a suitable condition for fieldwork when the same soil types even just a few miles further west are not (Hodge 1984, 33).

Towards the base of the long low ridge the soil type changes to Oxpasture Association soils. These predominately loamy soils overlie a clay layer and although they are not as naturally fertile as the adjacent Hanslope Clay Association soils they would have been easier to cultivate. Modern farmers still consider a loamy soil as easier to work and crop than clay soils, and this division could only be more marked in the past. Lying beneath the Oxpasture loams is a clay layer that tends to collect and retain water, and the location of this soil type at the base of the hill slope means the runoff from the adjacent slopes can exacerbate waterlogging, particularly in late winter. Despite these impediments the Oxpasture soils can be successfully planted during the autumn when the

7. *Northamptonshire and its open fields* 133

FIGURE 7.7. Soil types in the Central Nene Valley (Soil Survey of England and Wales 1983, Sheet 4).

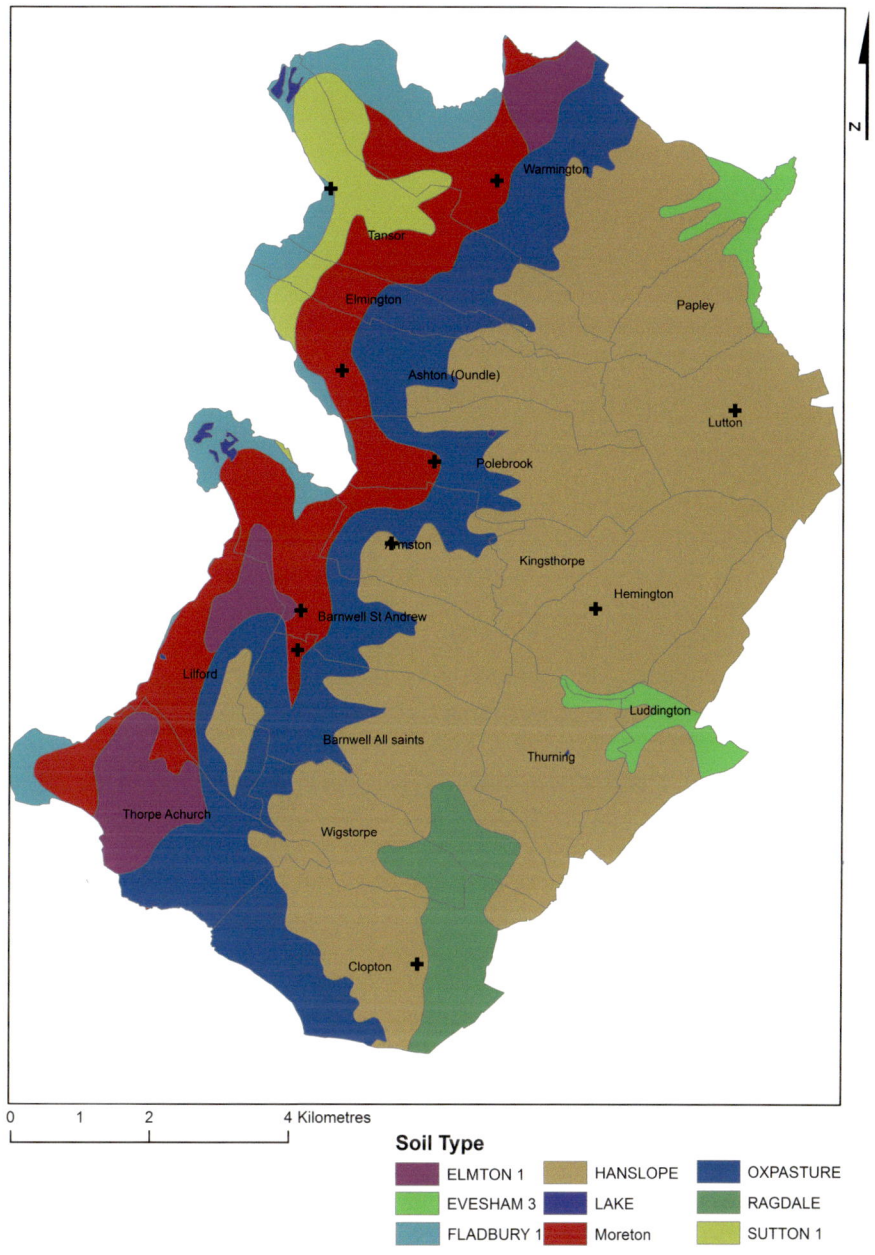

relatively dry conditions allow cultivation and sowing without damaging the soil (Hodge 1984, 288).

In the Central Nene Valley, the Oxpasture Association soils overlay the same Kellaways and Oxford Clay Formations as the Hanslope soils further up the slope. Closer to the river Nene the soils change once again to more permeable and lighter types that overlie the outcrop of the Great Oolite formation. Lying adjacent to the Oxpasture soils is the Moreton Soil Association, which is a permeable chalky loam. Several of the settlements, including Warmington, Polebrook and Wigstone, are situated at the junction of permeable Moreton and impermeable Oxpasture soils and, probably more critically, at a spring line where the Jurassic clay geology meets the permeable soils (Williamson 2013, 189).

The light and freely draining Moreton Association soils are easy to work at any time of year and require no artificial drainage (Hodge 1984, 253). Excess water drains freely into the underlying porous limestone bedrock, however, this also swiftly leaches away nutrients and as a result the soil retains little fertility. Towards the north end of the Central Nene Valley the village of Tansor is located upon a small outcrop of highly fertile Sutton Association loams, which are also easily worked. The light valley soils are free draining allowing year-round field cultivations, however, they are also prone to seasonal drought (Hodge 1984, 259). Finally, very close to the river is the floodplain, an area of loam and clay Fladbury soil, which has a high-water table and suffers seasonal inundation (Hodge 1984, 198). Although modern field drainage allows those fields least susceptible to flooding to be cultivated, much of this land lying close to the river Nene remains under grass. The high-water table even precludes anything other than hay making and summer grazing, due to the risk of poaching of the grass and the loss of vegetative cover (Hodge 1984, 199). In medieval times these areas would have provided valuable hay meadow.

The townships of the Central Nene Valley are fortunate in that they contain a variety of soils providing a range of possibilities for different farming practices; and although the soil map and classifications may be modern construction, it is inconceivable that the earlier generations of farmers who lived in the valley were unaware of the characteristics of their soils and climate, knowledge gained through years of farming the fields and waste.

In common with many other regions, the majority of Northamptonshire's prehistoric sites have been found to be located on the lighter and more easily workable soils. Although this distribution can be skewed by the visibility of crop marks in drought prone soil types, in the case of the Central Nene Valley the entire area has been extensively field walked and studied over several decades and few traces of prehistoric settlement activity have been found on the higher and heavier land.

The earliest sites within the Central Nene Valley, which have been dated to the Bronze Age, relate either to enclosures or burial mounds (RCHM 1975, xxviii). Iron Age settlement in the area appears to have been relatively minor (RCHM 1975, xxxiv). Despite the lack of archaeological evidence for late prehistoric human activity on the higher ground, it seems likely that these areas would have been utilised for grazing livestock and as a source of wood and timber. To date, little evidence for seasonal farmsteads has been found, suggesting that if such activity occurred it would appear to have been managed from settlements in the valley, which is not so very distant from the watershed.

The major continuous boundary found in many of the parishes and townships of the valley is, unsurprisingly, the river Nene itself. It forms the western boundary of all the townships from Lilford in the south to Warmington in the north. The only partial exception to this is Oundle, which originally contained land on both sides of the river; to the west was the major settlement, and on the opposite bank, the daughter townships of Ashton and Elmington, which later were combined to form the parish of Ashton.

Running roughly parallel around 4 km to the east of the river Nene is the broad watershed zone where many of the townships in the case study area have their easternmost boundary. A curious element of the major watershed feature in the Central Nene Valley is that although it was incorporated into the township boundaries in several short sections it was not followed by any of them for any significant length, in marked contrast to the situation in Orlingbury hundred. Instead, the parish territories tended to extend beyond the watershed, taking in areas of high ground lying within the next catchment, that of an unnamed tributary of the river Ouse. What makes this arrangement all the more surprising is the frequency with which the minor watersheds in the locality, dividing the catchments of tributary streams, were utilised as boundaries. Many of the townships and parishes are divided by the hill spurs that project out from the main ridge towards the river Nene and resemble teeth on a comb. The rough framework of rectangular parishes in the Central Nene Valley was therefore heavily influenced by the form of the major and minor topography, particularly the relationship between the minor slades and hill spurs, and the river Nene and the major watershed zone.

The main watershed may be overlooked by many of the parish boundaries but before Parliamentary Enclosure the broad interfluve zone contained evidence for a linear feature that appears to have followed its line. This sinuous feature was preserved in the furlong pattern of Warmington, Tansor and Kingsthorpe and in short sections of the township boundaries of Polebrook and Tansor. It continued for approximately 4.5 km from Warmington to Kingsthorpe. The Tansor Enclosure Map dated 1778 records that the feature was a lane called the 'Road to Ashton Wold' (Map/4608). It is notable that Tansor's township boundary followed the line of this road for a short stretch before it departed again, an action typical of the relationship between parish boundaries and watershed features found elsewhere in the country (Williamson 1986, 245).

The survival of the 'Road to Ashton Wold' as a post-enclosure lane in Tansor suggests that it preserved an earlier route or right of access that was not held only by the population of that parish. The road was on the hill-top and remote from the township, and it would appear to have provided little benefit to either the owners of the newly enclosed fields or the inhabitants of Tansor in general. Further evidence for the lane can be found on a seventeenth-century map of neighbouring Warmington, which shows it continuing through the parish open fields. As in Tansor, the route bypassed the settlement and was located on the hilltop. The watershed path did not appear to fit into the general pattern of lanes in Warmington that were otherwise focused upon the settlement. As it passed through Warmington's furlongs it was known as London Way, a name frequently given to north–south roads that did not link the local settlements and this further suggests that it did not originate with the early medieval vills (Field 1993, 151).

The same watershed feature was fossilised as a headland in townships lying further south, but unfortunately no early maps survive that record its name. Unlike the northern section of the watershed path townships, this portion did not appear to interrupt or influence any of the parish or township boundaries. Taking the area as a whole it appears possible that there was a ridgeway route that originally extended all the way from Clopton in the south to the modern county boundary in Warmington and possibly beyond, a total distance of 13 km.

During the first centuries of the Roman occupation of England, settlement in the area extended from the riverside terraces onto the clay slopes and probable farmsteads, field systems and roads have all been identified across the area (RCHM 1975, xxxiv). A large Roman Villa complex was found lying on the west bank of the river Nene in Cotterstock, and the large and opulent building must have been supported by a large agricultural estate. On the east bank of the river, roughly opposite the villa, was a small Roman town near the modern settlement of Ashton (RCHM 1975, 11).

Combining a programme of field walking with an analysis of the seventeenth-century map of Warmington, Stephen Upex identified a distinct group of small rectangular furlongs in the area between Broadgate and London Way shown on Figure 7.8 at point 'B' (Upex 2002). Field walking in the area indicated that one of these former furlongs contained a concentration of Romano-British and early medieval pottery. Upex identified a similar group of small rectilinear furlongs in Ashton, which also lay close to a scatter of Romano-British and early medieval artefacts found during field walking (Upex 2002, 90). Upex concluded that the correlation of the artefact scatter and the unusual size and shapes of the furlongs was evidence that the arrangement preserved the layout of Romano-British field boundaries. He further supposed that this was evidence that the fields must have been continuously cultivated through the fifth and sixth centuries, and then incorporated into the medieval open fields (Upex 2002, 99).

The local environmental conditions could provide an alternative explanation for the origin of these groups of small furlongs. Notably in both Warmington and Ashton they lie at the headwaters of minor slades. The complex nature of the streams close to their springs meant the orientation of the strips needed to change frequently to match the undulating landform, in order for the land to be effectively drained. Similar patterns of small rectilinear furlongs appear elsewhere in the Central Nene Valley usually associated with the headwaters of small watercourses. Local environmental conditions may also explain the presence of the associated artefact scatters, close to springs.

The principal settlements of the Central Nene Valley are located on lower ground, close to the river, and perhaps unsurprisingly their names do not

FIGURE 7.8. Detail of the furlong pattern in Warmington (Northamptonshire County Council 2008).

contain elements that suggest they were established in a woodland environment; instead, many place-names are associated with the local watercourses that they lay close to. Woodland place names are more commonly found closer to the watershed, for example Papley where the *–leah* element indicates a clearing from woodland. *Wold* place-names can also be found in Barnwell, Ashton and Tansor Wolds, which all lay close to the watershed. A map of Warmington dated to 1621 depicts a small green called Warmington Ould (Map/6433), likely to be a remnant of an earlier and more extensive area of common wood pasture.

The medieval settlement pattern in the Central Nene Valley was thus, as in Orlingbury hundred, one of valley-based settlements with access to the wooded uplands lying at no great distance: the river Nene and watershed typically lie just 3 to 4 km apart, with the settlements located about halfway between the two. Settlement remained primarily restricted to the original valley locations into the nineteenth century, with only a few scattered, post-enclosure, farms found on the clay slopes.

As in Orlingbury hundred, repetitive short-range movement of livestock from valley-floor settlements to wooded uplands created a direction of travel in the landscape that linked the valley and 'wold' and presumably cemented the rights to the outlying lands (Gardiner 2018, 116). These 'resource linkage routes' typically followed a direct route, ignoring the small-scale local topography. As the demand for arable land increased the general loose direction of travel became, as in so many other areas examined in this thesis, more and more restricted to a few parallel drove-ways preserved between the furlongs, which as

138 *How the Land Lies*

in Orlingbury hundred tended to follow, or at least share the orientation of, the hill spurs and tributary slades running at right angles to the Nene; indeed, it is possible that some of the hill spur boundaries discussed above may also have originated as resource linkage routes. As late as their final enclosure most of the townships in the Central Nene Valley retained at least one path, lane or headland that led from the settlement to the wold.

Evidence for how widespread such lanes might have been in the past can be found in the seventeenth-century map of Warmington, redrawn in Figure 7.9 (Map/6433). This shows a large number of long narrow commons lying between the furlongs, many of which ran roughly parallel to one another. One linear green, called Broadgate Way, linked the village of Warmington to the eastern township boundary and the wold commons. Its morphology suggests the gradual encroachment of an originally broader common drove, featuring as it does uneven or 'nibbled' edges.

This is also the case with other linear greens in the parish, particularly Broadgate Way. In this example, piecemeal extension of strips into 'waste' continued after the seventeenth-century map was surveyed. The earthwork plan from the Northamptonshire project (Figure 7.10) shows that Broadgate Way had almost completely disappeared by the time the open fields were converted to pasture. In the modern landscape Broadgate Way survives as a road until the junction with the former London Way, beyond this point it becomes a bridleway, but even in this much diminished form it still leads to the watershed and the former boundary with Papley.

With the exception of Warmington, few pre-enclosure maps survive for the townships of the Central Nene Valley and therefore the furlong pattern mapped

FIGURE 7.9. Detail of the *Map of the Manor of Warmington in 1621* by Richard Norwood (Map/6433).

FIGURE 7.10. Detail of the greens and furlongs of Warmington from The Northamptonshire Project (Northamptonshire County Council 2008).

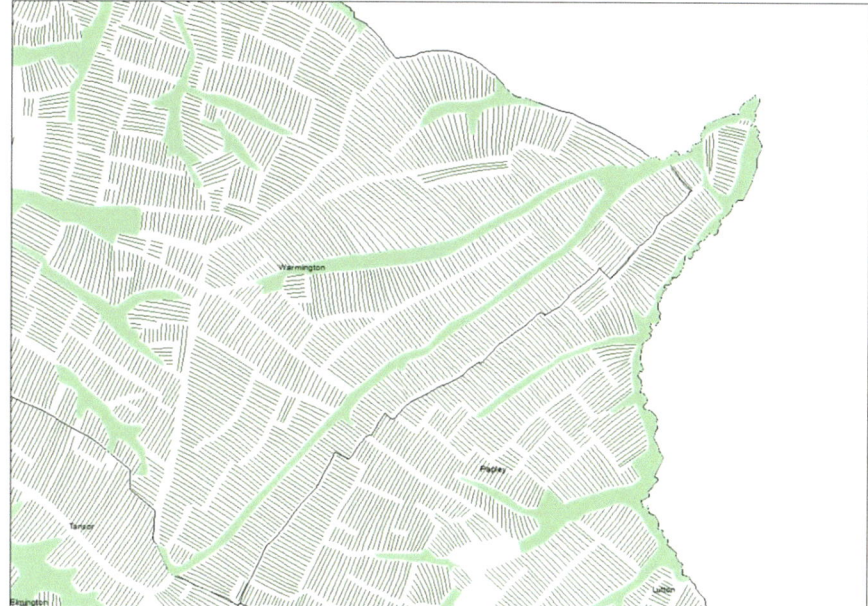

by the Northamptonshire project provides the best evidence for the layout of green lanes and narrow commons in the open fields, and for the pattern of strips and furlongs. The principal territorial boundaries within the Central Nene Valley reflected the local topography. The two major divisions were the river Nene and the hill formation that runs parallel to it. The townships were separated by boundaries that followed the characteristic path from watercourse to hilltop, but many of these appear to have been determined by the east–west aligned hill spurs and slades. The routes linking settlement and resources were also followed by boundaries and taken together this mix of natural and man-made features formed a sparse grid within which the townships, commons and open field furlongs fitted. Not all the linear greens, it should be emphasised, followed a vaguely co-axial path linking the valley and the watershed zone. Some ran at different angles, following minor slades or representing residual areas of 'waste' that had been left as the open fields expanded: many of the latter seem to have been removed in the course of the post-medieval period. Two seventeenth-century surveys of Papley, dated roughly 50 years apart show the presence and subsequent loss of several examples (Map/2221). The linear commons most likely to persist were those that lay along the minor watercourses.

While the sparse overall framework was primarily determined by the large-scale topography of the Central Nene Valley, the orientation of the individual open-field strips responded to the environmental conditions in their immediate area. Ridge and furrow was deliberately arranged so that it lay perpendicular to the slope in order to facilitate surface runoff. The orientation of furlongs therefore tended to ignore the large-scale topography when it was in conflict with the local slope. The furrows were angled to lead downhill and towards the nearest slade or stream that provided a means of draining the waters into the valley. Although at a large scale the landform in the Central Nene Valley appears to be relatively simple there are numerous minor slades and watersheds, many of which are aligned perpendicular to the principal hill formation. The result was a somewhat irregular looking furlong pattern, and in direct contrast to the situation in Orlingbury hundred where the relationship between the major and minor topography is more harmonious. Despite the visible difference in the regularity of the furlong pattern, the individual ridge and furrow strips were responding to the local environmental conditions in precisely the same manner.

Even those furlongs on the floor of the valley were arranged to reflect the local environment. They were orientated to follow the subtle changes in elevation, which led in places to the development of a ridge and furrow pattern that resembled a basket weave. It might appear that the strips were randomly aligned, when in fact the opposite was true. Close examination indicates that the furlongs that initially appear to be orientated in the 'wrong' direction, do in fact follow very small-scale gradients, with the land falling as little as 2 m along strips several hundred metres in length.[1] In view of the singular importance of drainage considerations on the orientation of open-field strips it is perhaps not surprising that the furlong pattern has the greatest regularity where the topography is the simplest. Close to the watershed the furlongs tended to be larger, reflecting both the planar formation of the main ridge and a relative lack of watercourses. In contrast, the furlongs located closest to the medieval villages are typically among the smallest in the township, reflecting more dissected topography and the presence of streams, springs and seepage lines.

In general, the complexity of the topography ensured that there were few places where strips in a succession of adjacent furlongs shared the same alignment – the kind of arrangement, that is, interpreted by Hall as resulting from the subdivision of long furlongs. In Barnwell St Andrew there was one example where the strips were clearly aligned downslope towards a watercourse and subdivided by transverse headlands, which evidently reflects the generally planar nature of the local topography. But for the most part slopes are interrupted by minor slades and valleys, and the arrangement of strips correspondingly varied and complex. The furlong pattern closer to the river Nene was more regular as the numerous slades of the hill slopes tended to combine into larger streams. With fewer watercourses the furlongs became larger as many of the furrows were aligned on the nearest watercourse, but in places small changes in elevation led to a 'basket weave' pattern, as already described.

Conclusion

This rather extended examination of the medieval landscape in two sample areas of Northamptonshire has demonstrated that the same types of topographic and environmental influences served to shape 'irregular' as much as 'regular' landscapes. These influences operate at a variety of spatial scales and it is interaction between the local and wider area topography that creates the illusion of regularity, or otherwise. This is important for understanding the origins of medieval fields because, as noted in the Introduction, their direct descent from prehistoric and Roman fields has not only been argued on the basis of topographic evidence. Recent research by Stephen Rippon, Ben Pears and Chris Smart as part of The Fields of Britannia project and published as the book *Fields of Britannia*, directly addressed the physical evidence for continuity between the late prehistoric and medieval open field landscapes. Rippon *et al.* argued that the orientation of excavated ditches of Romano-British date was generally shared by that of the field boundaries depicted on the First Edition Ordnance Survey 6-Inch maps found in the immediate area: most were either 'oriented', that is, the excavated feature shared an alignment with the historic landscape – within five degrees – but did not directly continue the lines of features within it; or 'aligned' where the excavated ditch visibly forms a part of the modern boundary system (Rippon *et al.* 2015, 100). Using excavation evidence to date boundary patterns was not in itself new. In the 1970s Taylor and Fowler found evidence that earlier ditches lay beneath some medieval open field headlands – but Rippon *et al.* employed a mass of data, much of it culled from the 'grey literature' and concluded that in the 'Central Zone', an area that roughly corresponds with the champion belt, '73 per cent of the excavated Romano-British field systems have a common orientation or alignment with historic landscape characteristic of former open fields' (Rippon *et al.* 2015, 330). This led them to believe that the open field furlongs had generally been fitted into or developed from fields originally laid out in or before the Romano-British period. Leaving aside doubts about how far excavated ditches can reliably be dated from material found in their fill, given that field boundaries were subject to regular de-silting and re-cutting, the evidence presented here throws considerable doubt on the argument that similarity of alignment indicates anything more than the continued utilisation of natural slopes in field drainage (Rippon 1991, 51).

Note

1   Such a small difference in land height could be interpreted as the effect of a ploughed out headland, many of which were originally at least of a comparable size.

CHAPTER EIGHT

Marshland: a planned landscape?

The discussion so far has largely focused on how field patterns are structured by environment and topography, mediated through systems of land use and resource allocation, which in certain circumstances can create highly regular patterns that have been interpreted by archaeologists as the consequence of deliberate planning. This chapter concentrates on a closely related yet different issue, already addressed in passing but now foregrounded: namely, the way in which highly organised landscapes can develop organically, rather than being the outcome of a single planning 'event'. The landscape of the Norfolk Silt Fen provides a unique opportunity to consider this question. The first detailed large-scale surveys of the area, the nineteenth-century Tithe Maps, show a highly regular field pattern, which, in its co-axial character, invites comparisons with the prehistoric field systems found in Co. Mayo and Dartmoor, although it is laid out on a much larger scale. But it cannot possibly have evolved from a prehistoric landscape. Environmental conditions sealed evidence of prehistoric and Romano-British settlement beneath a layer of silt flood deposits and effectively prevented re-colonisation of the area for several hundred years until the climate improved (Darby 1983, 38). An alternative explanation for the regular field pattern is that it derived from the fossilisation of the kind of early medieval long furlongs that have been detected in Holderness, Northamptonshire and elsewhere: that is, that the regularity in the landscape comes from planned open fields. On the First Edition Ordnance Survey 6-Inch map (Figure 8.1), many of the fields in the area had a narrow, 'strippy' appearance, sometimes displaying the long atrial curves of the long furlongs as seen in Middleton, North Yorkshire. The area covered by the regular field pattern in Marshland far exceeds any examples of supposedly planned open fields; instead of covering a field, or part of a parish or township, it incorporates seven parishes.

In reality, despite superficial resemblances the regular landscape in Marshland is the result of neither prehistoric nor medieval planning. This chapter will consider its true origins and will illustrate how environmental factors and utilisation of distant resources gradually created an extensive although sparse framework into which later strip fields were slotted. The environmental history of Marshland means that the colonisation of the former fenland landscape is both relatively recent and truncated in comparison to the development of more typical English lowland countryside such as that discussed previously in Cambridgeshire and Northamptonshire. Not only should this preserve more evidence for the development of the landscape, but it will also illustrate how apparent regularity can arise from organic and gradual expansion of fields and tracks into 'waste'.

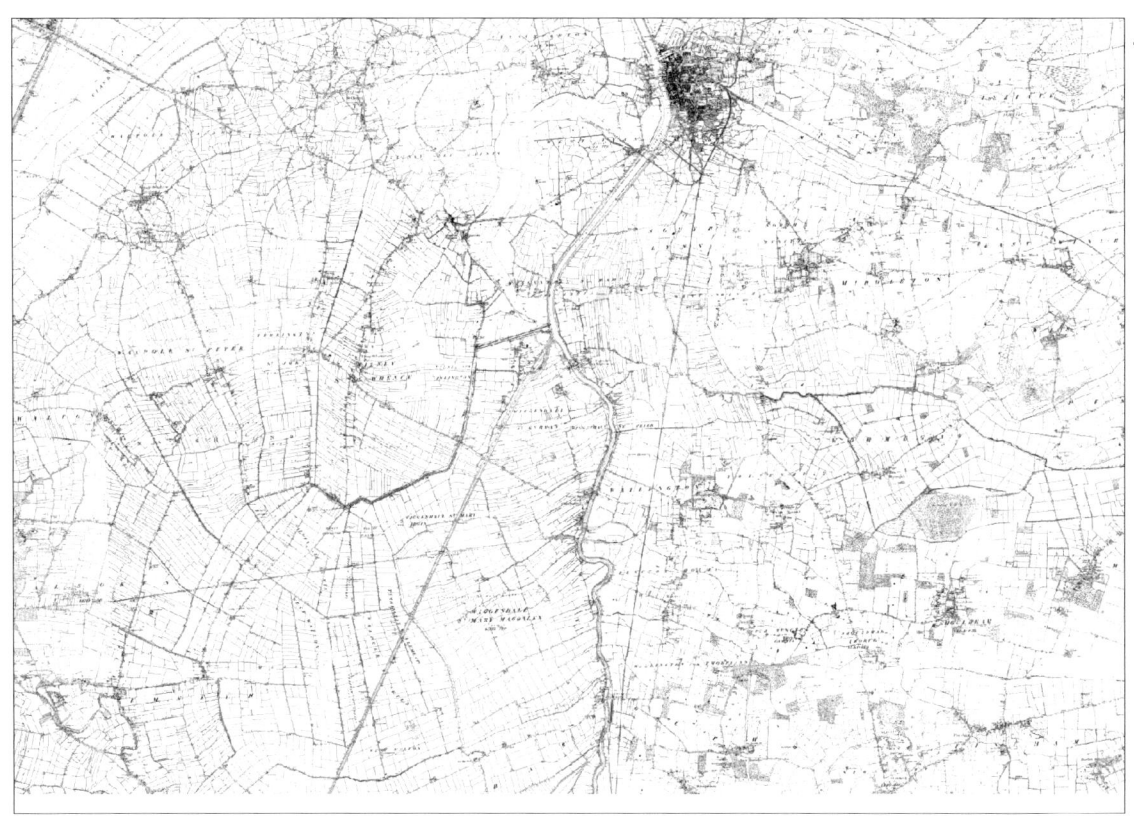

FIGURE 8.1. The landscape to the south of King's Lynn, Norfolk as mapped by the First Edition Ordnance Survey 6-Inch map.

The field pattern of Marshland has been recreated on a GIS map principally using a sixteenth-century plan of Marshland surveyed by William Hayward in 1591 (44CAM_ALMA), the First Edition Ordnance Survey 6-Inch maps for the area and a reconstruction of the medieval landscape created by Silvester (1988, fig. 124). The resulting GIS map allowed the pattern of dikes and ditches and boundaries to be overlaid on the relief and so highlighting relationships to both immediate local features and the wider pattern of topography in the region.

Using early secondary sources and archaeological reports a model for the development of the marshland landscape will be presented. This chapter will discuss the importance of the local environmental conditions to the final landscape form; but also highlight how Marshland remained an area susceptible to flooding into the Modern period, leading to a landscape that fossilised areas of both expansion and retreat. Particular attention will be paid to the development of fields and farming in the area, and the insight this provides into the creation of regular landscapes.

Before it was drained, a vast wetland landscape stretched from Norfolk, through Cambridgeshire and the former county of Huntingdonshire into Lincolnshire; known as The Fens, or Fenland, it was the largest area of its type in England. It was formed through a combination of topography and environmental changes. Glacial activity during the last Ice Age had left a shallow basin of low-lying land, much of it below the modern sea level through which numerous waterways flowed on their way to outfall into The Wash. Many of these rivers originated in the Midlands draining large catchment areas and as they flowed they carried silts washed from the distant uplands (Summers 1973, 13). The courses of these winding plains rivers frequently became silted up as they travelled slowly through the Fenland basin causing the waters to force a new route. The silted up former riverbeds of the old watercourses can still be traced as ribbons of silt that lay slightly higher than the surrounding soils and are known locally as 'Roddens' (Darby 1983, 33). During this period the Fenland basin was covered by woodland but increasing water inundation led to peat developing on the lower lying levels. Between 8000 and 3000 BCE the peat deposits were covered by a layer of clay (Darby 1983, 38). From 2000 BCE sea level rises and high tides hindered the outfall of the meandering rivers and led to the Fenland basin becoming a shallow mire once again, allowing peat to develop in the slowly moving freshwater (Darby 1983, 95). Not all of the land lay underwater; outcrops of higher ground remained dry and as the marshy vegetation developed on the waterlogged soils these became islands of dry land above the marshes.

Covering the largest area of The Fens was a vast expanse of inland peat, sometimes called the Black Fen (Astbury 1958). This developed over the lowest land levels and resisted attempts at draining and reclaiming the land until the early seventeenth century. The Black Fen is the most famous, or possibly infamous, part of Fenland, reaching the outskirts of Cambridge and Peterborough and surrounding the Isle of Ely. This area of The Fens was notorious for the loss of unwary travellers who missed the causeways and perished in the bogs, but it also contained the vital navigable rivers that allowed the inland communities to benefit from trade.

The Black Fen resisted the efforts of the drainers until recently but another area of Fenland, known as the Silt Fen, had been successfully reclaimed many hundreds of years earlier. The Silt Fen is found at the northern edge of Fenland, near the ancient coastline of The Wash. Environmentally the development of the Silt Fen began in much the same way as the rest of the Fenland basin but from the late third or fourth centuries CE repeated flood tides deposited layers of silt over the existing peat (Darby 1983, 38). Over time these repeated tidal silt deposits created a low narrow ridge, that shadowed the coastline from Norfolk to Lincolnshire. In places its surface was up to 5 m above sea level.

Lying on the seaward side of the Silt Ridge were salt flats and marshes similar to those found elsewhere across the wide shallow bay of The Wash. Inland from the ridge was an area that had experienced less frequent deposits of flood silts, which occurred only with exceptionally high tides thanks to the protection afforded by the natural bank. As a result, the depth of silt layer in this inland area was thinner than that found on the Silt Ridge, and the land surface was less elevated, perhaps lying only 1 or 2 m above sea level. The layers of tidal silts that overlay the peat soils became still thinner further inland and away from the coast before eventually petering out against the Black Fen (Silvester 1988, 7).

The inland area that was covered by the thinner layers of silt became known as the Silt Fen. The Silt Ridge, which protected the Silt Fen from tidal floods, acted as a barrier preventing the outfall of the waters from the Fenland rivers. Eventually repeated freshwater flooding of the Silt Fen caused another layer of peat to develop on top of the lower-lying land.

The Marshland environment and soils

The Silt Fen stretches from King's Lynn in Norfolk to Spalding in Lincolnshire, but this chapter deals primarily with Marshland in the strict sense, that is, the portion that is found in the hundred of Freebridge in the county of Norfolk.

The seven towns of Marshland were Clenchwarton, Tilney cum Islington, Terrington, The Walpoles, [West] Walton, Walsoken and Emneth (Figure 8.2). These parishes shared the large grazing commons found at the southern edge of the Norfolk Silt Fen, namely Smeeth Common and West Fen, later known as Marshland Common. The area of Marshland covers around 190 km² but as expected for an area in Fenland the topography is very subtle, the range in land height is from sea level to just 5 m OD.

In Marshland, the originally coastal settlements now lie several kilometres inland, the result of land reclamation in the nineteenth and twentieth centuries which has left the ancient sea wall redundant and surrounded by arable fields. To the south the Black Fen has been reclaimed and drained to produce farmland and is now cut through with new river channels, dikes and drains. Even Marshland's own peat Fen, formerly known as West Fen, and later as Marshland Common has been drained and converted to arable land. Famously the ground levels in the former peat fens of Eastern England have subsided many metres due to drying out of the soils and erosion (Darby 1983, 105). While the silt fens are generally thought to be much less affected by the falling water table, it is possible that the modern relief used in the GIS mapping included in this discussion may not preserve the precise topography of the medieval Marshland. The relative relationship between the higher and lower ground levels is, however, unlikely to have changed significantly.

The following discussion of Marshland soils is similarly based on modern post drainage data, although arguably providing some guide to the opportunities and challenges faced by early medieval farmers. Unsurprisingly the Silt Ridge is dominated by silt soils, the two most widespread are the Agney and Wisbech Associations, which underlie much of the ridge. Both are deep stoneless silt soils. Following reclamation Agney soils gradually become Wisbech soils as the original sedimentary layers are broken up through repeated cultivation. The soils are easy to work, although Agney is slightly heavier than Wisbech. They are fertile and rarely droughty, but in undrained situations the soils stay waterlogged for a period after winter (Hodge 1984, 88).

In the northwest of the Silt Ridge, and extending into the Silt Fen, is an outcrop of Tanvats Association Soils, which have both silt and clay elements, and as a result benefit from modern underdrainage, without which they have

FIGURE 8.2. The Norfolk Fens before Early Modern and Modern reclamation from the Sea.

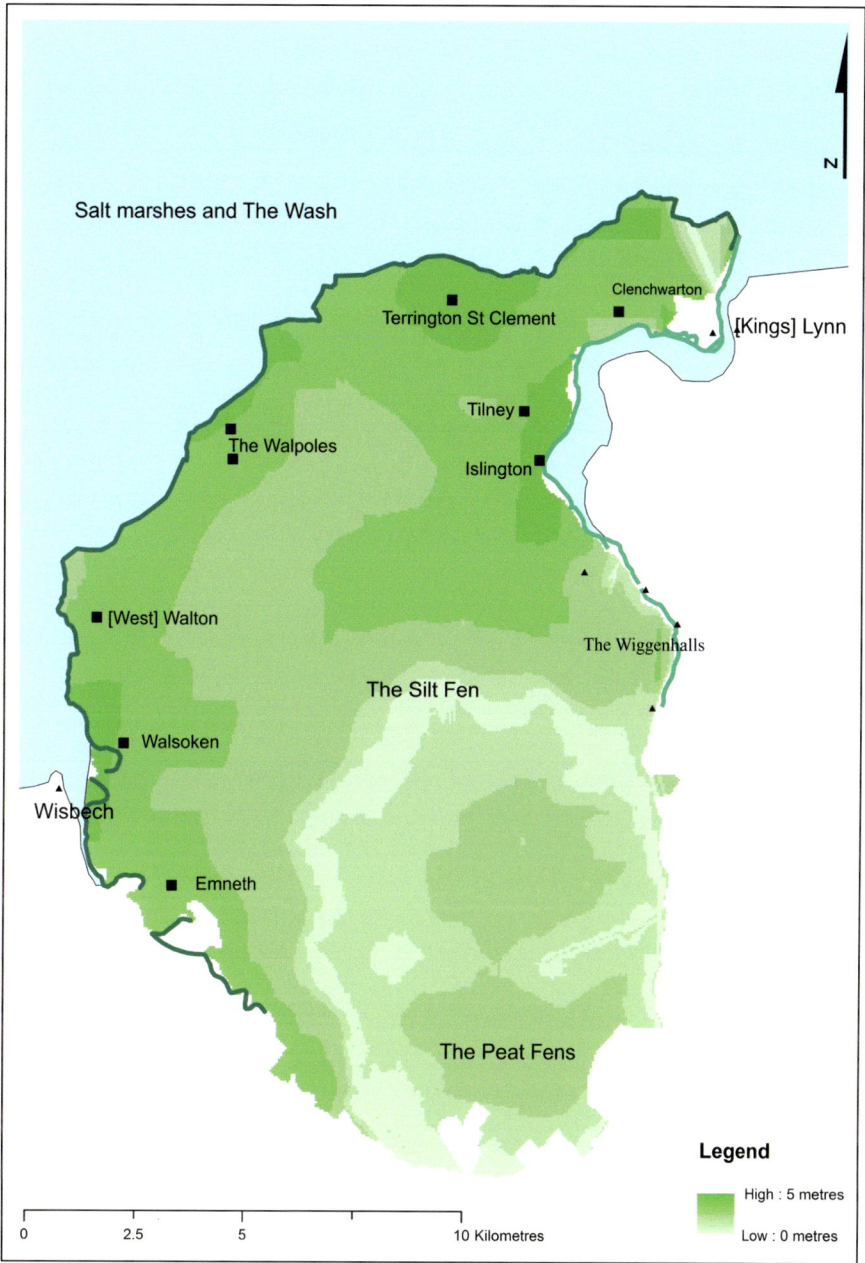

a tendency for prolonged waterlogging (Hodge 1984, 319). The remainder of the Silt Fen is covered with Wallsea 2 Association Soils, which are stoneless deep clays with naturally high groundwater levels. They similarly benefit from modern underdrainage and once improved are suitable for modern arable cropping in both spring and autumn (Hodge 1984, 338).

The earliest histories of Fenland tend not to distinguish between the peat and silt fens. They describe The Fens as a marginal landscape with all the inherent dangers of marshes and tides and as a region barely populated, an area popular with brigands and outlaws. Towards the end of the eighteenth century, William Dugdale wrote about the draining of Fenland and although much of his book focused upon the recent technological innovations and advances of draining the Black Fen, Dugdale also discussed the different settlement histories of the Black and Silt Fens. In common with contemporaries Dugdale accepted that Marshland's Sea Wall, the embankment running along the northern edge of the Silt Ridge, had been constructed by the Romans, but he also cited medieval charters and other records concerned with the construction and maintenance of the fen dikes. The term dike was used in Marshland and by Dugdale and Hayward, to mean a bank or barrier and not a ditch or drain as in modern parlance, and it is this historic meaning that will be used in the following discussion. Citing Hubert de Burgo's description of his holdings in Walsoken in 1181, Dugdale claimed that the majority of the region remained marsh in the late twelfth century (Dugdale 1605, 245). Later historians writing about the Fens, including Darby and Astbury in the second half of the twentieth century, tended to concentrate upon the reclamation of the peat fen (Astbury 1958; Darby 1983).

In the late twentieth century The Fenland Project was launched and attempted to collect together documentary sources and archaeological fieldwork and interpret the development of the entire Fenland landscape (Silvester 1988, 1). In the course of the project Robert Silvester combined documentary sources, particularly Hayward's map of Marshland from the late sixteenth century, with the results of his comprehensive archaeological field survey to examine the colonisation and expansion of settlement in the Marshland parishes (Silvester 1988, 12). In the resulting volume Silvester described the colonisation of the Silt Ridge during the Middle and Later Saxon periods for the purpose of salt manufacture and fishing as well as grazing of the fen. The results of the archaeological field survey showed that settlement was initially located on the Silt Ridge. From the thirteenth century settlement extended along the common drove-ways that crossed the lower lying former silt fens and linked the Marshland towns to their inland grazing marshes. Silvester concluded that the boundaries of many of the drove-ways became fixed only during the reclamation and enclosure of the surrounding land (Silvester 1988, 163).

Writing over a decade after completing the volume Silvester raised a note of caution over his use of Hayward's map of Marshland. At the time of writing the Marshland volume, Silvester believed that the maps that he viewed at the University of Cambridge and Wisbech Museum were firsthand copies of a map, since lost, that was drawn from an accurate land survey carried out by William Hayward around 1591 (Silvester 2002, 13). Silvester's subsequent research indicated that Hayward's survey had been carried out approximately a decade earlier and the resulting map had been drawn to show the former holdings of the Bishop of Ely. The 1591 map that was reproduced in the two copies viewed by Silvester, was itself redrawn or copied from the earlier map of the Ely holdings. As a result, although it remains a useful source, the accuracy of the depiction of the late sixteenth-century landscape in Hayward's 1591 map must be considered with caution (Silvester 2002, 14).

The Marshland study has been influential; David Hall accepted Silvester's conclusions despite suggesting an entirely different landscape history for the superficially similar field pattern in the neighbouring silt fens of Cambridgeshire and Lincolnshire (Hall and Coles 2014, 146). Recent archaeological fieldwork has supported Silvester's colonisation model, noting the importance of roddens as the locations for early medieval settlements (Crowson 2005, 54). This work has also confirmed Silvester's conclusion that the sea wall was constructed in the pre-Conquest period, early in the colonisation of Marshland (Silvester 1988, 160; Crowson 2005, 197). Only Silvester's suggestion that the initial Middle Saxon settlement was planned, with each of the six known settlements evenly spaced along the ridge and built upon artificial mounds, has been contested (Silvester 1988, 158; Crowson 2005, 293).

The combination of fresh and saltwater resources available in Fenland had long been attractive to humans and the former peat fens preserved many early sites particularly from the Bronze Age, however, little evidence of prehistoric activity has been found in Marshland to date (Silvester 1988, 154). Evidence for Romano-British settlement is found in the remains of several canals and the crop marks of probable farmstead sites on the roddens. Romano-British salt making sites or 'salterns' have also been identified (Silvester 1988, 156). Settlement became more marginal toward the end of the Roman centuries as the region began to experience the frequent sea floods that eventually deposited many layers of silt over the abandoned Roman settlements.

It is not clear precisely when the environment conditions in Fenland changed sufficiently to encourage the re-colonisation of Marshland. Environmental analysis indicates that regular tidal flooding in East Anglia took place between the fourth and sixth centuries CE, sealing evidence for Roman settlement beneath deposited silts (Crowson 2005, 10). A site in Tilney cum Islington contained some evidence for Early Saxon activity and has been interpreted as a temporary seasonal settlement. That this is the only site found so far from this early period implies that most of the surrounding landscape was still subject to regular flooding during this period and that this inundation of sea water prevented more widespread activity and colonisation (Crowson 2005, 48). It has, however, also been suggested that evidence for more Early Saxon activity in Marshland might be sealed beneath some of the later post-Roman silt flood deposits (Crowson 2005, 54).

By the Middle Saxon centuries, the incidence of sea flooding had reduced sufficiently to allow permanent settlements to develop upon the curving ridge of higher ground. They were located near the coast in what was to become The Walpoles and Terrington. As previously mentioned, early settlement sites were typically located on the highest naturally available land surface, usually roddens (Crowson 2005, 54). Analysis of the contents of the Middle Saxon middens has indicated that the farming activity of the settlements was not limited to grazing as might be expected in a wetland environment, although the amount of sheep bones found suggests that this was a primary activity. All the settlements excavated also contained evidence of cereal pollen, usually barley, indicating that the early farmers cultivated arable fields and grew salt tolerant crops probably upon the Silt Ridge (Crowson 2005, 146). Several of the early settlement sites appear to be associated with salterns, particularly those in Terrington St Clement and Walpole and this along with several field names that incorporate 'salt' suggests the presence of salt marshes on the Silt Ridge.

Crowson described the Saxon settlement in Marshland as 'critically dependent upon relief' and early settlements were located upon existing natural features, typically on the numerous roddens (Crowson 2005, 293). Environmental analysis of the fill from Middle Saxon ditches indicated that most creeks remained open to the tidal waters and confirmed that the settlements were not protected from the sea at this time (Crowson 2005, 146). The line of the sea defence is marked on the earliest map of Marshland and it remained the northern boundary of the Marshland towns until the seaward marshes began to be reclaimed in the Early Modern Period. Hayward labelled it as 'Roman bank' and the name persists in modern place-names, although in medieval records it is simply called the 'Sea Wall' (44CAM_ALMA; Darby 1983). Sections of the earthwork have survived although what remains does not reflect the scale of the earlier structure.

Despite the name recorded on Hayward's map the Sea Wall was not constructed during the Roman occupation. Archaeological excavation of a section of the old sea wall in Clenchwarton dated the construction of the earthwork to the tenth century (Crowson 2005, 204). This indicates that by this period the settlements on the Silt Ridge were sufficiently permanent for the inhabitants to expend the considerable effort required to construct an earth bank capable of protecting the farms and fields. Through landscape analysis of the tracks and banks in Clenchwarton and Terrington, Silvester concluded that at least two earlier phases of defensive sea walls were built before the so-called 'Roman Bank' was constructed in the tenth century (Silvester 1988, 41). This suggests that even at this early date the inhabitants of Clenchwarton and Terrington were expanding their territory through piecemeal intakes on the Silt Ridge. Even without the knowledge of the earlier sea defence walls identified by Silvester in Clenchwarton and Terrington the piecemeal nature of the entire construction is visible from the discontinuous line of the earthwork. The course of the Sea Wall (the dark green line following the coast in Figure 8.2) follows an indirect and convoluted route along the northern edge of the Silt Ridge with abrupt changes in direction at the boundaries of what later became parish territories.

There is no surviving boundary earthwork or clear line fossilised in the modern landscape that indicates that there was an inland equivalent to the Sea Wall which protected the settlements on the Silt Ridge from freshwater flooding. This was presumably due to a lower risk of inundation from the Silt Fen than the sea during the colonisation phase and recent environmental analysis of climate would appear to support this. In the years between 850 to 1150 CE, Marshland experienced a period of relatively low levels of inland flooding (Charman 2010, 1545). As will be seen these dates correspond with the early phases of Marshland settlement and expansion onto the Silt Fen, beginning in the Late

FIGURE 8.3. Late Saxon settlement activity in Marshland from archaeological fieldwork from *The Marshland Gazetteer*.

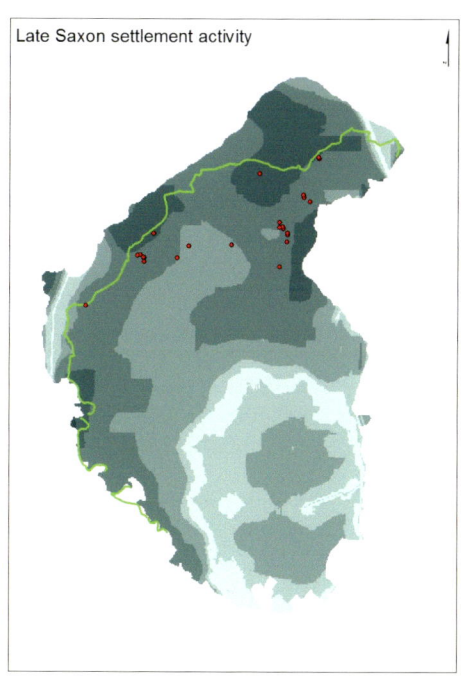

Saxon period, as illustrated by the red dots visible in Figure 8.3.

Despite the apparent lack of a physical boundary between the Silt Ridge and the lower lying Silt Fen there was a clear distinction in the field pattern of the two areas depicted on Hayward's map, which still survives in the modern landscape (44CAM_ALMA). The pattern of irregular fields, sinuous ditches and winding lanes on the Silt Ridge peters out as the land height falls away towards the Silt Fen. Once the land surface falls to 2 m or less the pattern of roads, ditches, dikes and fields appears to be much more regular in form and how this landscape developed will be discussed later in this chapter. In order to understand the Silt Fen we first need to consider the development of the irregular field pattern on the Silt Ridge.

The enclosures upon the Silt Ridge tend to be smaller and more irregular in form than those found on the former fen. On the higher ground the fields are bounded by sinuous lanes and winding ditches that may fossilise the course of natural creeks and roddons. The sea flood defences that surrounded the settlements and new intakes were pushed out into the open landscape both towards the sea but also inland (44CAM_ALMA; Silvester 1988, 166). Eventually expansion east and west was prevented when the intakes encountered the fields belonging to neighbouring communities leading to the township divisions and dikes. Hayward's sixteenth-century map includes a cartouche detailing the key for the symbols used in the plan, which states that the divisions between the Marshland towns are typically formed by dikes. On his map these township dikes were shown in red, to distinguish them from other boundary earthworks (44CAM_ALMA). Although not all survive as earthworks in the modern landscape, the path of most of the dikes has been fossilised as the parish boundaries (44CAM_ALMA).

Silvester noted that the township dikes appeared to pass around the fields on the Silt Ridge and interpreted this to mean the boundaries post-dated the reclamations (Silvester 1988, 166). An alternative explanation is to see the dikes as part of the method for reclaiming the land on the Silt Ridge, by clearing and canalising the natural creeks and creating dikes to protect the field from flood. Place-names can also provide some insight as to how the Silt Ridge was reclaimed for farming. A large proportion of the field names found on the Silt Ridge and particularly those found in Terrington and the Walpoles, incorporate personal names, suggesting they originated as intakes of marsh possibly carried out by an individual or kin group (Field 1993, 165). A field name element that appears frequently upon the Silt Ridge and Fen is 'new' in this context they can perhaps be interpreted as signifying land that is newly available for agriculture (Field 1993, 81).

Domesday Book indicates that many of the Marshland holdings contained plough lands for arable production and the value of the Marshland vills remained more or less constant from 1066 to 1086 and livestock numbers remained stable, except in the case of sheep where the passing of 20 years saw an increase in the size of the flock (Williams and Haward Martin 1992, 1138, 1162). Manorial landholding in eleventh-century Marshland was complex; most vills contained multiple manors, held by a variety of secular and seigneurial lords, with no indication for an individual who could have organised a large-scale planned landscape.

Medieval reclamation of the Silt Fen

Documentary evidence indicates that the wetland Silt Fen was undrained in the twelfth century; in 1181 Hubert de Burgo described his holdings in the Wiggenhalls, which lie east of Islington, as predominately marshland. Plotting the find locations recorded in *The Marshland Gazetteer* onto a map indicates that for those sites where the earliest evidence for habitation has been dated to the twelfth century there remained a clear preference for the higher ground, as can be seen on Figure 8.4. The GIS map further highlighted the continued importance of local topography in locating dwelling sites. The majority of the new farmsteads were constructed on ground that lay at least 3 m above sea level, with relatively few built on the land 2 m OD, but overall, most new houses were still being built on or close to the Silt Ridge. Two sites, one each in the parishes of Tilney and Terrington, were located further inland but as the topography shows, they both lay on a peninsula of higher ground that extended into the lower levels of the Silt Fen.

The new settlement sites on the Silt Ridge in the twelfth century had a tendency to cluster around the small greens that survived to be mapped by Hayward four centuries later (44CAM_ALMA). This is in marked contrast to the Late Saxon sites that were more typically located upon roddens, as can be seen in Figure 8.5 (Silvester 1988, 163). The preference for dispersed settlement continued and with the notable exception of the main towns, many communities upon the Silt Ridge were in the form of hamlets clustered around the numerous small greens. The commons, lanes and greens were surveyed by Hayward in the late sixteenth century, although it is likely that some of these features may have developed after the twelfth century, their relationships to the contemporary settlement sites suggest that many were already present in the earlier landscape.

The presence of habitation sites on the Silt Fen indicates that reclamation was already underway in the twelfth century. Furthermore, these newly inhabited areas must have been drained before houses were built. Logically it is likely that several years had passed between the draining of the land and the first habitation,

FIGURE 8.4. Twelfth-century settlement activity in Marshland from *The Marshland Gazetteer*. Greens and sea wall after Hayward's map of 'Marshlande' (44CAM_ALMA).

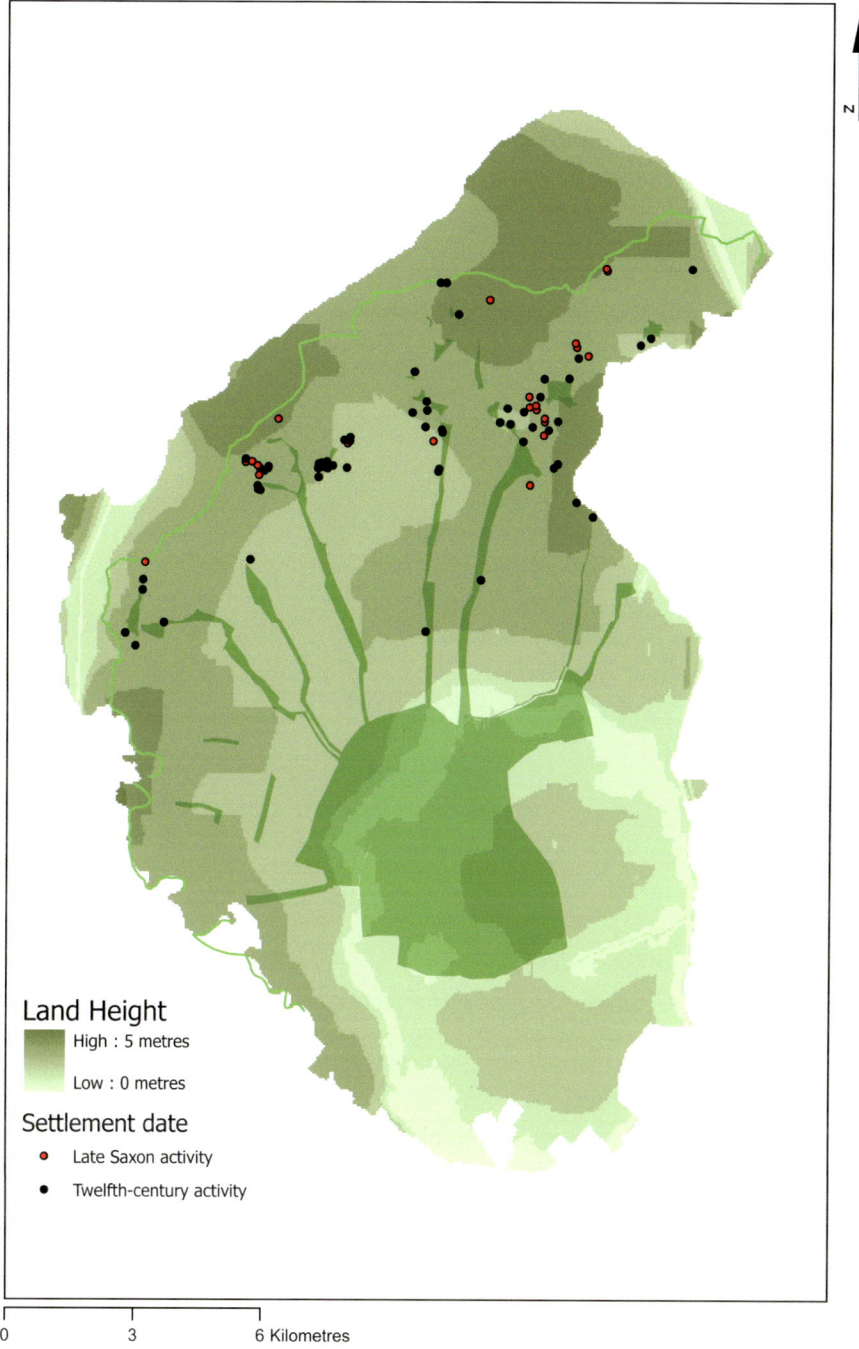

if only to ensure that the new inhabitants could be reasonably confident that they were unlikely to lose their homes and possessions to seasonal floods.

Notably a number of the new house sites in Terrington are found in an adjacent area of the Silt Fen called Jenkins Field, which was protected by a bank

FIGURE 8.5. The sixteenth-century landscape near Terrington St Clement (after 44CAM_ALMA), with dated probable habitation sites from *The Marshland Gazetteer* (Silvester 1988).

known as the New Fendike. This earthwork and the field it protected will be discussed later in this chapter, but the presence of the new farmsteads appears to indicate that Jenkins Field was already protected from inland flooding by the dike in the twelfth century. Furthermore, the correlation of house sites with the western edge of the Terrington Common Drove, shown in the centre of Figure 8.5, appears to indicate that this section of the common drove was also already present in the landscape.

Although settlement began to extend onto the former Silt Fen in the twelfth century, the archaeological record suggests that it was in the century that followed that the main secondary settlements were established. During the thirteenth century the previous critical dependence of settlement upon relief began to break down. New farmsteads were strung along the common droves that led from the towns on the Silt Ridge to The Smeeth Common (Silvester 1988, 163). This sudden expansion of settlement into the Silt Fen took place within a single century and can only reflect major changes to the local landscape that allowed permanent settlement on the former fenland to develop for the first time.

The population in England had risen hugely since the Conquest and the associated pressure upon resources to provide sufficient food for the people led to marginal land being cultivated and settled (Dyer 2000, 150). This pressure on available land might have similarly encouraged settlement upon recently reclaimed land in Marshland, which in earlier centuries might have been considered too precarious. Medieval Marshland was also home to vast flocks of sheep and the population were able to export wool through the neighbouring port of Lynn.

Another potential factor was climate change. As previously mentioned, three centuries of unusually dry weather, with relatively little evidence for fluvial flooding ended in the mid-twelfth century (Charman 2010, 1545). This short period may have provided a window of opportunity for the inhabitants of Marshland to extend farms and fields into the Silt Fen. This would also provide an explanation for the construction of the Old Podike, an enormous earthwork bank over 7 km long built in 1223 CE, ostensibly to protect the Marshland settlements from inland flooding (Dugdale 1605, 246). Dugdale stated that the earliest field intakes had taken place in advance of the construction of the Old Podike (Dugdale 1605, 283). The Old Podike was reputedly built to protect Marshland from freshwater flooding and it must have increased the attractiveness of permanent settlement onto the former Silt Fen (Dugdale 1605, 245).

Plotting locations from *The Marshland Gazetteer* onto a topographic map illustrates that the majority of the thirteenth-century sites for dwellings were located north of a curving lane called Castordike or the Oldfendike, as can be seen in Figure 8.6. Approximately half of the new house sites were built upon the Silt Ridge, many clustered around the small greens that had first attracted settlement in the previous century. The remainder were strung along the sides of the common droves that led from vills on the higher ground towards Castordike. The find sites recorded in *The Marshland Gazetteer* also indicate that both the Castordike and sections of the common droves that lay to the north and west of it, were already present in the landscape by the end of the thirteenth century (Silvester 1988).

Marshland's landscape framework

Having reviewed, at some length, the archaeological and topographic evidence for the expansion of settlement onto the Silt Fen, we can now turn our attention to the main subject of this chapter, the origins and significance of the area's distinctive regular landscape. With very few exceptions the house sites are located along the boundaries of the common droves, which implies the droves, and therefore the fields were already present in the landscape. The following section will discuss the reclamation of the Silt Fen and how a combination of transhumance and topography led to the development of the regular field pattern. By comparison to the Silt Ridge the former fenland appears emptier, the fields are larger and there are fewer lanes. Morphologically many of the features have a more regular appearance, the dikes, lanes and boundaries are straight, and the fields are frequently sub-rectangular. Overall, this gives the Silt Fen the appearance of a vast co-axial system not dissimilar to the so-called relict landscapes discussed in previous chapters, but the origin of Marshland's field pattern cannot be prehistoric planning. How then did the landscape of the former Silt Fen come to have so regular an appearance?

156 How the Land Lies

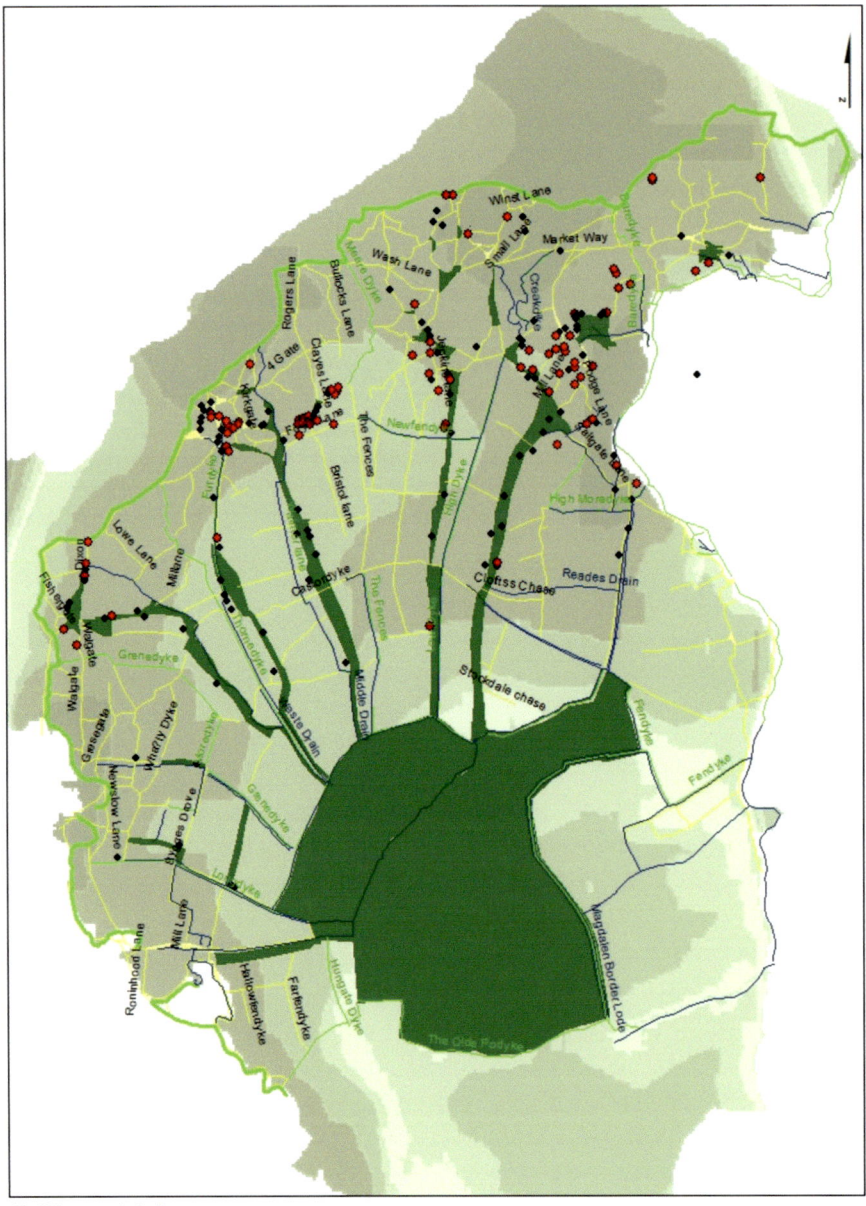

FIGURE 8.6. The thirteenth-century landscape (after 44CAM_ALMA), with dated probable habitation sites from *The Marshland Gazetteer*. Key after Hayward, lanes and minor dikes in yellow, Township dikes in red, common droves and greens coloured green and 'sewers' and drains shown in blue (44CAM_ALMA; Silvester 1988).

Piecing together the agricultural reclamation of the Silt Fen is fraught with difficulty not least due to the environmental changes and alterations wrought in subsequent centuries. The region was subject to devastating floods during the medieval and post-medieval period, furthermore the landscape was deliberately altered by both the inhabitants of Marshland and through changes to rivers and drainage wrought by communities far inland (Bond 2007, 185). In previous chapters we have seen how early transhumance routes formed loose frameworks in the countryside that were often respected and reinforced by later minor boundaries and roads. These examples have also shown how these routes linking settlements to distant resources typically responded to the large-scale topography, traveling up slope between valleys and wold resources, or along watersheds. In Marshland the curving silt ridge, and the low-lying basin that was Marshland or West Fen and The Smeeth formed a reverse to a typical 'river and wold' system, where the marginal land is on the highest ground.

Whilst the population of Marshland remained relatively low and located upon the Silt Ridge the livestock that belonged to the vills could be grazed over the undrained and undivided Silt Fen (Silvester 1988, 163). With few natural boundaries the early settlers were also able to utilise the more distant peat marsh called West or Marshland Fen (Silvester 1988, 32). Lying to the north of West Fen was an area known as The Smeeth. This marsh was on higher ground, a large rodden from a prehistoric fenland river (Silvester 1988, 32). The environmental conditions in The Smeeth encouraged plentiful grass that grew quickly providing abundant grazing.

Traces of several medieval paths that led into the middle of West Fen survived as soil marks in aerial photographs of the reclaimed fields. Similar loosely defined routes almost certainly crossed the un-reclaimed Silt Fen during the early medieval period leading to the grazing marshes. Over time the piecemeal draining of the Silt Fen began to restrict access across the Silt Fen into increasingly narrow zones of unimproved grassland retained as common droves for the livestock (Silvester 1988, 163). Precisely how Marshland's huge linear greens resulted from the reclamation of the adjacent fields will be discussed in detail later in this chapter, but they fossilised earlier transhumance between the Silt Ridge and the distant peat fen and formed spines in the sparse landscape framework within which the regular field pattern eventually developed (Figure 8.7). The linear greens have now all been enclosed but traces of their former size and importance can still be found in the modern road and settlement pattern (Silvester 1988, 166).

In Terrington and Tilney the common droves commenced at small greens that lay adjacent to the Silt Fen but at some distance from the main settlements, as can be seen in Figure 8.8. These small areas of common grazing had become the foci of settlement during the twelfth century. In West Walton and Walpole the long common droves similarly begin adjacent to smaller commons that lay at the edge of the Silt Fen. In these western parishes a continuous series of small greens and droves linked the settlement centres to the common drove in a defined, if indirect, path. The small irregular greens appear to have been formed during the piecemeal reclamation of the Silt Ridge, being retained as unenclosed common (Silvester 1988, 163). Their survival underlies the importance of access to the inland silt fen for grazing animals in these vills even at this early stage.

158 *How the Land Lies*

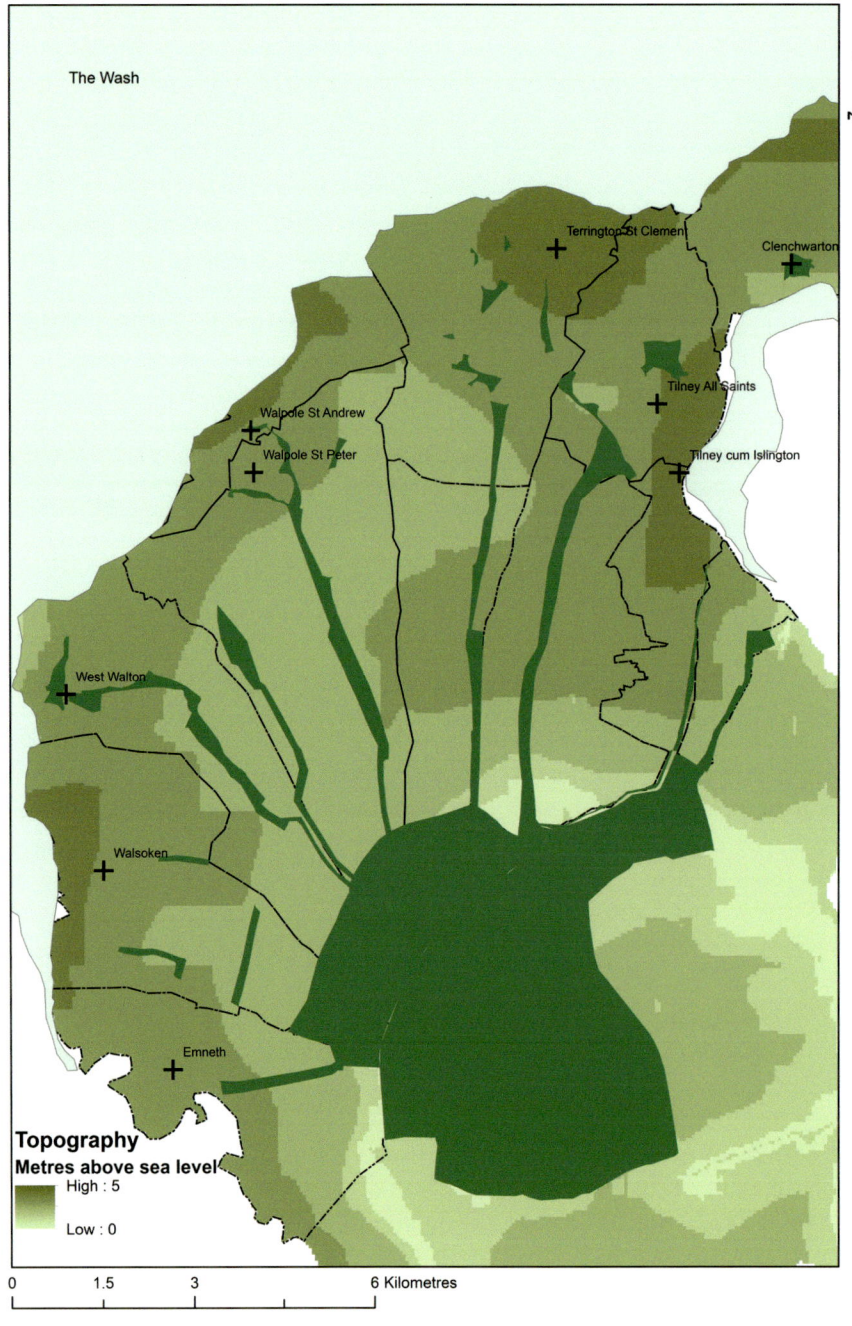

FIGURE 8.7. Topography of the Marshland vills, with greens and droves after Hayward and the 1851 parish boundaries.

The most curious arrangement for linking the settlement, common drove and the grazing marshes is visible in Walpole. The West Drove was connected to the centre of Walpole St Peter by a long narrow curving bank called Furdike. The Furdike ran for almost 2 km before it widened out into the more typical form of a common drove-way. Silvester reasoned that the narrow section of

FIGURE 8.8. The relationship of several of the common droves to the Silt Ridge settlement of Tilney, Terrington and the Walpoles. Key after Hayward, lanes and minor dikes in yellow, Township dikes in red, common droves and greens coloured green and 'sewers' and drains shown in blue (44CAM_ALMA).

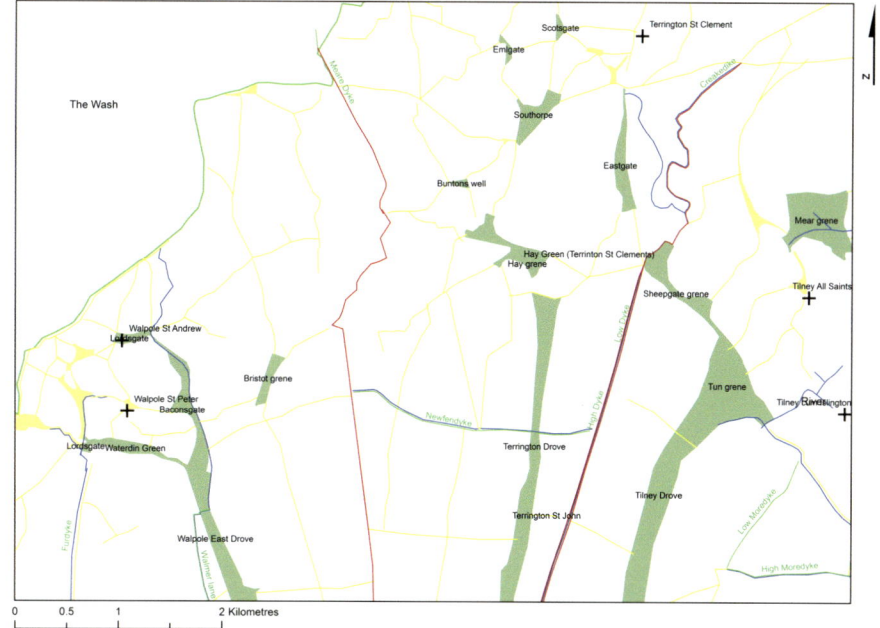

drove that survived to be mapped by Hayward resulted from modifications during the medieval period, at a time when he believed that a large portion of the upper common drove-way was enclosed and cultivated (Silvester 1988, 80).

Silvester concluded that the Marshland droves became established through the piecemeal reclamation of the Silt Fen (Silvester 1988, 163). Examination of maps, even the modern Ordnance Survey 1:25,000 maps support this as they show that the outline of the former droves altered when they met field boundaries and former fen dikes. However, Silvester also concluded that two of the common droves showed signs of deliberate planning, namely the Walpole East Drove and the southern section of Tilney Drove (Silvester 1988, 65, 80). His evidence for both arguments included a combination of apparent 'slighting' of the field strips and place-names that indicated that the common droves split pre-existing fields (Silvester 1988, 65, 80).

Silvester's strongest argument was for the late insertion of Walpole East Drove. This was the most important route to the Marshland commons for the inhabitants of Walpole by the thirteenth century (Silvester 1988, 80). Silvester highlighted several features as supporting his conclusion that it resulted from a later planned imposition on the field pattern. His evidence included the long section of the drove that ran parallel with the western parish boundary, the fact that there was no alteration in the form of the drove as it intercepted Old Fendike, and finally the apparent 'slighting' of East New Field (Silvester 1988, 80). Each of his arguments will be considered in turn.

The parallel relationship between the drove and the western parish boundary and township dike that separated Walpole and Walton is visible in Figure 8.9a. The eastern edge of the drove does indeed run roughly parallel to the parish boundary, which lies over 2 km to the west, and both follow a mostly straight course for several kilometres. Curiously the western edge of the drove, which lies closer to the supposedly influential township dike has little relationship with either the parish division or the eastern edge of the East Drove. There are further problems with the presumed relationship between the drove and the parish boundary, not least that the supposed alignment of the 'parallel' eastern edge of the drove actually begins almost half a kilometre before the parish boundary straightens to follow a direct course to The Smeeth.

Silvester's second piece of evidence was that when Walpole East Drove and Old Fendike met they both appeared to be unaltered (Silvester 1988, 80). In his analysis Silvester apparently overlooked the slight deviations of the same drove when intercepting dikes and lanes that lie to the north of Old Fendike; these are particularly visible at Cobblers Lane and March Lane. It is difficult to conceive of a reason why an important and planned new drove that would cut, presumably inconveniently, through existing arable fields would be deflected and altered by these minor lanes.

Silvester's final piece of evidence would initially appear to be the hardest to argue against. To the south of Oldfendike the drove appears to split East

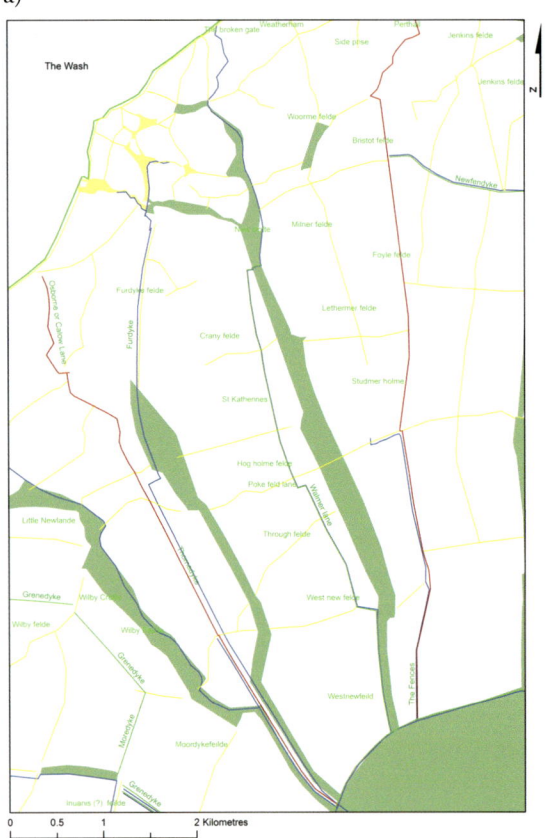
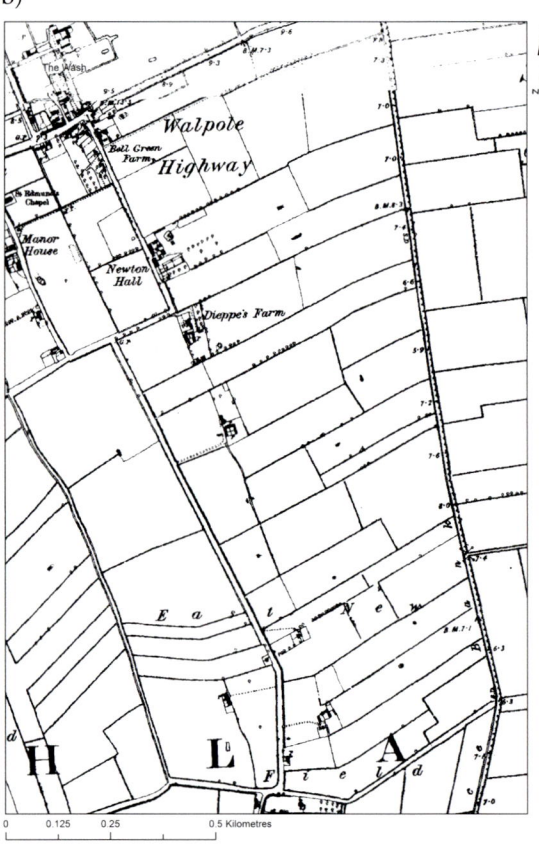

FIGURE 8.9. a) Walpole East Drove after Hayward (Key after 44CAM_ALMA), lanes and minor dikes in yellow, Township dikes in red, common droves and greens coloured green and 'sewers' and drains shown in blue; b) detail of the First Edition Ordnance Survey 6-Inch map showing the field divisions in East Field, Walpole.

New Field into two (Silvester 1988, 80). East New Field is a tongue of land bounded on the east by the parish boundary dike, and the west by New Field Bank, and later, the common drove visible in Figures 8.9 a and b. From the strip pattern, it appears that the southern section, also called East New Field was reclaimed separately; this section is divided from the northern portion by a kinked road, which appears to influence the formation of the drove-way. Closer examination of the strips on the First Edition Ordnance Survey Map in Figure 8.9b indicates that although they follow a similar orientation on each side of the narrow common, the fields are not truly 'slighted'; the boundaries do not match up on either side of the drove, as they should if the common drove was the later feature.

Silvester suggested that the East Drove was inserted into the landscape to provide better access for the populous but now deserted hamlet of Bristot Green in Walpole, which lay approximately half a kilometre east of the top of the drove (Silvester 1988, 81). As previously noted, there is a more compelling relationship between the East Drove and the local settlement pattern in that it commenced at two minor Silt Ridge commons, namely Waterkin Green and Baconsgate. These minor greens were part of a group of small commons that together formed a route between the principal Walpole settlements and the edge of the former Silt Fen.

Although visually arresting when viewed on Hayward's map, the common droves were not part of a planned landscape framework of towns, droves and commons. Rather they came into existence gradually as the surrounding marshland was reclaimed (Silvester 1988, 163). Another spine in the sparse framework of Marshland's landscape was provided by the township dikes. On the Silt Ridge the township dikes followed sinuous paths but once they reached the Silt Fen their morphology changed entirely. The township dikes took direct, straight paths, which stretched from the edge of the Silt Ridge to the limits of the common grazing marshes, as can be seen in Figure 8.10 (Silvester 1988, 166).

The divisions between Islington, Terrington, Walpole and West Walton stretch for more than 6 km across the former Silt Fen. Silvester concluded that the Marshland township dikes arose from planned apportionment of the Silt Fen, which he dated to the twelfth century as a time when many parish boundaries were finalised elsewhere in England (Silvester 1988, 166). In the Polders on mainland Europe similar long features, typically droves, have been identified, stretching miles from the original village deep into the marshes to sites of secondary settlement. These lines have been shown to utilise the church as a sightline in the open landscape when planning the expansion into the wetland (Knotterus 2013, 250). Examination of the locations of Marshland's township dikes suggests there is no evidence for a similar practice in Norfolk. Although at first glance the long township boundaries appear to be straight and unbroken, even the modern Ordnance Survey 1:25,000 map illustrates that the dikes are not as straight as they may initially appear. Instead, they are

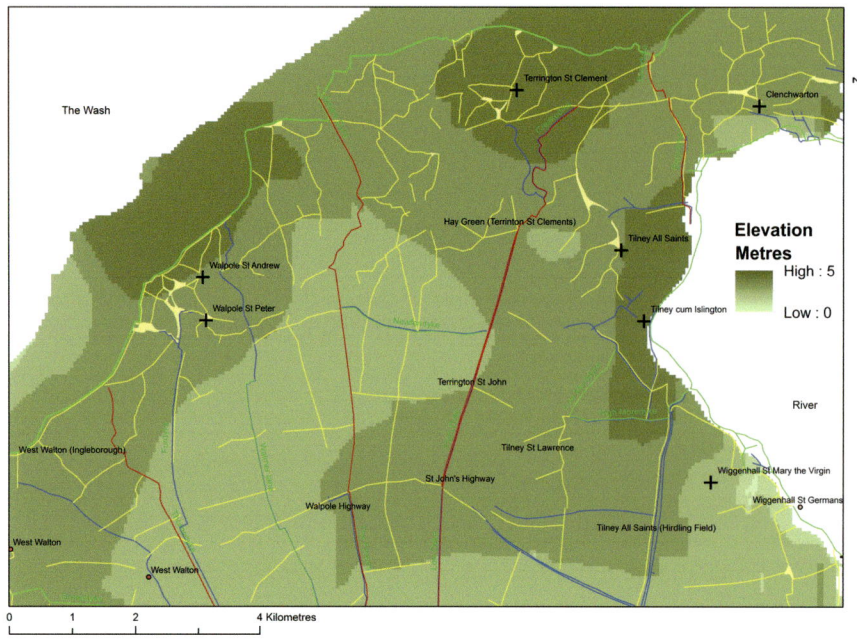

FIGURE 8.10. Township banks (shown in red) in Marshland (after 44CAM_ALMA).

made up of numerous shorter banks, which continue along the same orientation, but they contain slight shifts in alignment, which suggests interruptions in construction.

The same subtle broken morphology can even be seen in the High and Low Dikes that divided Terrington from Islington cum Tilney which Silvester described as 'arrow straight' (1988, 166). The fragmented make-up of the township boundary earthworks indicates that the course of the dikes was not planned and executed in a single endeavour as Silvester suggested; the construction appears to have taken place in stages and while this doesn't necessarily preclude planning, neither does it imply it.

Furthermore, as visible in Figure 8.11, the straight sections of the dikes that cross the former Silt Fen all begin at the edge of the Silt Ridge at the point where the pre-existing township dikes, on the Silt Ridge end. This relationship to the earlier township boundaries suggests that expansion into the Silt Fen was undertaken only after the Silt Ridge had been fully exploited, as suggested by the previous analysis of settlement patterns.

Together the common droves and the township dikes created a fan-like pattern of north–south aligned features on the former Silt Fen and the framework, visible in Figure 8.11, also incorporated several transverse features. The most significant was a lane and dike called Castordike or the Old Fendike and mentioned previously in relation to settlement expansion. It lay approximately halfway between the Silt Ridge settlements and The Smeeth Common and it disrupted the path of both the township dikes and common droves. The name of the lane and dike is curious, 'castor' would suggest a Roman origin for the feature, but as with Roman Bank there is no archaeological evidence for this. Its other name, 'Old Fendike', needs little explanation, particularly given that it appears to have been the southern extent of the settlement during the thirteenth century. The name implies that the transverse earthwork may have been constructed originally as a flood defence between the remaining marshes and the reclaimed fields.

The Old Fendike utilised the regional topography. Despite being located several kilometres south of the Silt Ridge and deep into the former fen, for much of its length the lane runs along a peninsula of higher ground, as can be seen in Figure 8.11. To the east of the Tilney Drove a possible earlier path of the Old Fendike is fossilised as a lane and ditch, which matches a dead-end lane in the neighbouring parish of St Mary Wiggenhall. It is also notable that Tilney Drove contains two slight shifts in alignments comes close to the feature, once as it intersects the Old Fendike, and again a few hundred metres to the north where it met the probable earlier phase. Silvester concluded that the Old Fendike may have been planned and constructed in a single regional agreement (Silvester 1988, 164). An alternative explanation is that it was formed piecemeal. The replacement of one route with another in Tilney suggests that the Old Fendike was constructed separately in much the same way as the township dikes. Furthermore, the distances from both The Smeeth and the Old Fendike to the Marshland towns varied considerably, which led to an uneven distribution of the former Silt Fen. This seems to be an unlikely arrangement if the Old Fendike were part of a regional plan.

The township dikes on the Silt Fen appear to have prevented or at least hindered east–west travel and very few lanes or bridges linked the drove-side communities to one another. Only the Old Fendike allowed the inhabitants of the former fenland to travel between the neighbouring fen communities without having first to travel up to the Silt Ridge. The Old Fendike is the site of another subtle change in the field pattern. Hayward's map of Marshland (44CAM_ALMA) depicts many more minor lanes and dikes in the area that lay to the north of the curving earthwork, than are shown amongst the fields to the south. This pattern persisted into the nineteenth century as shown by the First Edition Ordnance Survey 6-Inch map.

In his Marshland volume, Silvester surmised that the medieval drainers built the dikes and ditches, or sewers to protect the newly reclaimed fields from the surrounding high-water levels (Silvester 1988, 164). It is perhaps more probable that the construction of ditches and dikes was fundamental to the process of reclaiming land. The amount of the parish territory located on the Silt Ridge varies markedly between the Marshland towns. The populous western vills had relatively little land that lay above 3 m OD and this must have resulted in early pressure to exploit the adjacent Silt Fen. Silvester concluded that the western parishes had reclaimed the fen to the borders of The Smeeth by the thirteenth century, and documentary sources appear to confirm this with the mention of Emneth Hungate which lay at the edge of the former common, in a 1223 description of the region (Silvester 1988, 86). Elsewhere in Marshland evidence for timing of the reclamation activity comes from the expansion of settlement onto

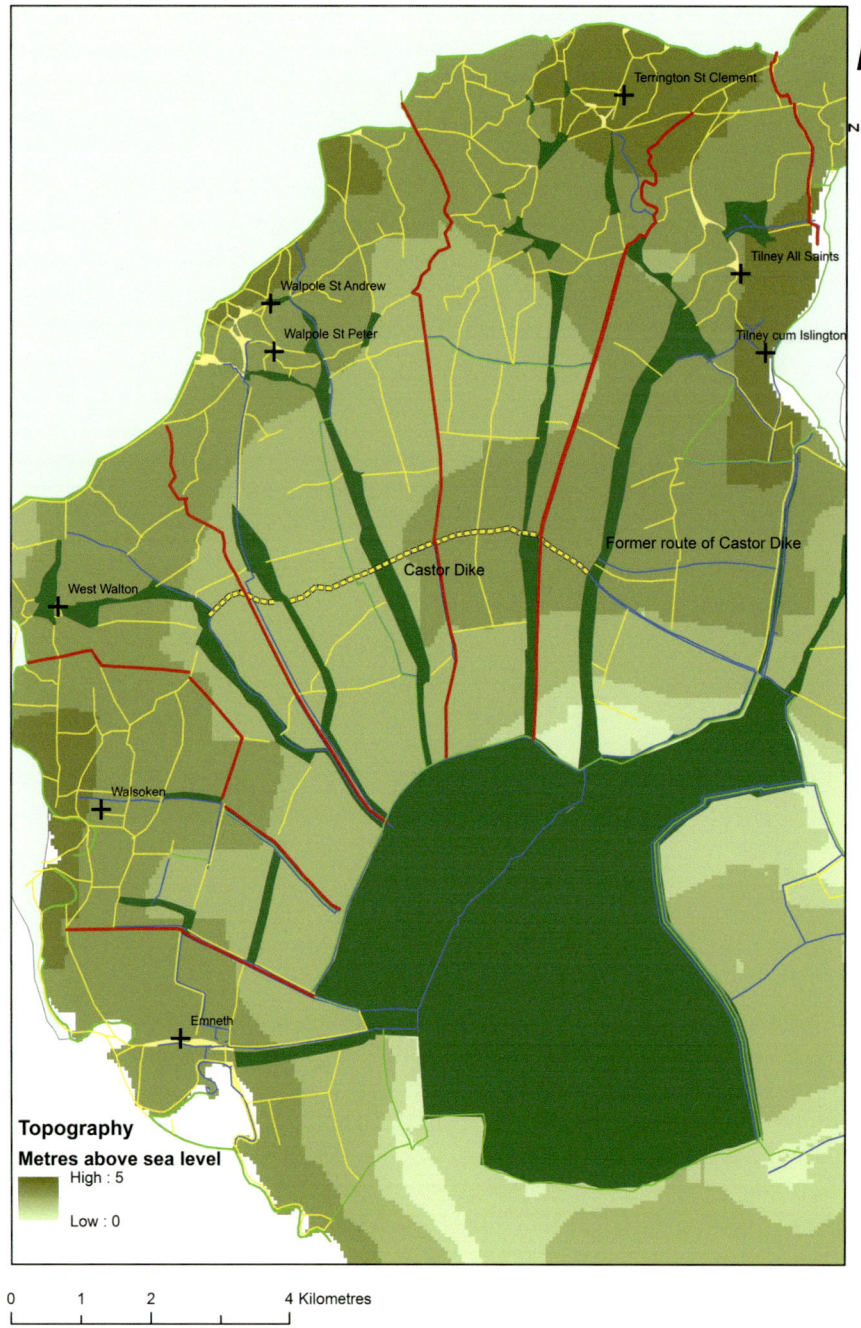

FIGURE 8.11. Castor or the Old Fendike (after 44CAM_ALMA).

the former marshes. As touched upon previously an early intake took place in Terrington St Clement, as confirmed by the location of several twelfth-century house sites on the low land protected by the Newfendike. This transverse earthwork ran west between the two township dikes and on Hayward's map is shown to intersect with Foyles Lane in Walpole in Figure 8.12 (44CAM_ALMA). The connection with Foyles Lane is almost certainly a later adjustment and the probable earlier course of the dike was preserved in a field ditch that survived into the early nineteenth century. The original dike continued the general curving path to meet the end of the township dike that divided Terrington and Walpole. This section of ditch was realigned during the nineteenth century to create rectangular fields, and it disappeared before the First Edition Ordnance Survey map. Newfendike presumably predated the twelfth-century expansion of settlement onto the former Silt Fen that it protected, and its original form provides clues to the piecemeal reclamation of the fen.

On the west the dike appears to have originally terminated at the edge of the Silt Ridge. This indicates that while the division between Walpole and Terrington was present on the higher ground, neither vill had extended their territory into the freshwater fens when Newfendike was constructed. By contrast, at the east end Newfendike terminated on High Dike, the township dike dividing Terrington and Islington, and this indicates that Newfendike must post-date that boundary earthwork. Newfendike would have been a large undertaking; it was 3 km long in its original form, and enclosed approximately 280 ha of the former Silt Fen. Hayward recorded that the resulting field and the lanes crossing it all incorporated 'Jenkins' in the place-names (44CAM_ALMA). This might imply that this intake was carried out by an individual family or kin group, although the scale of the endeavour makes this less likely (Field 1993, 166). For most of its length the course of the Newfendike follows the division in soil types between the workable Agney silt soil and the waterlogged Wallasea clay to the

FIGURE 8.12. Newfendike with greens and droves after Hayward and twelfth-century settlement sites from *The Marshland Gazetteer*.

south. It is inconceivable that the builders of the dike were unaware of this, and it provides a justification for the unusual sinuous form of the dike and drains. The later alteration of the course of the Newfendike provides a useful reminder that even substantial earthworks could be adjusted and remade if they were no longer useful or had become inconvenient.

The curving path of the Newfendike in Terrington St Clement is atypical; elsewhere on the former Silt Fen transverse field boundaries tended to be straight. Most of them were classified by Hayward as 'lanes or lesser droves' (44CAM_ALMA). Their origin as routes is unlikely, not least because most do not extend beyond the parish boundaries, and end when they reach the common droves. They appear to demarcate the extents of piecemeal intakes from the Silt Fen and possibly functioned as field access ways. Terrington contains four of these unequally spaced dividing lanes, Newfendike in the north and three more to the south, one of which is Old Fendike, and this arrangement is typical. In all cases the relationship between the extent of the reclaimed field, the transverse boundaries and the township dikes implies they are contemporary.

The areas of the land enclosed by these former field dikes is not consistent even within parishes, in Terrington the largest is the field enclosed by Newfendike at approximately 280 ha, but the smallest field contains around half that at 150 ha. Overall, there is little indication of a pattern that could suggest that the intakes fitted into a large-scale landscape plan. Terrington and the Walpoles contained some of the lowest land levels in the Silt Fen and reclamation would have been especially challenging, requiring a level of communal cooperation to undertake the task. Rather than small fields originating from kin group assarts, as seen on the Silt Ridge, in the former fen the groups of husbandmen worked communally to embank and drain large intakes.

In his 'History of the County of Norfolk', Francis Blomefield discussed the draining of the Wiggenhall parishes that border the eastern edge of Marshland. He noted that in 1181 the land to the south of Wiggenhall St Mary had been described as uninhabited waste, which was subsequently reclaimed by the efforts of 'divers inhabitants in the neighbourhood' (Blomefield 1808). According to Blomefield the Wiggenhall reclamation was carried out by the inhabitants of the vill who undertook the activity on their own behalf. However, once the former fenland had been reclaimed 'that they might the more securely enjoy the same, were content to be tenants for it unto such great men [...] of whom they held their other lands' (Blomefield 1808). While this may initially seem a curious choice, surviving documentary sources indicate that the maintenance and repair of small dikes and drains were managed by the manorial courts. By holding the land as freehold tenants, the husbandmen could ensure that any individuals shirking their responsibilities would be compelled to carry out their obligations or face the consequences in the local manorial court. Records of the Abbey of Ely's holdings in the Cambridgeshire and Norfolk Silt Fens indicate that most of the land was held in freehold by the middle of the thirteenth century, which appears to support Blomefield's description (Miller 1951, 131). The Ely Abbey records also appear to confirm that the draining of the Silt Fen was not taking place at a parochial or manorial level; if it were, the land would be expected to be divided among the copyhold inhabitants of the vill, and the manor in the form of equal portions, and there is no evidence for this.

Blomefield suggested that the success of the late twelfth-century draining in Wiggenhall directly inspired inhabitants in the neighbouring Marshland towns to attempt to drain their own silt fenlands (Blomefield 1808). This is a late date as other documentary sources indicate that significant reclamation of the Silt Fen had already occurred. In 1207 an agreement was made between the principal landholders of Marshland, including the Bishop of Ely and the Prior of Lewes, that the West Fen would remain as common land forever (Dugdale 1605, 245). The 'West Fen' was described as the area of pasture and turbary stretching from Chancellors Dike in the west and is almost certainly the area later known as Marshland Fen. That an agreement was required suggests that at least some of the vills had already extended their reclaimed land to the edges of the common by this early date. The West Fen agreement included a provision that should the common ever be enclosed, it would be divided between the towns according to defined but unequal amounts 'in proportion to their fiefs as of old'.

The field dikes and lanes were the final elements of the landscape framework in Marshland. The common droves and township dikes provided the principal axis as they travelled roughly north–south from the Silt Ridge to the grazing marshes. The linear greens fossilised the older transhumance ways that linked the farms with the summer commons. The dikes provided both a continuation of the township boundaries into the fen, and a way to reclaim the lower-lying land, as the accompanying ditches drained into the lower levels of the fen. The transverse field dikes constructed between the township dikes completed the flood defences of the newly reclaimed land. The location of a number of these, including Newfendike in Terrington and the Old Fendike appear to have either reflected soil conditions, or made use of higher land levels. Together they created a sparse but regular framework, determined by both topography and transhumance and which influenced the field pattern in the later landscape.

Silvester concluded that while much of the Silt Ridge was farmed for arable, the Silt Fen was used primarily for pasture and meadow during the medieval period (Silvester 1988, 165). Silvester also observed that whilst fields in the former salt marshes closest to the vills were heavily manured, this was less common elsewhere (Silvester 1988, 165). Reclaiming the Silt Fen to create more pasture in a region rich in grassland might initially appear not to repay the considerable effort of the draining. However, the Marshland towns were famous for their enormous sheep flocks (Silvester 1988, 165). The Smeeth and Marshland commons provided plentiful grazing during the summer months, but the livestock of the vills still needed to be fed during the potentially long periods when the common grazing marsh was inundated.[1] As population increased much of the land on the Silt Ridge was reclaimed for arable cultivation and this may have left little land for winter grazing (Silvester 1988, 163). The reclaimed fields may have also been used as meadows to provide winter fodder in the form of hay. The subdivision of meadows into narrow strips or doles is not uncommon and Mark Gardiner has argued that the long strip fields found in former fenlands originated as 'dales' for the production of hay (Gardiner 2009, 3). How this may have led to the strippy field pattern in Marshland will be discussed later in this chapter.

The regular field pattern

In his Marshland volume Silvester created a putative medieval map of Marshland, based in part on Hayward's survey but also showing individual strips found within the larger fields obtained from nineteenth-century maps (Silvester 1988, 14). Unfortunately, Hayward's map does not include the small detail of individual strips and neither does the late eighteenth-century survey by William Faden. The Ordnance Survey Surveyors' drawings from 1819 are similarly lacking in detail about the strip divisions and frustratingly there are very few estate or farm maps for the region that might provide insight into the layout of the fields before the mid-nineteenth century. Eighteenth-century estate maps survive for several neighbouring parishes and do contain strip fields, but within Marshland the first map evidence showing that the larger fields were split into smaller strips comes from the parish tithe maps.

There is landscape evidence that at least some of the strips must have already been in existence prior to Hayward's survey. The township boundary between Emneth and Walsoken appears to have picked its way around individual strip fields, not all of which had survived to be included in the tithe maps. To the extent that they can be compared, the parish boundary line is comparable with the township boundary shown in Hayward's map, suggesting that a pattern of strip fields must have been established by the sixteenth century. Silvester suggests the evidence of the parish boundary pushes the date of origin of the strip fields far earlier to the eleventh century when he concluded the parish boundaries became fixed, but as has been seen in previous chapters, it was not unusual for these divisions to be agreed much more recently (Silvester 1988, 166).

Although the first map evidence for the strip fields dates from the nineteenth century, there are other clues to their antiquity. The Cartulary of Lewes Priory dating to the thirteenth century contains many references to holdings of apparently discrete parcels of land within larger fields on the Silt Fen, for example, 'four acres in the Newfield of Walpole between the land of John and his own land' (Bullock 1939, 223). There is evidence, therefore, that the large fields on the Silt Fen, along with many on the Silt Ridge were subdivided into separate units by the thirteenth century. Although the husbandmen held lands in strips in larger fields, and shared obligations to maintain the dikes and drains, there is no evidence for open field farming in Marshland.

Within Midland open fields the individual strips could vary in width. As discussed in previous chapters this was generally around a mean of 6 to 7 m. As a result, fields created by piecemeal amalgamation and enclosure of former open field lands tend to have widths that relate to multiples of this original measurement, and many represent the grouping together of only a handful of strips. This is not the case on the Silt Fen. Using Rednewland Field in Terrington as an example, the narrowest strip is 30 m wide, but the widths increase until they reach well over 100 m. A similar pattern is found in New Sibley Field where again the smallest strip is 30 m wide, but this measurement only occurs once, and as in Rednewland Field the strip widths increase incrementally with no clear indication for a single base multiplier.

It would appear likely that a method of proportional allocation not dissimilar to that described in the 1207 charter was used to divide the newly reclaimed and embanked fields. The West Fen agreement included a provision that should the common ever be enclosed, it should be divided between the towns according to defined but unequal amounts 'in proportion to their fiefs as of old' (Dugdale 1605, 245). If a similar proportional allocation applied to the land reclaimed within the new fields this could explain the variations found in strip widths. If this should be the case it would be interesting to know whether the amounts of new land were allocated based upon previous holdings and rights belonging to the individual, or whether it was more directly linked to the investment of labour or coin made during the reclamation activity.

Although some combining, and presumably subdivision, of earlier holdings must have occurred, evidence from aerial photographs suggests this was not widespread. Crop or soil mark shadows of lost field ditches are relatively rare although this assumes that the strips were always bounded by drains. Overall, the evidence suggests that the large fields were not initially divided into equal sized strips, but that the reclaimed lands were shared unequally from the beginning.

FIGURE 8.13. Orientation of the strip, First Edition Ordnance Survey 6-Inch map, greens after Hayward (44CAM_ALMA).

As discussed in the earlier chapters, on poorly draining land medieval arable strips tend to follow the natural topography, in order to take advantage of surface drainage. This relationship does not occur with any great regularity upon the Silt Fen, where in many cases the strip boundaries appear to cut across the topography. The orientation of the narrow strips instead appears to have been primarily concerned with providing access to the land holdings from an adjacent lane or common drove and the First Edition Ordnance Survey provides a clue of why that was important. In Marshland, most features, whether they be lanes, dikes or droves, are bounded by drains. The First Edition Ordnance Survey records that the lanes provided access to the strips, usually by way of a single culvert or bridge, usually one for each strip field. Culverts leading between the strips themselves appear to be rare, presumably only required if the adjacent land was held by a single farmer. Although the short edge of the strip typically abutted on a lane or other access way, the strips were not always arranged at 90 degrees to the path (and drain), as can be seen in Figure 8.13.

Across the former Silt Fen the strips appear to be primarily laid out in relation to another and presumably pre-existing landscape feature, whether it be drain, drove or lane. This even led to some curved strips, particularly east of the Tilney drove where the strips have a sinuous 'S' shape, rather than the reverse 'S' one would expect from a ploughed strip as they follow the alignment of Reeds Drain. This is reminiscent of the pattern of former open field strips in Middleton in North Yorkshire, where the morphology of the stream was repeated in the field pattern and presumably reflects the same origin as the width of the fenland strips were measured from the natural feature.

The lack of relationship between the orientation strips and local topography would be explained if the small fields originated as meadow doles that were converted into arable fields at a later date (Gardiner 2009, 5). We have previously seen how fundamental topography was to arable farming in the similar low-lying fen landscape of Holderness and although this also led to a regular strip pattern, it was determined by different factors. The arrangement of the minor field boundaries on the former Silt Fen supports Silvester's conclusion that the land was not initially reclaimed for arable farming. It also suggests that the enclosure and conversion of the strips to arable land was likely to be piecemeal, which prevented the strips being realigned to better fit the natural slope.

Conclusion

This chapter has discussed the origins of the distinctive regular landscape of Marshland by examining it within its wider historical context. Colonisation of the area began in the seventh century with the greatest expansion of settlement taking place during the twelfth and thirteenth centuries; the organised field systems are associated with areas settled in this latter phase. On the Silt Fen the importance of remote grazing to the Marshland vills was indicated by the long common droves that provided access to the summer pastures in the shared fens that lay to the south. In scale Marshland's common droves dwarf the linear greens seen in previous chapters, but their functionality was the same. They provided routes for the livestock through the fields to reach distant resources but were also themselves commons that could be grazed. The less noticeable but equally important township dikes formed another component to the loose framework of field dikes and reclamation.

The regular field pattern of the Silt Fen developed according to many of the same general principals as the irregular landscape found on the Silt Ridge. The use of dikes and ditches to drain the former fen was similar, but on the Silt Ridge this appears to have taken the form of canalising existing creeks and utilising natural roddens. On the Silt Fen perhaps it was the relative scarcity of similar environmental features which led to the creation of the straight township dikes and ditches, but more probably it was the scale of the undertaking, which required cooperation. Undoubtedly the individual intakes on the Silt Fen had to be organised and planned to a degree, but there is no evidence to suggest this was as part of a large-scale design. The frequency with which the field dikes correspond to natural features in the landscape suggest that the reclamations were based upon sound knowledge of the former fen. Barring natural barriers, a straight course is always shorter than a curved one and given the scale of the undertaking of digging new ditches and constructing dikes, a strong preference for a straight course is understandable.

The somewhat straight lines of the township dikes, common droves and field dikes created large sub-rectangular enclosures. The division of the large Marshland fields into ditched strips has only added to the appearance of regularity, particularly when viewed at a large scale. Documentary evidence suggests that the reclamation of the fen was undertaken by husbandmen, and the new land shared unequally. The pattern of small, ditched enclosures depicted on the nineteenth-century maps adds to the impression of a highly organised landscape, but this does not indicate a planned origin. The evidence for the gradual expansion of fields into the former fen is preserved in the slight adjustments to the field and township dikes and the morphology of the common droves. The Marshland landscape is a classic instance of how large-scale landscape regularity can arise from gradual, piecemeal, organic development.

Note

1. Although it should be remembered that sheep faming was of considerable benefit to arable land, particularly through close folding.

CHAPTER NINE

Conclusion

The assumption that regular landscapes containing seemingly ordered arrangements of boundaries and lanes could only arise through deliberate planning has been a central pillar of theories about relict field systems as it argues for the survival of organised prehistoric and Romano-British field systems in the framework of the medieval and modern landscape. Similar ideas also underpin arguments for the planned origins of open fields. In the preceding chapters I have argued that the notion that regularity must indicate landscape planning is flawed without careful consideration of the environmental context.

The connection between the principal or large-scale topography and the development of patterns of drove-ways that can form a powerful framework for the subsequent development of the landscape is not new. Previous research by Tom Williamson and Sarah Harrison into relict landscapes has illustrated how tracks linking valley-based settlements and watershed resources have created a 'grain' in the landscape preserved in modern parish boundaries, lanes and paths (Williamson 1998; Harrison 2002). But in most examples of regular landscapes any discussion of the local topography is brief and limited. In the first section of this thesis, I demonstrated that this approach risks overlooking topography and the natural environment as fundamental influences in the development of regularity in historic agricultural landscapes. All the published examples of planned landscapes considered in this thesis can be explained as the result of such influence, albeit in many cases multiple, and interacting in complex ways. There is, I would contend, a consistent relationship between features that fossilise historic resource utilisation and their immediate local environment.

Undoubtedly my review of the regular field patterns identified in relict field systems has benefited considerably from the modern availability of LiDAR, which allows a closer examination of minor topography on a wider scale than would otherwise be possible. This illuminated the relationship between what could appear to be insignificant changes in land height, as well as the influence of location and course of many of the apparently regular boundaries even while they conformed to the model of a typical 'resource linkage track' (Harrison 2005). I would argue that the evidence suggests a very similar relationship between landforms and the lesser boundaries that were also frequently located upon the watersheds of hill spurs and contours of dry valleys. I suggest that these same topographic influences were found to underlie the regularity in all the examples of relict landscapes discussed. Furthermore, there was a correlation between examples where the major and minor topography were more or less in alignment and landscapes that were especially regular.

The early chapters also touched upon another element of regular landscapes that rarely receives attention, and that is scale. Most examples of relict field systems have been identified using the First Edition Ordnance Survey maps, which allowed large areas to be scrutinised from above, a viewpoint that was unlikely to be available to the individuals who lived and farmed within it. It can be surprisingly difficult to observe regularity at ground level, but when viewed on a large-scale map the widespread repetition of manmade features on the same general orientation is arresting. In practice much of the regularity so apparent at a large scale is significantly less convincing at a local level. I would also suggest that the importance of scale has tended to be overlooked when comparing the morphology of 'relict field systems' to examples of the prehistoric field that they are supposedly characteristic of. In general, both the regular landscape and the enclosures within it are vastly larger in the historic field pattern.

Tom Williamson has argued that a large-scale landscape grain is determined primarily by sparse transhumance tracks. While I agree with his interpretation, I would also contend that the location and direction of long boundary patterns frequently involves the opportunistic use of natural features as boundaries. Furthermore, the impression of regularity is enhanced where a second axis lies approximately perpendicular to the principal valley and watershed alignment, as in the square field pattern located on the Dengie peninsula in Essex (Williamson 2016). Similar arrangements were identified in several of the so-called relict field systems discussed in the first section, but as before the location and course of the tracks and boundaries appeared to correspond with minor contours in the natural landscape.

While the landscape grain generally reflected the major topography of the area, I have suggested that the principal influence on the small detail of the field boundary was (and is) drainage. This might seem a rather prosaic and even mundane explanation, especially when compared to grand designs and regional resource planning. The supposition that the minor boundaries were determined by the local drainage patterns was confirmed as over and over again the field drains were shown to be constructed in order to facilitate the drainage of the soils. As I have argued throughout the preceding chapters in areas where the landform is planar the resulting landscape pattern is especially regular. Further confirmation of the relationship was provided by examples where the landscape grain or grid appeared to contain an irregular field pattern due to the undulating nature of the topography.

In the second part I argued that the same underlying importance of local drainage patterns was as visible in the open field furlongs, as it was in the relict landscapes. The alignment of ridge and furrow was determined by the slope, and the proximity of a ditch or natural stream. In many cases the open field strips ended at watersheds or on contours, creating furlongs in which many if not all of the boundaries were determined by the natural topography and features. This highlights another key tenet of regular landscapes, namely that regularity could not arise organically such as through the gradual expansion of farmland over centuries. I have argued in the preceding chapters that not only can the appearance of regularity derive through piecemeal expansion over many years, but analysis of numerous open field furlongs with reference to the local environment demonstrates that this took place. Furthermore, I have suggested that the response to the same underlying influences in differing environmental and landscape situations can lead to both regular and irregular furlong patterns. Examples in the Northamptonshire open fields demonstrated this. In the Central Nene Valley the furlong patterns ranged from large regular furlongs that lay near the major watershed and on the hill spurs to the small irregular blocks close to the headwaters of minor streams. Despite the difference in scale and location, the same factors governed the strip arrangements, namely the requirement to orient the furrow down the slope and to the nearest brook or stream.

As in Northamptonshire the field pattern in the Marshland towns varied, from the irregular pattern on the Silt Ridge to the organised field grid visible on the former fenland and which I have argued was due to the differing environmental challenges in expanding agricultural land. The relatively late colonisation of the Silt Fen in Norfolk preserved documentary evidence for organic development of the regular field pattern that has not survived elsewhere. They record that the Silt Fen fields were created through piecemeal intakes undertaken by groups of landholders. Putting the landscape in its topographic and environmental context indicates that rather than conforming to a grand agricultural design, many of the intakes were opportunistic and made use of existing man-made and natural features where they could benefit the undertaking. Although the environmental challenges of intakes from the former Silt Fen would have been extreme, I would argue that there was a similar degree of opportunistic incorporation of natural features in boundaries and intakes.

The importance of topography, drainage and environment to the location and direction of boundaries has implications when using landscape morphology and field patterns in order to identify a date of origin of a feature. I have argued throughout the preceding chapters of the importance of topography and drainage in the organic development of regular boundary patterns; so fundamental in the optimising of soil for farming that interpreting a relict landscape simply on the basis of morphology is unreliable. We have seen the consistent relationship between field and boundary patterns and the local environment, in particular the topography. The relationship between watersheds and major boundaries is well accepted, but I would argue that there is a similarly strong correlation between the orientation of field ditches and topography. This has implications for the use of slighting to date regular landscapes. The inconvenience of an angle ended strip or field is easily outweighed by the continued effectiveness of the furrow or field ditch. This association between slope and drainage is so compelling that evidence of the morphological relationship between a modern field boundary and an excavated section of historic ditch with which it shares an alignment or orientation implies only that water still drains downhill.

This statement will undoubtedly be seen as overly deterministic by those who would prefer to believe that people need not be limited by such seemingly prosaic environmental concerns. Anyone who doubts of the importance of surface drainage to generations of husbandmen should surely be persuaded by Gervase Markham's direction that understanding the way the water drained from the land was essential to farming, but if not then perhaps the fact that even with all our modern agricultural technologies, field ditches still tend to reflect the local topography may convince them.

Bibliography

Primary sources

Cambridge Record Office

K124/P/80 Smith, W. *Toft, Cambridgeshire. Draft Inclosure Map.* c. 1812.

Cambridge University Library

44CAM_ALMA Hayward, W. *The Description of That Parte of Norfolke Wch Lieth on Ye Weste Side of Ye River Ouse: Wherein Is Contained the Countrie of Marshlande Beinge Severed from the Reste (Lyinge More into the South) with a Red Line … / Guilielmus Haiwarde Descripsit 1591.* [England], [between 1680 and 1702], 1680.

East Riding Archive

DDCC/155/2 Bland, J. and T. Smith. *A Map of Certain Lands at Skefling … Part of the Estate of Edward Bee Gent.* 1721.

DDCK35/1/b Iverson, J or W. *A Copy of the Enclosure Plan of Skeffling in Holderness.* 1765.

DDCK 35/1/f Iverson, J or W. *A Copy of the Enclosure Plan of Preston in Holderness.* 1774.

IA/126 *Preston Enclosure Map.* 1774.

Northamptonshire Archive

Map/705 *Walgrave, Northamptonshire. Walgrave, Langham Estate.* 1778.

Map/2221 Banks, T. *The Plot of the Lordship of Papley in the Parish of Warmington. For William Elmes Esqr., Lord of the Same. Surveyor: Thomas Banks. October 1632. W.R. 82.* 1632.

Map/6433 Norwood, R. *Composite Colour Map of the Manor of Warmington in 1621 by Richard Norwood. Reconstructed from Maps in a Survey by Norwood for Thomas Elmes Now in Oundle School Archive. Inset Showing Pages with a Plan of the Village. Misc. Photostat 1108 Is a Complete b/w Copy of the Survey. Acc. 2006/76.* 1621.

Map/4608 *Tansor, Northamptonshire. Inclosures Award.* 1778. Scale 6 Chains to 1 inch.

North Yorkshire Record Office

I MIC 280 *Cropton Enclosure Records, 3 Awards.* 1766.

MIC 2046/118-24 & 1982/276-79 *A Plan of the Tyth Land at Middleton in the County of York Belonging to Sr Danvers Osborn Bart. Distinguished by the Yellow Colour Containing about 153 Acres, and in Dunsmire There Is One Oxgang and Two Acres More besides the Swaiths in the Lyth Ings &c. Surveyed Oct. 1730.* 1730. Scale 4 chains to 1 inch.

Secondary sources

Albion Archaeology. 2005. *A428 Caxton to Hardwick Improvement Scheme, Cambridgeshire. Intrusive Archaeological Field Evaluation.* Bedford, Albion Archaeology.

Allerston, P. 1970. English Village Development: Findings from the Pickering District of North Yorkshire. *Transactions of the Institute of British Geographers* 51, 95–109.

Astbury, A.K. 1958. *The Black Fens.* Cambridge, Golden Press.

Ault, W.O. 1972. *Open Field Farming in Medieval England A Study of Village By Laws.* London and New York, Routledge.

Baker, A.R.H. and R.A. Butlin, eds. 1973. *Studies of Field Systems in the British Isles.* Cambridge, Cambridge University Press.

Blair, J. 2005. *The Church in Anglo-Saxon Society.* Oxford, Oxford University Press.

Blair, J., S. Rippon and C. Smart. 2022. *Planning in the Early Medieval Landscape.* Liverpool, Liverpool University Press.

Bond, J. 2007. Canal Construction in the Early Middle Ages: An Introductory Review. In *Waterways and Canal-Building in Medieval England*, edited by J. Blair, 153–206. Oxford, New York, Oxford University Press.

Bowen, H.C. 1978. 'Celtic' Fields and 'Ranch' Boundaries in Wessex. In *The Effect of Man on the Landscape: The Lowland Zone*, edited by S. Limbrey and J.G. Evans, 115–23. London, Council for British Archaeology Research Report 21.

Brown, T. and G. Foard. 1998. The Saxon Landscape: A Regional Perspective. In *The Archaeology of Landscape: Studies Presented to Christopher Taylor*, edited by P. Everson and T. Williamson, 67–93. Manchester, Manchester University Press.

Bryant, S., B. Perry and T. Williamson. 2005. A 'Relict Landscape' in South-East Hertfordshire: Archaeological and Topographic Investigations in the Wormley Area. *Landscape History* 27(1), 5–16.

Bullock, J.H., ed. 1939. *The Norfolk Portion of the Chartulary of the Priory of St. Pancras of Lewes*. Norwich, Norfolk Record Society Publications 12.

Caulfield, S. 1978. Neolithic Fields: The Irish Evidence. In *Early Land Allotment*, edited by H. Brown and P. Fowler, 137–43. BAR British Series 116. Oxford, British Archaeological Reports.

Caulfield, S. 1983. The Neolithic Settlement of North Connaught. In *Landscape Archaeology in Ireland*, edited by T. Reeves-Smyth and F. Hamond, 195–215. BAR British Series 116. Oxford, British Archaeological Reports.

Caulfield, S., R.G. O'Donnell and P.I. Mitchell. 1997. 14 C Dating of a Neolithic Field System at Céide Fields, County Mayo, Ireland. *Radiocarbon* 40(02), 629–40.

Charman, D.J. 2010. Centennial Climate Variability in the British Isles during the Mid to Late Holocene. *Quaternary Science Reviews* 29, 1539–54.

Christy, M. 1926. On Roman Roads in Essex: Second Supplement. *Transactions of the Essex Archaeological Society* 2, 17, no. Part III, 85–100.

Compton, A. 2014. A Practical Arrangement: Territorial Organisation in the Southeast Midlands. Unpublished Masters Dissertation, University of East Anglia.

Compton, A. 2018. A Reassessment of the 'Relict Field System' in Tadlow, Cambridgeshire. *Proceedings of the Cambridge Antiquarian Society* 107 (2018), 119–28.

Crawford, O.G.S. and A. Keiller. 1928. *Wessex from the Air*. Oxford, Clarendon Press.

Crowson, A. 2005. *Anglo-Saxon Settlement on the Siltland of Eastern England*. Sleaford, Heritage Trust of Lincolnshire.

Darby, H.C. 1983. *The Changing Fenland*. Cambridge, Cambridge University Press.

Drury, P.J. 1978. *Chelmsford Excavations I: Excavations at Little Waltham, 1970–71*. CBA Research Report 26. Norwich, Chelmsford Excavation Committee and the Council for British Archaeology.

Drury, P.J. and W. Rodwell. 1980. Settlement in the Later Iron Age and Roman Periods. In *Archaeology in Essex to AD 1500: In Memory of Ken Newton*, edited by D.B. Buckley, 34, 59–75. London, Council for British Archaeology Research Report 34.

Dyer, C. 2000. *Everyday Life in Medieval England*. Hambledon and London, A&C Black.

Everitt, A. 1977. Reflections on the Historical Origin of Regions and Pays. *Journal of Historical Geography* 3(1), 1–19.

Field, J. 1993. *A History of English Field Names*. Singapore, Longman Group.

Fleming, A. 1988. *The Dartmoor Reaves: Investigating Prehistoric Land Divisions*. London, Trafalgar Square Publishing.

Fleming, A. 2008. *The Dartmoor Reaves: Investigating Prehistoric Land Division*. Oxford, Windgather Press.

Fleming, A. 2010. *Swaledale: Valley of the Wild River*. Oxford, Windgather Press.

Foard, G. 1977. Systematic Fieldwalking and the Investigation of Saxon Settlement in Northamptonshire. *World Archaeology* 9(3), 357–74.

Fowler, P.J. 1981. *The Farming of Prehistoric Britain*. Cambridge, Cambridge University Press.

Fox, H.S.A. 1981. Approaches to the Adoption of the Midland System. In *The Origins of Open-Field Agriculture*, edited by T. Rowley, 64–111. London, Croom Helm.

Gardiner, M. 2009. Dales, Long Lands, and the Medieval Division of Land in Eastern England. In *Agricultural History Review* 57(1), 1–14.

Gardiner, M. 2018. The Changing Character of Transhumance in Early and Later Medieval England. In *Historical Archaeologies of Transhumance Across Europe*, 109–19. London, Routledge.

Gelling, M. 1993. *Place-Names in the Landscape*. London, Dent.

Gover, J.E.B., A. Mawer and F. Merry Stenton. 1933. *The Place-Names of Northamptonshire*. Vol. 62. Cambridge, Cambridge University Press.

Gray, H.L. 1915. *English Field Systems*. Vol. 22. Cambridge, Harvard University Press.

Hall, D. 1981. The Origins of Open-Field Agriculture – The Archaeological Fieldwork Evidence. In *The Origins of Open-Field Agriculture*, edited by T. Rowley, 22–38. London, Croom Helm.

Hall, D. 1982. *Medieval Fields*. Aylesbury, Shire Publications.

Hall, D. 1995. *The Open Fields of Northamptonshire*. Vol. 38. Northampton, Northamptonshire Record Society.

Hall, D. 2014. *The Open Fields of England*. Oxford, Oxford University Press.

Hall, D. and J. Coles. 2014. *Fenland Survey: An Essay in Landscape and Persistence*. Swindon, English Heritage Publishing.

Harrison, S. 2002. Open Fields and Earlier Landscapes: Six Parishes in South-East Cambridgeshire. *Landscapes* 3(1), 35–54.

Harrison, S. 2005. A History of Evolution and Interaction: Man, Roads and the Landscape to c.1850. Unpublished PhD Thesis, University of East Anglia.

Harvey, M. 1978. *The Morphological and Tenurial Structure of a Yorkshire Township: Preston in Holderness 1066–1750*. London, Department of Geography, Queen Mary College, University of London.

Harvey, M. 1980. Regular Field and Tenurial Arrangements in Holderness, Yorkshire. *Journal of Historical Geography* 6(1), 3–16.

Harvey, M. 1981. The Origin of Planned Field Systems in Holderness, Yorkshire. In *The Origins of Open Field Agriculture*, edited by T. Rowley, 184–201. London, Croom Helm.

Harvey, M. 1983. Planned Field Systems in Eastern Yorkshire: Some Thoughts on Their Origin. *The Agricultural History Review* 31(2), 91–103.

Harvey, M. 1985. The Development of Open Fields in the Central Vale of York: A Reconsideration. Geografiska Annaler. Series B. *Human Geography* 67(1), 35–44.

Hinton, D.A. 1997. The 'Scole-Dickleburgh Field System' Examined. *Landscape History* 19(1), 5–12.

Hodge, C.A.H. 1984. *Soils and Their Use in Eastern England*. Harpenden, Lawes Agricultural Trust, Soil Survey of England and Wales.

Homans, G.C. 1941. *English Villagers of the Thirteenth Century*. Cambridge MA, Harvard University Press.

Hooke, D. 2013. Old English Wald, Weald in Place-Names. *Landscape History* 34(1), 33–49.

Hoskins, W.G. 1988. *The Making of the English Landscape*. London, Hodder & Stoughton.

Hunn, J.R. and C. Turner. 2004. *Tyttenhanger: Excavation and Survey in the Parish of Ridge, Hertfordshire*, Undertaken by Archaeological Services and Consultancy Ltd. Vol. 381. Oxford, Archaeopress.

Hunter, J.M. 2003. *Field Systems in Essex*. Essex, Essex Society for Archaeology and History.

Johnston, R. 2005. Pattern Without a Plan: Rethinking the Bronze Age Coaxial Field Systems on Dartmoor, South-West England. *Oxford Journal of Archaeology* 24(1), 1–21.

Knotterus, O.S. 2013. Reclamations and Submerged Lands in the Elms River Estuary (900–1500). In *Landscapes or Seascapes?*, edited by A.M.J. de Kraker, T. Soens, D. Tys, L. Vervaet and H.J.T. Weerts, 241–66. Comparative Rural History of the North Sea Area 13. Turnhout, Brepols.

Lewis, C., P. Mitchell-Fox and C. Dyer. 2001. *Village, Hamlet and Field: Changing Medieval Settlements in Central England*. Oxford, Windgather Press.

Liddiard, R. 1999. The Distribution of Ridge and Furrow in East Anglia: Ploughing Practice and Subsequent Land Use. *The Agricultural History Review* 47(1), 1–6.

Maitland, F.W. 1907. *Domesday Book and Beyond: 3 Essays in the Early History of England*. Cambridge, Cambridge University Press.

Margary, I.D. 1964. *Roman Roads in the South-East Midlands*. London, V. Gollancz.

Martin, E.A. and M. Satchell. 2008. *'Wheare Most Inclosures Be' East Anglian Fields: History, Morphology and Management*. East Anglian Archaeology Report 124. Ipswich, Suffolk County Council Archaeological Service.

Matzat, W. 1988. Long Strip Field Layouts and Their Later Subdivisions: A Comparison of English and German Cases. Geografiska Annaler. Series B, *Human Geography* 70(1), 133–47.

Miller, E. 1951. *The Abbey & Bishopric of Ely; the Social History of an Ecclesiastical Estate from the Tenth Century to the Early Fourteenth Century*. Cambridge, Cambridge University Press.

Molloy, K. and M. O'Connell. 1995. Palaeoecological Investigations towards the Reconstruction of Environment and Land-Use Changes during Prehistory at Céide Fields, Western Ireland. *Probleme Der Küstenforschung Im Südlichen Nordseegebiet* 23, 187–225.

Nitz, H.-J. 1988. Introduction from Above: Intentional Spread of Common-Field Systems by Feudal Authorities through Colonization and Reorganization. Geografiska Annaler. Series B, *Human Geography* 70(1), 149–59.

Oosthuizen, S. 2006. *Landscapes Decoded: The Origins and Development of Cambridgeshire's Medieval Fields*. Vol. 1. Hatfield, University of Hertfordshire Press.

Orwin, C.S. and C.S. Orwin. 1938. *The Open Fields*. Oxford, Clarendon Press.

Partida, T., D. Hall and G. Foard. 2013. *An Atlas of Northamptonshire: The Medieval and Early-Modern Landscape*. Oxford, Oxbow Books.

Postgate, M.R. 1964. The Openfields of Cambridgeshire. Unpublished PhD Thesis, University of Cambridge.

Pryor, F. 2013. *The Flag Fen Basin: Archaeology and Environment of a Fenland Landscape*. London, English Heritage.

Rackham, O. 1986. *The History of the Countryside, the Classical History of Britain's Landscape, Flora and Fauna*. London, J.M. Dent.

Rippon, S. 1991. Early Planned Landscapes in South-East Essex. Essex Archaeology and History, *The Transactions of the Essex Society for Archaeology and History* 22, 46–60.

Rippon, S., B. Pears and C. Smart. 2015. *The Fields of Britannia*. Oxford, Oxford University Press.

Roberts, B.K. 1982. The Anatomy of the Village: Observation and Extrapolation. *Landscape History* 4(1), 11–20.

Rodwell, W. 1978. Relict Landscapes in Essex. In *Early Land Allotment in the British Isles. A Survey of Recent Work*, edited by P.J. Fowler and H.C. Bowen, 89–98. British Series 48. Oxford, British Archaeological Reports.

Royal Commission on Historical Monuments (RCHM). 1968. *An Inventory of Historical Monuments in the County of Cambridge Vol. 1 West Cambridgeshire*. Vol. 1. London, HMSO.

Royal Commission on Historical Monuments (RCHM). 1975. *An Inventory of the Historical Monuments in the County of Northampton. Volume 1 Archaeological Sites in North-East Northamptonshire*. Vol. 1. HMSO.

Seebohm, F. 1883. *The English Village Community*. London, Longmans, Green & Co.

Silvester, R.J. 1988. *The Fenland Project Number 3: Marshland and the Nar Valley, Norfolk*. East Anglian Archaeology, Report 45. Gressenham, Norfolk Archaeological Unit.

Silvester, R.J. 2002. Some Early Maps of Marshland. In *Through Wet and Dry: Essays in Honour of David Hall*, edited by T. Lane and J. Coles, 10–17. Lincolnshire Archaeology and Heritage Reports Series, 5 WARP Occasional Paper 17. Sleaford, Heritage Trust of Lincolnshire and WARG.

Spratt, D.A. 1991. Recent British Research on Prehistoric Territorial Boundaries. *Journal of World Prehistory* 5(4), 439–80.

Summers, D. 1973. *The Great Ouse: The History of a River Navigation*. Newton Abbott, David & Charles.

Taylor, C. 1973. *The Cambridgeshire Landscape: Cambridgeshire and the Southern Fens*. London, Hodder & Stoughton.

Taylor, C. 1978. Roman Fields into Medieval Furlongs. In *Early Land Allotment in the British Isles. A Survey of Recent Work*, edited by P.J. Fowler and H.C. Bowen, 159–62. British Series 48. Oxford, British Archaeological Reports.

Thirsk, J. 1964. The Common Fields. *Past & Present* 29, 3–25.

Thirsk, J. 1966. The Origin of the Common Fields. *Past & Present* 33, 142–7.

Thirsk, J. 1973. Field Systems of the East Midlands. In *Studies of Field Systems in the British Isles*, edited by A.R.H. Baker and R.A. Butlin, 232–80. Cambridge, Cambridge University Press.

Titlow, J.Z. 1965. Medieval England and the Open-Field System. *Past and Present* 32, 86–102.

Upex, S.G. 2002. Landscape Continuity and the Fossilization of Roman Fields. *Archaeological Journal* 159(1), 77–108.

White, P. 2003a. *The Arrow Valley, Herefordshire: Archaeology, Landscape Change and Conservation*. Hereford, Herefordshire Archaeology.

White, P. 2003b. *The Leen, Pembridge: A Whole Farm Archaeological Survey*. Herefordshire Archaeology Report 103. Hereford, Herefordshire Archaeology.

Whitefield, A. 2017. Neolithic 'Celtic' Fields? A Reinterpretation of the Chronological Evidence from Céide Fields in North-Western Ireland. *European Journal of Archaeology* 20(2), 257–79.

Williams, A. and G. Haward Martin. 1992. *Domesday Book: A Complete Translation*. London, Penguin.

Williamson, T. 1986. Parish Boundaries and Early Fields: Continuity and Discontinuity. *Journal of Historical Geography* 12(3), 241–8.

Williamson, T. 1987. Early Co-Axial Field Systems on the East Anglian Boulder Clays. *Proceedings of the Prehistoric Society* 53, 419–31.

Williamson, T. 1998. The 'Scole-Dickleburgh Field System' Revisited. *Landscape History* 20(1), 19–28.

Williamson, T. 2013. *Environment, Society and Landscape in Early Medieval England: Time and Topography*. Vol. 19. Woodbridge, Boydell Press.

Williamson, T. 2016. The Ancient Origins of Medieval Fields: A Reassessment. *Archaeological Journal* 173(2), 264–87.

Williamson, T., R. Liddiard and T. Partida. 2013. *Champion: The Making and Unmaking of the English Midland Landscape*. Liverpool, Liverpool University Press.

Wrathmell, S. 2021. Sharing out the Land of the Northumbrians: Exploring Scandinavian Settlement in Eastern Yorkshire through-Bý Place-Names and Township Boundaries (Part Two). *Medieval Settlement Research* 36, 4–17.

Wright, J., M. Leivers, R. Seager Smith and C.J. Stevens. 2009. *Cambourne New Settlement: Iron Age and Romano-British Settlement on the Clay Uplands of West Cambridgeshire*. Wessex Archaeology Report 23. Salisbury, Wessex Archaeology.

Yates, D.T. 1999. Bronze Age Field Systems in the Thames Valley. *Oxford Journal of Archaeology* 18(2), 157–70.

Online resources and websites

Blomefield, F. 1808. An Essay Towards a Topographical History of the County of Norfolk, Vol. 9. London. *British History Online*, http://www.british-history.ac.uk/topographical-hist-norfolk/vol9 [accessed 3 December 2022].

Dugdale, W., Sir. 1605. The History of Imbanking and Drayning of Divers Fenns and Marshes, Both in Forein Parts and in This Kingdom, and of the Improvements Thereby Extracted from Records, Manuscripts, and Other Authentick Testimonies / by William Dugdale. Oxford Text Archive. http://hdl.handle.net/20.500.14106/A36795 [accessed 20 August 2022].

Landis. 2020. Cranfield University 2020. The Soils Guide. http://www3.landis.org.uk/soilsguide/mapunit_list.cfm [accessed 30 October 2020].

Lock, G. and I. Ralston. 2017. Atlas of Hillforts of Britain and Ireland [ONLINE]. https://hillforts.arch.ox.ac.uk [accessed 30 October 2020].

Markham, G. 1613. The English Husbandman. Vol. The First Part: Contayning the Knowledge of the true Nature of euery Soyle within this Kingdome: how to Plow it; and the manner of the Plough, and other Instrumentse within this Kingdome. Project Gutenburg. https://www.gutenberg.org/cache/epub/22973/pg22973-images.html [accessed 13 August 2022].

Northamptonshire County Council. 2008. The Northamptonshire National Mapping Programme [Data-Set]. York, Archaeology Data Service. https://doi.org/10.5284/1000366 [accessed 29 August 2022].

Page, W. 1923. Parishes: Middleton. In *A History of the County of York North Riding: Volume 2*, edited by W. Page. London. *British History Online* https://www.british-history.ac.uk/vch/yorks/north/vol2/pp453-461 [accessed 24 January 2022].

Norfolk County Council. 2012. Tithe Maps of Norfolk, circa 1840. http://www.historic-maps.norfolk.gov.uk/tithe.aspx [accessed 4 December 2022].

Published maps

Soil Survey of England and Wales. 1983. *Sheet 1: Soils of Northern England*, Ordnance Survey, Southampton.

Soil Survey of England and Wales. 1983. *Sheet 4: Soils of Eastern England*, Ordnance Survey, Southampton.

Index

Page numbers in *italic* refer to illustrations.

aggregate field systems 5, 8, 32
Arkley, Hertfordshire 14, 78–82, *80–2*
Arrow Valley, Herefordshire 14–15, 66–75, *66*, *69–71*, *73–4*, 84
axial reaves 5–6
    see also co-axial systems

Belderg Beg field system, Co. Mayo 7–8
Blair, John 92, 95
Blomefield, Francis 166
Bourn Valley 16, 23, *24*, 92
Bourn Valley relict field systems, Cambridgeshire 27–31, *29–30*, *38*, 39, 83
Bronze Age period 4, 5, 8, 9, 13
    see also Tadlow Bronze Age field system
brooks see watercourses
Brown, T. 89, 122
Bryant, S. 76, 78

Cambourne Development Area, Cambridgeshire 31–8, *31*, *33–7*
Cambridgeshire 15–16, 18, 83
    see also Flag Fen; Western Clay Plateau
Caulfield, Seamus 7, 8
Caxton, Cambridgeshire 40–4, *41–4*, 84
Céide field system, Co. Mayo 6–7, 17
Central Nene Valley, Northamptonshire 130–40
    furlongs 136, *137*, 138–40
    resource-linkage routes 137–8, *138–9*, 139
    settlement patterns 131–2, 134–5, 136, 137
    soils 132–4, *133*
    topography 131, *131*, 140
    watersheds and linear features 135–6
    woodland 136–7
Centuriation 10, 11–12
champion belt 15–17
    see also open fields
Christy, Miller 10
co axial field systems 6, *7*, 9, 11, 12
Co. Mayo, Republic of Ireland 6–7, 7–8, 17

cohesive field systems 4–5, 8
confirmation bias 49
county boundaries 50–1, 52
Cressing Temple, Essex 20
Crowson, A. 150

Dartmoor reaves 5–6, 9, 17–18
Dengie peninsula, Essex 10, 11, 18–19
ditches 43–4
    Arrow Valley field ditches 14–15, *66*, 68–9, 74, *74*
    Flag Fen droveways 8
    Late Iron Age farmsteads 32
    Marshland 150, 163, 171
    post-Roman continuity of 16, 17
    purpose of 43–4
    Romano-British farmsteads 32, 33, 34, *35*, 38, 141
drainage 174–5
    modern changes 97
    open fields 87, 98, 104, 106, 118, 122–3, 129, 140
    relict field systems 35–6, 42, 44, 57, 65, 74–5, 81–2, 84
drove-ways 8, 14, 76–7, *77*, *79*
Drury, P.J. 53–5, 56, 57
Dugdale, William 148, 155

East Yorkshire 103–4
enclosure maps
    Preston, East Yorkshire 97, *97*, 99, *99*
    Skeffling, East Yorkshire 103–4, *104*
    Toft, Cambridgeshire 47–9, *48–9*
    Walgrave, Northamptonshire 128–9, *128*
enclosures 15
Essex 10–13, 18–19, 19–20, 53–7

Fens see Marshland
field lynchets 4
Fields of Britannia 16–17, 141
Flag Fen, Peterborough 8, 9
Fleming, Andrew 5–6
Foard, Glenn 89, 122
Fowler, Peter 15
Fox, Harold 89
furlongs 42–3, *43*, 87
    see also long furlongs

Gardiner, Mark 18, 20, 83, 168
Germany 91
Gray, H.L. 88
Grimms Ditch, Suffolk *58*, 59

Haddon, Northamptonshire 16
Hall, David 90–1, 105, 108–9, 110, 115, 122, 149
Harrison, Sarah 18, 20
Harvey, Mary 89–90, 95–6, 98–100, 103–4
Hayward, William 148–9, 150, 151, 168
headlands 87, 90, 105, 106–7, 108
Herefordshire 14–15
 see also Arrow Valley
Hertfordshire 14
 see also Arkley; Wormley
Hinton, David 13, 19
Hunn, Jonathan 14, 79, 80, 81
Hunter, John 19–20

Iron Age farmsteads 31–2, *31*, *33*–5
Iron Age period 11, 13, 28, *29*, 38

Johnston, R. 18

lands 87
Landscape Stratigraphy 10
landscape types 15
Lea Valley see Wormley
LiDAR 173
 Arkley, Hertfordshire 81–2, *82*
 Arrow Valley, Offa's Dyke 73–5, *73*–*4*
 Arrow Valley, Rowe Ditch 70–1, *70*–*1*
 Bourn valley, linear commons 46, *46*–*7*, *47*, *49*, 49
 Bourn Valley, northwest 39, *39*
 Bourn Valley, pre-Roman boundaries 42, *42*
 Caxton, Cambridgeshire 43, *44*
 Little Waltham *56*, 57
 Middleton in Ryedale, North Yorkshire 115–16, *115*
 Preston, East Yorkshire 101, *101*
Liddiard, Robert 92, 122
linear commons 29, 44–50, *46*–*9*
linear greens 78–9, 128–9, 138, *138*–*9*, 139, 157, 167
Little Waltham, Essex 53–7, *54*–*6*
long furlongs 90, 91, 104, 105, *106*–*7*, 107, 108
lynchets 4

Maitland, F.W. 88
maps see Ordnance Survey maps; Tithe maps; Toft Draft Inclosure map
Markham, Gervase 122–3
Marshland 143–71

Black Fen 145
droves 157–61, *159*–*60*, 170–1
environmental change 149, 150, 155
Fenland Project 148
field patterns 151–2, 157, *158*, 162, 163, *164*, 171
field strips 168–70, *169*
formation of 144–6
historical records 148–9
landscape framework 167
linear greens 157, 167
location 146, *147*
maps 144, *144*, 168
Newfendike and other field dikes 164–6, *165*, 171
reclamation 146, 163, 166–7
Sea Wall *147*, 150
settlement patterns 148–50, *151*, 152–4, *153*–*4*, 155, *156*, 163
Silt Fen 145–6, 154, 156–7, 161, 163–7, 170–1
soils 146–7
township dikes 161–4, *162*, *164*, *165*
Martin, E.A. 19
Matzat, W. 91
medieval ridge and furrow 34–7, *34*, *36*, 87, 101–2, *101*
medieval transhumance 18
Mesolithic period 3
Middleton in Ryedale, North Yorkshire 108–17
 curving field pattern 108–10, *109*, 111–14, *112*–*13*, 115–16, *115*, 117
 soils 110–11
 topography 110, 116, *117*
 village crofts and adjacent fields 114–15, *114*
Midlands 15
Molloy, K. 17
moorlands 6

Nene Valley see Central Nene Valley
Neolithic period 3–4, 7–8
Norfolk 12–14, 19
 see also Marshland
North Yorkshire 108–17
Northamptonshire 89, 92–3, 121–41
 background 121–3
 Central Nene Valley 130–40, *131*, *133*, *137*–*9*
 Haddon 16
 Orlingbury hundred 123–30, *124*–*5*, *127*–*8*, *130*
 Raunds 91, 105–7, *106*
 Wollaston 90, 107–8, *107*
Northmore, Thomas 5

O'Connell, M. 17
Offa's Dyke 67, 73–5, *73*–*4*
Old, Northamptonshire 129–30, *130*

Oosthuizen, Susan 16, 23, 27–30, 39, 40, 44–5, 49–50, 83, 92–3
open fields 15, 16
    chronology of 88–9, 90, 91–2
    farming methods 88–9
    other explanations 92–3
    planned open fields 89–92
    see also North Yorkshire; Northamptonshire; Preston, East Yorkshire
Ordnance Survey maps 10, 17
    Arkley, Hertfordshire 78–9, 80, *80*
    Arrow Valley *66*, 67, 68, *69*
    Bourn Valley, northwest *38*, 39
    Caxton, Cambridgeshire 41, *41*
    Little Waltham, Essex 55
    Marshland 144, *144*, 160, 161, *169*, 170
    Middleton in Ryedale, North Yorkshire *109*, 110, *114*, 115, 116, *117*
    Preston, East Yorkshire 102, *102*
    Tadlow, Cambridgeshire 50–1, *50*
    Wormley, Hertfordshire 76, *77*
    Yaxley *58–9*, 59, 60, 61–2, *61–2*, 63–4
Orlingbury hundred, Northamptonshire 123–30
    furlongs 128–30, *128*, *130*
    phases of landscape 126–7, *127*
    settlement pattern 126
    soils 124–6, *125*
    topography 124, *124*
    woodland 127–8
Orwin, C.S. and C.S. Orwin 88, 122

parish boundaries 10, 11, 12–13, 50–1, *50*, 52
Partida, Tracey 92, 122
Pears, Ben 16, 141
Perry, B. 76, 78
Petrie, Flinders 10
Pike, John 5
ploughing 4
post-Roman continuity 16–17
prehistoric fields 4–10
Preston, East Yorkshire 89–90, 95–105
    historical records 98–100, *99*, 103
    maps *99*, 100–1, 102, *102*
    open-field system 95
    organisation and reorganisation 103
    ridge and furrow 101–2, *101*
    settlement pattern 95, *96*
    soils 97–8
    topography 95, 97, 103, 104–5
proto-common fields 28–30, *29*, 44–50, *46–9*
Pryor, Francis 8

Rackham, Oliver 12, 13, 15, 50, 53
Raunds, Northamptonshire 91, 105–7, *106*
relict field systems
    definition of 3
    first identifications 10–15
resource-linkage routes 18, 40, 51, 52, 78, 83, 129, 137–8
retrogressive analysis 49
ridge and furrow 34–7, *34*, *36*, 87, 101–2, *101*
Rippon, Stephen 16, 141
rivers see watercourses
Rodwell, Warwick 10–12, 53, 54, 57
Roman Centuriation 10, 11–12
Roman roads
    Cambridgeshire (Ermine Street) 40–4, *42–4*
    Essex 10–11, 53, *54–6*, 55, 57
    Norfolk (Pye Road) 12
    Suffolk (Pye Road) *58*, 59, 61, *61*, 62
    see also Rowe Ditch
Romano-British farmsteads 32–4, *33–5*, 37–8
Rowe Ditch *66*, 67, 68, 70–3, *70–1*

Satchell, M. 19
Saxon period 16
Saxon proto-common fields 28–30, *29*, 44–50, *46–9*
scale of field systems 9, 14, 20, 139–40, 171, 174
Scole–Dickleburgh field system, Norfolk 12–14, 19
Seebohm, F. 88
selions 87
short perch 92
Silvester, Robert 148–9, 150, 151, 158–61, 162, 163, 167, 168
Skeffling, East Yorkshire 103–4, *104*
slighted field boundaries 83–4, 175
    Arrow Valley 70–2, *70*
    Bourn Valley 40–4, *41–4*
    Essex 10–11, 53
    Marshland droves 159, *160*, 161
    Scole–Dickleburgh field system, Norfolk 12
    Yaxley, Suffolk 63–4, *63*
Smart, Chris 16, 141
soil associations
    Agney 146
    Banbury 125
    Bearstead 1 26
    Beccles 59, 75
    Burlingham 2 97–8
    Denchworth 125–6
    Elmton 2 111
    Essendon 75, 79–80
    Evesham 3 26
    Fladbury 134
    Foggathorpe 2 111

Frilford 26
Hamble 75
Hanslope 25–6, 106, 124–5, 132
Holderness 97–8
Melford 59
Moreton 106
Morton 125, 134
Oxpasture 126, 132–3
Rivington 1 111
Rowton 67–8
Sutton 134
Tanvats 146–7
Wallsea 97
Wallsea 2 147
Wantage 26
Windsor 75, 79–80
Wisbech 146
soils
 Arkley, Hertfordshire 79–80
 Arrow Valley 67, 68
 Central Nene Valley, Northamptonshire 132–4, *133*
 Middleton in Ryedale, North Yorkshire 110–11
 Norfolk Fens 146–7
 Orlingbury hundred, Northamptonshire 124–6, *125*
 Preston, East Yorkshire 97–8
 Raunds, Northamptonshire 106
 Western Clay Plateau, Cambridgeshire 25–6
 Wormley, Hertfordshire 75
 Yaxley, Suffolk 59–60
South Downs 4–5
South Elmham, Suffolk 13
stone walls 5, 7
streams *see* watercourses
strips 87
Suffolk 13
 see also Yaxley

Tadlow Bronze Age field system, Cambridgeshire 50–2, *50*
Taylor, Christopher 15, 24–5
terminal reaves 5, 17–18
Thames Valley 9
Thirsk, Joan 88, 89
Tithe maps 61–2, *61*, *111*, *112–13*, *115*, 116
Titlow, J.Z. 88
Toft Draft Inclosure map, Cambridgeshire 47–9, *48–9*
topography 83, 84, 173
 Arrow Valley *66*, 67, *71*
 Fens 152, *153*
 Little Waltham *56*, 57
 Middleton in Ryedale, North Yorkshire 110, 116, *117*
 Northamptonshire 124, *124*, 131, *131*, 135, 139, 140
 Preston, East Yorkshire 95, 97, 103, 104–5

Western Clay Plateau, Cambridgeshire 24–5, *24*, 39–40, *39*, 42, 43
 Yaxley, Suffolk *63*, 64–5
transhumance 18
transhumance routes 13, 14, 18
 see also linear commons; linear greens
triangular fields 42, 43, *43*, *61*, 63, 64

Upex, Stephen 16, 136
uplands *see* moorlands

Walgrave, Northamptonshire 128–9, *128*
Warmington, Northamptonshire 136, *137*, 138, *138–9*
watercourses
 Arrow Valley 72, 73–4, *73–4*
 Caxton, Cambridgeshire 42, *42*
 Raunds, Northamptonshire 106, *106*
 Yaxley, Suffolk *63*, 65
watersheds 13, 14
 Arkley, Hertfordshire 80–1
 Bourn Valley settlement 27
 Cambridgeshire 77–8
 Central Nene Valley, Northamptonshire 135
 Orlingbury hundred, Northamptonshire 124, 125, 126, 128–9
 Raunds, Northamptonshire 106, *106*
 resource-linkage routes and 40, 51
Western Clay Plateau, Cambridgeshire
 archaeological investigations 26–7
 Bourn Valley relict field systems 27–31, *29–30*, *38*, 39
 Bronze Age field system, Tadlow 50–2, *50*
 Cambourne Development Area 31–8, *31*, *33–7*
 environmental analyses 27
 geology 25
 location 24, *24*
 Roman roads and slighted field boundaries, Caxton 40–4, *41–4*
 Saxon proto-common fields, Toft 44–50, *46–9*
 settlement pattern 26
 soils 25–6
 topography 24–5, 39–40, *39*, 42
White, Paul 14–15, 67, 68–9
Williamson, Tom 12, 18–19, 20, 59, 60, 61, 62, 64, 76, 78, 92, 122, 174
Wollaston, Northamptonshire 90, 107–8, *107*
woodland 15, 127–8, 136–7
Wormley, Hertfordshire 14, 75–8, *75*, *77*, *79*, 83
Wrathmell, Stuart 109–10

Yates, David 9
Yaxley, Suffolk 58–9, *59*–65, *61–3*